About the author

Michael Bhaskar is a writer, researcher and digital publisher. He is Co-Founder of Canelo, a new publishing company.

Michael has written and talked extensively about the future of media, the creative industries and the economics of technology for newspapers, magazines and blogs. He has been featured in and written for *The Guardian*, the *Financial Times*, *Wired* and the *Daily Telegraph*, and on BBC 2, BBC Radio 4, NPR and Bloomberg TV amongst others. He has worked as a digital publisher, an economics researcher, a book reviewer, and founded several web initiatives.

Michael has a degree in English Literature from the University of Oxford, where he won the University Gibbs Prize. He has been a British Council Young Creative Entrepreneur and a Frankfurt Book Fair Fellow. He is also author of *The Content Machine* and co-editor of a forthcoming book about publishing. He can be found on Twitter @michaelbhaskar.

CURATION

THE POWER
OF SELECTION
IN A WORLD
OF EXCESS

*MICHAEL
BHASKAR*

piatkus

PIATKUS

First published in Great Britain in 2016 by Piatkus

1 3 5 7 9 10 8 6 4 2

A CIP catalogue record for this book
is available from the British Library.

ISBN 978-0-349-41250-4

Typeset in Sabon by M Rules
Printed and bound in Great Britain by
Clays Ltd, St Ives plc

Papers used by Piatkus are from well-managed forests
and other responsible sources.

MIX
Paper from
responsible sources
FSC® C104740

Piatkus
An imprint of
Little, Brown Book Group
Carmelite House
50 Victoria Embankment
London EC4Y 0DZ

An Hachette UK Company
www.hachette.co.uk

www.improvementzone.co.uk

Curation: *using acts of selection and arrangement (but also refining, reducing, displaying, simplifying, presenting and explaining) to add value*

Everything in excess is opposed to nature.

HIPPOCRATES

*In a few hundred years, when the history
of our time will be written from a long-
term perspective, it is likely that the most
important event historians will see is
not technology, not the Internet, not e-
commerce. It is an unprecedented change
in the human condition. For the first time –
literally – substantial and rapidly growing
numbers of people have choices. For the first
time, they will have to manage themselves.
And society is totally unprepared for it.*

PETER DRUCKER

Weniger aber besser.

DIETER RAMS

Contents

Contents

Introduction

IBM estimates that the world now produces over 2.5 quintillion bytes of data – that is, 2,500,000,000,000 megabytes – every day.[1] If you wrote out all the ones and zeros of just one megabyte in longhand, the line would be five times longer than Mount Everest is high. Facebook alone deals with at least 2.7 billion items of content and 600 terabytes each day. In the past two years humanity has produced more data than the rest of human history combined, and this extraordinary rate of production is still growing by 60 per cent a year. By the time you read this the figures are likely to be bigger. Computation is increasing in parallel. According to McKinsey the world added five exaflops of computational capacity in 2008; in 2014 alone it added forty exaflops.[2]

For comparison, the Library of Congress in Washington DC holds around twenty-three million books. Let's assume the average book is 400 pages long. According to LexisNexis, in its most basic form 677,963 pages of text is equivalent to one gigabyte of data.[3] This means the entire book collection of the Library of Congress holds around 13,570 gigabytes of data or 13.5 trillion bytes, forty-five times less than Facebook's daily churn. Sophisticated new routers can transfer such an amount in seconds. This data pile represents the accumulated wisdom, knowledge and culture of humanity.

Information used to be rare. Creating, collecting, storing and transmitting data was time-consuming, expensive and difficult. Mostly those processes relied on laborious copying. The materials to do so were fragile and scarce – books were written on clay tablets, papyrus or vellum in isolated islands of learning. Even after the invention of the printing press, books were a relative rarity, and finding, let alone verifying, data was incredibly difficult.

The Library of Alexandria was by far the largest store of information in antiquity. It was the pinnacle of learning for a society that spanned the 'known world', whose trade routes, roads and aqueducts crossed continents, which maintained a standing army over half a million strong and which could mobilise millions more, whose cities were the biggest ever seen, and whose culture, engineering and economy would not be matched for 1,500 years. Based around the Nine Muses, the library was a hotbed of scholarship – here the heliocentric nature of the solar system was discovered many centuries before Copernicus. Containing hundreds of thousands of scrolls, it was invaluable and unrivalled, unique and, when it burnt to the ground, irreplaceable, the very summit, the limit, of what had been thought and known.

Now we carry the equivalent in our pockets, accessible at any second. This is a kind of miracle. It is also a problem.

We have, in the space of a few years, gone from information scarcity to a tsunami of data. Information that used to be private, forgotten, disregarded or simply unknown is instantaneously available and public. But are those 2.5 quintillion bytes worth more than the much smaller collection in the Library of Congress or even the Library of Alexandria? No: much of it is CCTV footage; meaningless keystrokes; spam emails. We have more than solved the problem of transmitting and recording information. In fact, we've solved it so well there's a new kind of problem: not information poverty, but information overload. The question now isn't about how we can produce or transmit more information – the question is how we will find what matters?

We don't always need more information. Instead, value today lies in better curating information. This is a lesson tech companies have rapidly learned, but one whose ramifications extend far beyond the world of digital media.

Why 'curation'?

Why has curation become a buzzword? Why does it provoke as much eye rolling as enthusiasm? Once the preserve of a few specialists, curation is now applied to practically everything. Music festivals, shops and shopping malls, websites of all kinds, the news, TED conferences, venture capital portfolios, gala openings, dinner parties, music playlists, vacations, personal identities, fashion shows and wine lists all claim to be curated. Curation is ubiquitous.

We're all curators now, whether 'curating' our look, our mini-break, our TV on a night in ... Reporter and investor Robert Scoble calls curation 'the next $1bn opportunity'. Barack Obama is called the 'chief curator' of George W. Bush's legacy, while in very different contexts the power broker of Russian politics and the Italian Prime Minister are also called curators. Pep Guardiola was called the curator of Bayern Munich FC. Leonardo DiCaprio is the curator of a charity art auction. Director Danny Boyle is the curator of a film festival. Satya Nadella, the Microsoft CEO, wants to be the curator of a company culture. A glamorous restaurant doesn't just have a chef, it has a 'chef-curator' (Nuno Mendes of the Chiltern

Firehouse, in case you were wondering). The *Financial Times* has a Head of Curated Content while *Wired* magazine refers to a genetic scientist as 'curator of the gene pool'.

Over the past few years I've collected examples of newspapers or celebrities talking about curation: Gwyneth Paltrow curating her website Goop, Kim Kardashian curating a fashion store, Madonna curating Art for Freedom. David Bowie, Pharrell Williams and Johnny Depp have all curated one thing or another. In *Doctor Who*, one of the baddies is known simply as The Curator. The list continues … open a newspaper or magazine and you will find someone referring to curation.

What's going on?

It's rarely made clear what curation means in these contexts. Many in its traditional heartlands aren't happy. One top commentator on curation sees it as 'absurd' that the word should be so used.[4] Another famous curator argues that this new use of the word 'has to be resisted'.[5] Yet another argues that more commercial uses are 'corrupting' the original sense.[6] In general the art and museum worlds look on in horror as a prized concept is ripped from their grasp.

At the same time, many of us feel an instinctive distrust. There seems something frivolous and self-indulgent about the idea. The comedian Stewart Lee calls it a 'dead word'.[7] CNBC thought it was one of our most overused words.[8] The spoof news website The Daily Mash ran a brilliant article about someone curating their tea, getting to the heart of the pompousness that so often seems to accompany curation ('The tea-making process is an ongoing dialogue between water, milk and tea that requires careful curation').[9] In a *Press Gazette* survey of PR terms journalists hate, 'curate' was beaten only by the delightful trinity of 'reach out', 'growth-hacking' and 'onboarding'.[10] Caught between some of the more bizarre uses it's popularly ascribed and those in the art world who shun its new-found popularity, curation presents an easy target: something for people in self-appointed 'creative hubs' like Williamsburg, the Mission District, East London and East Berlin; a self-serving and self-regarding art world reject adding false dignity to a host of everyday practices.

We should change how we think about curation; challenge our easy assumptions and knee-jerk reactions that curation is nothing more than a hipsterish accoutrement. Dismissing or mocking it is all too simple – and tempting. But ... under the surface curation is powerful and interesting – an approach that recognises how our problems have evolved. We've missed too much of this big picture because we've been distracted by the conceptual legacy and all those celebrities. We get that curation is a buzzword. Happens in art galleries and the more modish eateries of San Francisco. But then we ignore the context. We don't join the dots, for example, between the term curation, the wider business environment, the new insights from psychology, science, economics and management, the impact of technologies of all kinds.

The more I looked the more it was apparent that the things we call curation were happening long before we called them that. If we think that curation spread from the art world, we've got it backwards. It was taking place already, in a bewildering variety of contexts. We just started calling those things curation because it was a handy word. Whether we accept it as curation or not, the businesses, trends and activities described here are playing an increasingly prominent role in the economy. Applying the word 'curation', let us catch up with a changing reality. It was a way of encapsulating a newly prominent idea or a loose set of processes and activities. Despite being stretched, scorned and, in the minds of some, misappropriated, for many others it just *worked*.

My view on the word itself is that although we can take

or leave it, the horse has bolted. People already use it in new ways. Language isn't static; words evolve and take on new meanings every day. Rather than resist, we should accept that curation is now a broader and deeper term than it used to be, with relevance beyond the limited contexts of either celebrity stunts or gallery exhibitions. The genie is out of the bottle, and however much we may scoff at what seems like a ridiculous poseur, it's not going to be put back.

Why curation? Because, despite careless and excessive use, it is the best we have. We need to reclaim 'curation' from those who curate their dog's breakfast. It might not always sit right, but curation is the best word available for this ensemble of activities that goes beyond selecting and arranging to blend with refining and displaying, explaining and simplifying, categorising and organising. Those that decry the spread of curation are already much too late: it's at work everywhere, from the art gallery to the data centre, from the supermarket to our favourite social networks. It's to these newer and at times more controversial uses that this book is directed.

A different kind of problem

Curation is misunderstood because it's rarely looked at in its full context. Curation became a buzzword because it was one answer to a new set of problems; the problems caused by having too much. For two hundred years we've lived in a world that champions creativity, pursues growth above all else, relentlessly increases productivity and always wants more: more people, more resources, more data, more everything.

With each passing day though, it's becoming clear we're overloaded. In the West we have everything that previous generations hoped for. Clothes at Primark available for less than a cup of coffee (itself, of course, once a product only for the wealthy). The world's information at our fingertips. All the gadgets and toys we want. We can raise mountains, go into space and generate nuclear power. Yet we don't know what, or who, to believe; worst of all, we are seemingly incapable of action in the face of our systemic problems from financial crises to environmental catastrophe.

We no longer go hungry, but we face an obesity pandemic. We generate more data but also more noise. We're constantly entertained, but ever more distracted. We are richer, but more indebted, and we are working longer hours. Excess choice is a daily feature of our lives. I used to go shopping at a hypermarket in France so large staff were equipped with rollerskates to get from one end to another. While this profusion of choice may have started with fast-moving consumer goods, really it is the oxygen of capitalism; media, utilities like power and water, our romantic partners, jobs, pensions. Areas like health, finance (insurance, pensions) and education – which carry enormous personal risks and responsibilities – are now based on market choice. In all of them, options have proliferated faster than consumer understanding. Businesses need to find a new way of working.

Luckily, the nature of this problem suggests an answer – we are already seeing a revolution in how we approach value. If value, pecuniary or otherwise, used to be about primary production, now, in a world no longer dominated by scarcity, it has shifted. Value today lies in solving these problems, cutting down complexity. Curation is about how we build companies and economies built on *less* – more tailored, more appropriate – choice. This is the key difference and the big underlying trend that we are still only beginning to understand.

Curation answers the question of how we live in a world where problems are often about having too much. Acts of selecting, refining and arranging to add value – my working definition of curation – help us overcome overload. This book highlights numerous places in which this simple but forceful definition of curation is increasingly felt: in art and on the web, yes, but also in retail and manufacturing, communications and media, even policy and finance.

It's a way of changing ingrained attitudes to production and creativity in order to allow for a more sustainable future. It's the next roadmap for moving to higher-value areas. It's gone from an afterthought to a prime USP. A response to 'too much' that says let's not just stop, let's not wait for a magical fix, but let's make the job of sorting it valuable in and of itself.

A new generation of web curators and engineers are fixing the problems of information overload. Rather than just putting out more product, mature creative industries are becoming more choosy as a growth strategy. Retail businesses are realising that their value lies in curation, not in stocking and shifting. Consumers don't blindly take whatever's on offer. They want to be curators of their lives. We have built a vast services and financialised economy based on this principle, only we don't realise it. Banks are once again becoming curators of our money, not gamblers with it.

All of this takes place amidst a series of social, business, economic and cultural transformations one commentator has labelled 'the Great Disruption'.[11] They include the advent of a new post-digital era of information abundance, pervasive connectivity and the blurring of offline and online environments; the substantial movement of our culture, business and relationships into this new realm; changing patterns of production and distribution; new economies centred on experiences, luxury goods and high-end services and, above it all, a craving for simplicity. We've heard about them so often it's become a cliché; but it doesn't mean they aren't real.

Curating, doing less, whittling down excess, works because it follows major trends in the economy and argues that market forces will push them on. We have been conditioned for hundreds of years to put primacy on activities and businesses that create more stuff. Where business used to want more, now they should want better. Abundance was the goal, now it's the problem to be solved. When the problems change, so should we.

And we are. Many businesses from bars to banks are already in the business of doing less. But it's only just beginning. We solved the problem of insufficiency, only to find it was replaced by abundance. As a result we'll have to curate far more effectively. In order to prosper we'll start to appreciate the value of less, of simplicity in a complex world. Understood and used correctly, curation can be an essential principle over the coming decades. It will allow organisations to unlock stores of value they never knew they had in saturated markets and a ferociously competitive climate.

About the book

This book discusses both curation as we are familiar with it, and that more hidden, longer-term view. It sees them both as part of the same equation. It wants to get beyond the debates about what is or isn't or should or shouldn't be curation; there have been plenty of those, and meanwhile, people carry on using the word regardless. To understand business and culture in the context of too much. To see how expertise and taste have become new currencies.

Several caveats are in order. This book is by no means comprehensive. Much is left out for the sake of space. It won't convince everyone. For some, the whole idea will be a debasement of an elevated practice from the get-go. For others it will be the height of pretension to even touch upon the subject. I happen to believe neither is the most useful or interesting path, but readily accept both views will remain.

Nor do I in the slightest see the view of curation offered here as complete and definitive – it's only in the last forty or so years that even art exhibitions were curated, so we really are at the beginning of where this idea is going. Curation is still contested, uncertain and up for grabs. This book is part of a conversation, a series of suggestions that I hope are instructive and useful. Technology and business alike move with unprecedented speed. Today's commonplace wisdom becomes yesterday's naivety. Making predictions is asking for trouble; I am looking for the tendencies.

With all that in mind, the structure is as follows:

Part I looks at how we ended up with problems of too much. It examines the engines of our rising productivity. Digital technology is the most obvious example of abundance today, but in fact most goods are, in some contexts, abundant – material products as well as informational ones. This is the result of a Long Boom beginning with the Industrial Revolution and continuing over the last two hundred years. Beyond that Part I looks at two symptoms of this abundance – the idea of overload, when too much of a good thing causes problems, and the creativity myth, our unwavering faith that creativity is always a positive.

Part II discusses the history of the term curation and looks to define its contemporary use in more detail. Why do I think selection in particular, but also concepts like arrangement, are so significant, the core principles of curation today? What do they mean, and how can we understand them in the context outlined in Part I? Along the way I look at related questions – how the Internet transformed curation and the impact made by algorithmic models of selection; the changing nature of retail; and then a host of 'curation effects' – both positive side effects and principles of curation. Understanding these principles hints at how curation can be seen as part of the arsenal deployed to combat overload.

Part III surveys prominent examples of businesses, organisations and individuals curating today. Given the sheer range of such activity it makes no claims to be encyclopaedic; instead I want to highlight interesting examples and tease out consequences. It also introduces some refinements and a new vocabulary of curation – implicit and explicit curation, thick and thin curation, a broadcast model and a consumer-curated model of media.

Running a shop or a newspaper has always involved what we now call curation. What has changed is that curation has become ever more central to the activities and identity of those organisations. Hidden from view, even at times to those curating, it has become essential to their bottom lines. How much is curation already within and integral to our business model without us fully acknowledging that fact? How has the world changed so that we need new kinds of cultural and business intermediaries?

We already live in a curated world. Walk around not just Paris or New York, but Buenos Aires, Bangalore and Beijing and you will be surrounded by curation; the shops, galleries, hotels, restaurants of course, but also homes and workspaces, work itself and leisure: if you are lucky enough to be even moderately wealthy in global terms, careful, expert selection is everywhere around you wherever you live. And whoever you are, on the Internet you cannot help but be confronted by a curated offering – of things to read, photos to look at, videos to watch, apps to download or people to follow – and to be a curator yourself in turn.

The Japanese have a word – *tsundoku* – for the act of

constantly buying more books but never actually reading them. Most of us have been there. It's this kind of feeling that is now spreading at a societal level. Typically the Japanese have an answer for *tsundoku*. In Tokyo's Ginza district there is a bookshop that sells only one book at a time.[12] It's a start.

Patterns of selection and arrangement are, gradually, sometimes quietly and sometimes obviously, becoming more prevalent parts of our lives. Ignoring that isn't an option. Mastering it means mastering the context of the twenty-first century.

Part I
THE PROBLEM

First World Problems

Remember #firstworldproblems? Complaints on social media about a minor problem – the difficulty of choosing between the Scottish smoked salmon and the USDA prime steak, the stress of getting dressed for a night out, the affliction of a fundamentally worthless gadget going momentarily wrong – were suffixed with the hashtag #firstworldproblems. It soon became a craze. Buzzfeed catalogued its favourites, which included such gems as 'I can't eat ice cream in my convertible as my hair keeps whipping into it' and 'I spent too long taking a picture of my plate and now my food is cold'. Ah yes, problems indeed. The phrase became so commonplace that it even found its way into the Oxford English Dictionary.

Of course, first world problems are both embarrassing and tongue in cheek. The notion recognises that, for much of the planet, we no longer have to contend with problems such as famine, disease and war, as many still do. It's an attempt to forestall guilt about some of the undoubted nuisances of the modern world, a deflection tactic, the perfect way of balancing those competing contemporary demands of irony and registering annoyance via social media. Now, #firstworldproblems are the faux whining of the overprivileged who know, deep down, they've won the birth lottery. But there is nonetheless an interesting angle.

For many, the situation has changed. In an age of abundance, #firstworldproblems quite simply *are* the problems some people face. The question with first world problems is, of course, not whether they are ridiculous and self-indulgent – that much should go without saying. The question is how we ended up in a world where, even in jest, these problems could exist at all.

This is uncomfortable but important. It doesn't mean that deep-seated issues to do with poverty and conflict have gone away, although in large parts of the world they are receding, it simply recognises that, although we are living through an age of Great Recessions, austerity and stagnation, it is often the problems of too much, not too little, that define life in the West. It doesn't always feel that way – after all, who doesn't want, even need, more money? – but the reality is that compared to our ancestors we live amidst superabundance.

The psychologist Abraham Maslow's hierarchy of needs makes the point. Maslow argued (see Figure 1) that our needs formed a pyramid.

Each layer in the pyramid rests on those below. So once we've taken care of basic physiological requirements like food and water, we worry about a different set of concerns: are we safe from violence? Do we have the ability to sustain our livelihoods and our health? Then at the top of the pyramid we come to the higher-level functions, self-esteem and making the most of our lives. Do we have control? Can we express ourselves? What Maslow's pyramid indicates is that, in the twenty-first-century West and many other parts of the globe, we aren't principally worried about the lower levels of the pyramid. This isn't to say life is perfect and we can forget

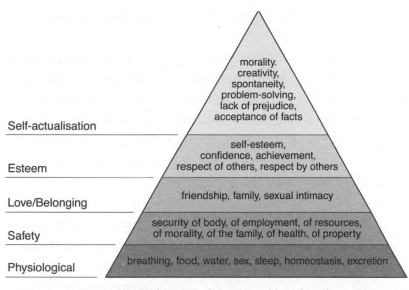

Figure 1. Abraham Maslow's hierarchy of needs

about them, just to point out that for large swathes of the population they are taken for granted. Day-to-day problems have gone upstream.

This then is the biggest irony of all about #firstworldproblems. It's all a big joke and shows quite how vacuous we have become. Yet it also reflects something significant. That problems really have changed. That more is not always more. That there is a tipping point after which simply adding in extra no longer works. This matters. First because for the last two hundred or so years we have engineered society and businesses to keep growing; to keep adding more. Second because we are now reaching overload, when incremental additions cause more harm than good. Lastly it is important as we have an idea, whether in business, the arts or our general lives, that creativity is always a net positive. Perhaps it is. If, however, problems arise from creating more, aren't there grounds to question that assumption?

Let's go back to the tsunami of data we identified in the Introduction. For most of history information was incredibly difficult to find, but even so people still felt there was too much. Plato thought writing would make us lazy thinkers. Seneca the Elder thought books were a distraction and there were too many of them. In 1860 a young doctor called James Crichton Browne spoke to the Royal Medical Society of Edinburgh in language we would recognise today: 'We live in an age of electricity, of railways, of gas, and of velocity in thought and action. In the course of one brief month more impressions are conveyed to our brains than reached those of our ancestors in the course of years, and our mentalising machines are called upon for a greater amount of fabric than was required of our grandfathers in the course of a lifetime.' The roots of information overload run deep.

Yet if people have often felt there was too much data in the past, nothing compares with now. The amount of digital data is doubling every three years or so, growing more than four times faster than the world economy, and the rate of change is constantly increasing. By the end of 2013 there were 1,200 exabytes of stored data in the world. Less than 2 per cent of this was non-digital, whereas in 2000 75 per cent of information was non-digital.[1] As Big Data specialists Kenneth Cukier and Viktor Mayer-Schönberger argue, this is equivalent to the entire USA being covered in fifty-two layers of encyclopaedias. If they were transferred to CD and stacked up the pile would stretch to the moon five times over. Each person alive now has 320 times as much information available to them as in the whole Library of Alexandria which would have so concerned Seneca. If James Crichton Browne worried about information overload in 1860, it's difficult to sense what he would make of it today.

Our technology is a vast machine for creating data. It comes from a huge variety of places – not just tweets, pictures, videos on YouTube, but also sensors (such as humidity sensors in vineyards or temperature sensors in cars), web clicks, company accounts, health data, mobile phone geolocation, streams of CCTV images. The world is being 'datafied', turned into raw data one bit at a time. In practical terms this is both a problem and an opportunity. A problem because all this excess data is unusable in its raw form. An opportunity as companies are learning to process and harness this data into actionable insights.

To get a sense of the problem side of the equation I went to speak to a trader at a major US bank, who had been introduced through a friend. Let's call her Lisa. Dark-haired, expensively accessorised and quick-talking, Lisa gets up every day at 5.30 a.m. and immediately checks her iPhone (back in the day it was a BlackBerry). So begins the overload. She then reads through emails and instant messages (she uses WhatsApp to talk to friends and family), checks any financial data that's come through overnight and scans the news. However, it's at her desk that the overload becomes fully apparent. She has eight screens, like many traders. 'At first I thought it was great,' she tells me, sipping a fizzy water in an anonymous Starbucks. 'This was the real deal. This was trading, it's on the frontline.' Bloomberg fed through real-time market data, emails flooded in, analysts' reports jammed her inbox, the ticker feeds of market movements sped before her eyes. The sheer amount of data the average trader has access to on a second-by-second basis is extraordinary. Moreover they are under great pressure to respond to this data correctly and at lightning speed. Automated trading programmes are able to instantaneously comprehend and act on the total available set of market data. The

NASDAQ stock exchange alone sees over two billion shares traded every day.

The pressure increases. 'The main thing I feel now is . . .' she pauses, thinking for the right word, 'paralysis. I guess that's it, paralysis. So much going on, so much to take in that you don't know where to look anymore. Knowing what to pay attention to is my job, but it seems to get more difficult.' She hasn't told anyone else on the trading floor she is seeing a therapist to try and overcome these problems – 'It's not like it's Wolf of Wall Street but it is a tough place.' She strikes me as being hard as nails. Our brains today are roughly the same as those of our ancestors on the savannah. They are designed to hold about seven pieces of information in our working memory at any one time. Beyond that we hit cognitive capacity. With eight screens overflowing with complex information, each catching Lisa's eye, each potentially important, it's no wonder she or anyone else struggles to keep up. And the long days take their toll. Lisa is cash rich in a way few of us ever will be. But she is chronically time poor. Work swallows her entire day and most weekends. Forget about taking a real vacation.

So, how do we tie these strands together? In many respects Lisa is the embodiment of #firstworldproblems. She has a large salary, an enviable apartment and a high-powered job. Yet she is breaking down at work amidst the pressurised flood of data and two relationships ended because she doesn't have the time. No one is crying into their coffee about Lisa's problems and nor should they. But as James Crichton Browne recognised, 'our mentalising machines are called upon for a greater amount of fabric'. This is where the value of curation starts to become clear. In a world of too much data, having the right data is valuable. In a world where we don't have any time, choosing the right thing to do is valuable.

In a world of too much, selecting, finding and cutting down is valuable.

In the context of excess, curation isn't just a buzzword. It makes sense of the world.

But how did we get here in the first place?

1

The Long Boom in Everything

When he died in 1792 Richard Arkwright, the son of a tailor who couldn't afford to send him to school, was the richest non-aristocrat in Britain. His fortune of £500,000 was immense by any standards – but in an age of low social mobility, virtually unheard of. How did this humble Preston-born man generate so much wealth? In answering that question we also begin to answer where the problems of too much came from. As much as any individual, Arkwright was responsible for the Industrial Revolution, an event which fundamentally changed the direction of history and explains the roots of modern excess.

Textiles are a prominent part of any pre-industrial economy – everyone needs clothes and they are labour-intensive to produce. Buying a shirt before the advent of industrial technology was hugely expensive, costing at least $3,500 (or £2,500) in today's money compared with the few dollars we could now spend at a budget store.[1] The problem for consumers was this – home-grown English cotton was high-quality and relatively cheap. But the labour costs of spinning the cotton fibres into threads were prohibitive. The result was that clothing and other textiles were scarce and expensive. This, then, was the general condition – scarcity defined people's lives. One shirt entailed a significant outlay, with the according ramifications for a household's annual budget.

Arkwright was among those who saw an opportunity. James Hargreaves, a weaver and carpenter from Lancashire, saw his spinning wheel fall over, and, watching it spin on its side, realised that if a spindle could move from vertical to horizontal and back again, it could do the job much more quickly than a human. This insight led to the development by 1764 of the spinning jenny – a seminal instance of machine power augmenting human labour which kick-started a productivity revolution. What's more, by lining up several of these machines in a row, you could increase overall production.

Arkwright himself took a different tack. A born entrepreneur, he sank an enormous amount of money, £12,000, into developing his tech, patenting the spinning frame in 1769 and the carding engine in 1775. The water frame, as the spinning frame was also known, was powered by river water and used a system of rollers to spin its basic material. It could produce a strong twist for the warp threads, which the jenny could not. But it wasn't just the technology that Arkwright envisioned; he also needed a new system of organisation – the factory – to fulfil its potential. At Cromford in Derbyshire from 1771 Arkwright brought all the elements together – the new technology for which he had taken out patents; an army of workers; a factory specially built with machinery in mind, designed to facilitate maximum productivity in design and situation; and a working practice that was dictated not by natural light or the rhythms of the day but by machines (from 1772 they ran twenty-four hours a day). Arkwright even built housing and bussed in workers, thereby creating the template for the industrialised city. The spinning frame was simple to use and manufactured a high-quality product. By 1785 the factory had been coupled with steam power and the Industrial Revolution was about to hit full swing.

You can still visit Cromford today and see the heavy bricks and orderly ranks of square windows spread throughout the complex. Compared with anything that went before it was the cutting edge. Although it feels quaint now, this was a hard place pioneering new forms of organisation and technology. This grey and huddled ensemble changed the world.

The impact on textiles was dramatic. In the twenty-seven years from 1760 to 1787 imports of raw, unspun cotton leapt from 2.5 million pounds to 22 million pounds. By 1837, when Britain was the workshop of the world and Manchester was becoming 'Cottonopolis', imports of cotton had ballooned to 366 million pounds. As the volumes went up so the prices came down, from 38 shillings per pound in 1786 to just 7 shillings per pound in 1807.

Arkwright became one of the richest men in Britain by doing something new. For most of history, economies had grown slowly. Technology changed at a glacial pace measured in lifetimes. It was Arkwright and those like him, many of them – including industrialists like Matthew Boulton and technologists like James Watt – members of the Lunar Society of Birmingham, an informal but prolific group of likeminded inventors, scientists and business executives, who transformed one of the drivers of the modern world: productivity.

Arkwright combined three things. First he harnessed energy in new ways, converting for his own purposes the water power of streams and then the stored energy in coal. Humankind's capability was immediately improved. By using fossil fuels our capacity for action was transformed. One barrel of oil contains energy equivalent to 25,000 man hours of work. Given that we have used 944 billion barrels of oil since 1870, that represents an awful lot of work, and it was around this time that the potential of energy resources began to be systematic- ally exploited.[2] Then Arkwright changed the nature of work. For better or for worse, work became regimented, tightly controlled and process-driven. Tasks were divided, rather than lumped together. Lastly Arkwright applied principles of science and engineering to the mass production of objects. Automation and technology would ramp up the productive capacity of the firm.

The Industrial Revolution was a productivity revolution. And it was this change in productivity that meant that shirts could go from being a major purchase in the eighteenth cen- tury to a trivial one in the twenty-first. Material objects which had always been scarce started to become widely available. The Long Boom in everything had begun.

The very short answer to the question of how we arrived at a situation where we have too much of everything is that productivity has been growing for over two hundred years. Every year we can make more than the year before. Eventually things accumulate. Eventually the scale tips from scarcity to excess. A new set of problems – and opportunities – arises. Marx and Engels described this change relatively early on and clearly saw its magnitude. The Industrial Revolution

> created more massive and more colossal productive forces than all preceding generations together. Subjection of Nature's forces to man, machinery, application of chemistry to industry and agriculture, steam-navigation, railways, electric telegraphs, clearing of whole continents for cultivation, canalisation of rivers, whole populations conjured out of the ground – what earlier century had even

a presentiment that such productive forces slumbered in the lap of social labour?[3]

Like James Crichton Browne, these mid-Victorians would no doubt have been astonished at the continued transformations since their own time.

Technology has always played a crucial role in change. It was the spinning jenny and the steam engine which kick-started the Industrial Revolution. However the less well known second Industrial Revolution, one hundred years after the first, again underscores how technology constantly transforms productivity. A new set of technologies and the businesses pioneering them would once again reorder the world.

The Bessemer process and then the Siemens-Martin process gave the world steel, and in turn a host of new applications from bridges to skyscrapers. Innovation in this area continued for decades. In 1920, for example, it took three worker hours to produce a ton of steel. By 2000 this was just 0.003 worker hours per ton.[4]

Then came the electrification of factories and goods. Emil Rathenau's AEG pioneered electrical engineering, as did Werner von Siemens, who produced telegraph technology, dynamos, electric trains and light bulbs. Siemens created the self-excited generator – a dynamo that converts mechanical energy to electrical energy. This meant that steam- and water-driven turbines could produce significant amounts of cheap electricity, which could power factories and other innovations in a virtuous circle. Companies like Siemens had their great American counterparts like Edison's General Electric. If one invention, alongside the Bessemer process, could be said to have ignited the second Industrial Revolution, this generator was it.

If Arkwright had applied science, the second Industrial Revolution did so in a far more focused and systematic way. Chemicals and synthetic dyes, for example, were propelled by German firms like BASF and Bayer, who made enormous strides pursuing their own research agendas. By 1914 German firms had nearly 90 per cent of the world market in dyestuffs. A multitude of other technical improvements were happening around the same time: the creation of dynamite; the use of rubber and lubricants to ease and speed up manufacturing; the rollout of nitrogen fertilisers.

There was also a boom in transportation and infrastructure. The 1880s witnessed more rail construction than any decade before or since. Mass adoption of steam shipping and the telegraph shrank the planet. If the first Industrial Revolution had launched the Long Boom, it was the technological innovations of the second – the use of electromagnetism, say – that turbocharged it. A raft of technological improvements led to a clear step change in productivity over those years. The early Industrial Revolution saw productivity growth climb to 0.5 per cent per year. This may sound small, but compared with centuries of near-stagnation it was unprecedented. From 1870 to the present day, however, global productivity growth has been 1.7 per cent per year. According to Jeffrey Kaplan, US productivity per hour worked doubled between 1948 and 1991 and rose a further 30 per cent from 1991 to 2006.[5] The use of technology made the difference.

Since the 1970s there has been some debate about what economists call the secular decline of productivity growth. Put simply, some commentators argue that productivity has stopped growing. As we will see, this does not mean the world economy has stopped growing. Far from it. Nor is it even certain to be the case. Part of the issue is that as productivity grows in manufacturing, so the overall position of manufacturing shrinks: one factory which used to employ a hundred people now only needs ten. Productivity improvements are harder to achieve in services. The classic example is hairdressing – hairdressers can only give so many haircuts, whereas thanks to technological improvements factories can usually squeeze out additional productivity gains.

Regardless of whether productivity has stalled – and there is evidence that digital technology and the Internet have given it a considerable boost – we are still witness to productive capacity on an awe-inspiring scale. Today the cumulative effects of all those technological improvements are jaw-dropping. Take the Taiwanese manufacturing firm Foxconn.

If you own an iPhone or a BlackBerry, have played on a PlayStation or an Xbox or read on a Kindle, chances are it will have been assembled by Foxconn, quite possibly at their (in)famous Longhua campus in the Chinese city of Shenzhen. If you want to see the frontline of productivity today, this hulking, walled presence is it. Calling it a factory is a stretch. Really Longhua is a kind of city, a sprawling 2.5 square kilometre powerhouse employing up to 300,000 people, housing not just assembly halls but dormitories, kitchens, food halls, banks, bookstores, gyms, playing fields and even an onsite McDonald's.[6] Everything at Longhua is about maximising efficiency and productivity. Foxconn is a manufacturing behemoth, China's largest private employer with 1.4 million employees spread across fourteen sites. Its largest factory at Zhengzhou in Henan province can reportedly make 500,000 iPhones a day in addition to other product lines. Producing millions upon millions of complex consumer goods a year, Foxconn has revenues of above $130bn. The human cost can be high and has not escaped notice.

Yet this is only the beginning. Now the colourful chairman Terry Guo has announced a campaign to build 'one million robots'. Hiring a team of MIT robotics researchers in 2006, he has set about building the Foxbot, a robotic arm which will theoretically be capable of undertaking the difficult assembly tasks in which Foxconn specialises. This being Foxconn he wants one million of them; one million tireless, precise, incredibly fast robots building phones and tablets twenty-four hours a day. That means a lot of phones and tablets.

Not everything has gone to plan. So far each Foxbot costs around $20–25,000 to produce and there are only around 30,000 of them.[7] They are only working on a few lines – reports suggest HP's ink cartridges and the iPhone 6 may be among them. They will not replace the human workforce but augment it, reducing costs and increasing productivity. Foxconn pushed the old factory model as far as it would go, building the biggest factories on earth. Like Arkwright or Siemens before them though, they are using technology to boost productivity and profit, the motors of industrialisation. By using new technology Foxconn shows that the secular decline in productivity is not a foregone conclusion. As a leading part of one of the great stories of our time – the opening of the Chinese economy and its vast productive capacity – they are also part of the wider story of how technology has pushed productivity; and how productivity has produced abundance.

The economist W. Brian Arthur argues, 'the economy is an expression of its technologies.'[8] In other words the character, growth and structure of an economy are dependent on its technologies, which goes some way to explaining our present condition. For the past two hundred and fifty years our technologies have been directed at boosting productivity. To producing more. More goods, more food, more data, more stuff.

And the story doesn't end there.

*

Danica May Camacho was born on Sunday 30 October 2011 at Manila's Jose Fabella Memorial Hospital. She was another healthy, happy baby; another human miracle. Except unlike most newborn babies, Danica came into the world amidst the flash of photographers and the world's media. Danica May was, according to the UN, the seven billionth human being alive on planet Earth. By way of congratulations she received a woolly hat and a scholarship fund, although they could equally have gone to another of the estimated 220,000 babies born that day. Twelve years earlier Adnan Nevic was born in Bosnia-Herzegovina. He had the distinction of being the six billionth human being. In twelve years, one billion people had been added to the net total of humans, at a time of rising life expectancy. It's not just productivity that has been growing – so has humanity.

The sheer number of human beings alive has an enormous impact on our economic capacity. Humans at once generate both demand and supply. The more of us there are alive, the more we can consume and produce; the more choice there is and the more our resources are, in theory, stretched. If productivity and technology power abundance, so too does the sheer abundance of people. Around four or five thousand years ago the total population of humanity was still in the tens of millions. By 1700 CE it had climbed to around 600 million, with the one billion figure arriving by around 1820. So it took all of human history up to 1820 before a billion people were alive at one time.

Thereafter things sped up. The geographer Danny Dorling argues that 1851 was the pivotal year, after which the growth rate in the population shot up thanks to rapid industrialisation.[9] It took only 106 years (in 1926) to reach the second billion, hundreds and hundreds of times quicker than the time it took to reach one billion. The third billion was

attained in 1960, just thirty-four years later, while the fourth
billion took another fifteen years, coming in 1975; the fifth
billion took thirteen years, arriving in 1988. Six billion then
took twelve years, coming in 2000; seven billion took a further twelve years. During the twentieth century countries like
China or Iran at times pushed the limit of human reproduc-
tivity, their populations growing at 4 per cent a year, close to
the biological maximum. This rate of growth is unsustain-
able and there is a large body of evidence to show that the
rate of growth has been slowing since the 1970s – but we
are still feeling the lag. In countries like Japan, Germany and
Italy the slowdown has even turned into a reverse, balancing
some of the extraordinary growth seen in places like sub-
Saharan Africa. The eighth billionth human will probably
be born sometime in 2026, fifteen years after Danica May
Camacho. Although forecasting population in the long term
is beset with difficulty, many demographers think it likely
that the population will reach nine to ten billion by the end
of the century.

While indicating a slowdown, that is still an awful lot of
people. Most of us have moved from living in societies of at
most a few million – and they were a rarity – to living in cities
of millions or tens of millions; in societies and international
blocs much larger than that; and, to an unprecedented degree,
in a single globalised world of billions. Quantitatively speaking the difference is obvious, but it also creates a qualitative
difference. The scale and range of human activity is now far
beyond our grasp, changing the scope of the economy, the
diversity of things on offer and the pressure on resources. All
those people have aspirations and needs that drive, power and
tax the world.

Technological development and population explosion are
obvious manifestations of how we have created conditions of

too much. It's not just about people or technology though, but about the way the two interact.

Take the humble pin. Adam Smith, the great eighteenth-century economist, was extremely interested in this 'very trifling manufacture', as he called it. For Smith pins showed the key to rising wealth by demonstrating the value of the division of labour. Smith saw that by breaking tasks down into small components you could improve them more easily. On a societal level it was much better to have one person focused on making candles and another on making tables, rather than everyone producing their own candles and tables. Moreover, even within an activity like making a pin, you could break the process down into stages to increase efficiency, boost productivity and generate more profits.

Smith argued that discrete tasks could be improved more easily than a bundle of interlinked processes. Workers could become quicker and better. Transition costs of moving from one activity to another could be eliminated. Above all, discrete tasks were much more amenable to automation, as Arkwright, Smith's contemporary, was already showing. One worker alone could produce perhaps twenty pins a day, navigating a series of fiddly tasks in a tricky sequence. But dividing the production into various sub-processes meant that a ten-person unit could produce 48,000 pins in a day – 4,800 per worker, a vast increase. This was the power of the division of labour and technology.

Economist Ha-Joon Chang records what happened next. In 1832, forty-two years after Smith died, the father of computing, Charles Babbage, studied pin manufacture and estimated 8,000 pins could now be produced per worker per day, a near doubling in productivity thanks to improvements in technology *and* workflow.[10] By 1980 a study estimated that modern factories could produce 800,000 pins per worker per day: a 100-fold increase in productivity over 150 years. Today that figure might be much higher thanks to ever-increasing automation. Here then is where technology meets organisation. Now imagine this applied across almost every area of endeavour and we are starting to see the formula behind the Long Boom.

In the two hundred years after Arkwright built his factory and Smith sketched the division of labour and the foundations of capitalism, methods of organising to increase productivity and wealth underwent continuous refinement. In the early twentieth century Fordism suggested a production-line approach to manufacturing that was far more efficient than the stop-and-go process that came before. Car production stayed on the frontline with, for example, Toyota's *Kaizen* method of continuous improvement and just-in-time logistics. Taylorism sought to make a science of working, supposedly maximising the output of office workers. Today executives and engineers in Silicon Valley spend large amounts of time analysing their own productivity and that of others, the better to build tools and workflows that can be rolled out in-house and offered as services.

Adam Smith laid down the 'Goldilocks' formula of the Long Boom, the elixir of classical economics: technology creates productivity improvements, which then create economic growth, which leads to more demand, more production and further technological change, and so on. Build this on the back of a constantly rising population and an increased emphasis on getting the most out of things and you have the recipe for sustained expansion. Of course there were and are many other elements to economic growth. Access to energy and capital for example, and the infrastructure around them, have been critical to growth of all kinds. Geography has played a role as well, although some countries without natural resources like Japan have become rich and some with them, like the Democratic Republic of Congo, have ended up poor. Rising wealth meant rising demand and lively markets for all those new goods and services. At the heart of the story, though, is how new technologies and an ever-growing population drive growth. We still see the effects today. China has grown so fast because it has played catch-up by quickly adopting Western technology and methods.

Quantifying the scale of the Long Boom is not easy. We can look at any number of measurements – population is one, productivity another. The size of the global economy is useful as well. Angus Maddison was an economist whose life work was studying long-term trends. Growth used to be very slow, only a tiny fraction of 1 per cent a year, if there was any growth at all. During the period from 1000 to 1500 Western Europe only grew as much as it took China six years to grow between 2002 and 2008.[11] From 1820 growth was super-charged and rose at an annual rate of 1 per cent. However this was put in the shade by the 'Golden Age of Capitalism', the *Trente Glorieuses*, the *Wirtschaftswunder* of 1945–1973, when Western European per capita income grew on average at 4.1 per cent each year. Japan and China have experienced even faster periods of growth. Maddison estimates the global economy grew fifteen-fold in the ninety years between 1913 and 2003.[12] The UK government claims that British productivity grew seven-fold over the twentieth century – an impressive result except that productivity growth was even stronger over the same period in France, Germany, Japan and the United States, for example.[13] Despite recessions, depressions, reversals, revolutions, wars, panics, shocks and slumps, more was produced, whether films or food, in almost every year of the last two hundred than in the preceding year. And this clearly translates into ever more consumption. Jeffrey Kaplan cites figures suggesting that US household spending in 2005 was twelve times greater than in 1929, while the spending of those same households on durable goods rose thirty-two times over the same period.[14]

Moreover, despite worries about recessions and productivity gains the Long Boom has not slowed down. Indeed since the fall of the iron and bamboo curtains, when Eastern Europe and China opened their economies, the world economy has been boosted by the biggest growth of the labour force and the widest rollout of technology and technological catch-up ever seen. Not just in those nations but everywhere from Mexico to Brazil, Turkey to Indonesia, industrialisation, productivity boosts and labour increases have been enormous – one estimate suggests 1.7bn workers were added to the global labour force in the years 1980–2010.[15] Workers moved from rural areas to cities, family farms to factories, while – as we saw with Foxconn – those factories and businesses reached new levels of productivity. Over the past century transaction costs associated with communication, transport, logistics and tariff barriers have fallen. Investment capital has grown more liquid and mobile. At various times the Long Boom has been powered by financial engineering: the transition to fiat money from the gold standard with the collapse of the Bretton Woods agreement in 1971; creative monetary policy from then on; expansion of business and consumer credit.

We think of digital technology, among other things, as leading to a huge boost in data storage and data creation. This is true, but it is far from the only way digital technology has transformed conditions of scarcity into conditions of abundance. Digital tech has led to vast supply increases and price falls in communications, access to markets, inventory space, content creation and publishing, software, consumer choice, services and processing power. In each of these areas the past twenty years have seen the dominant trend switch from scarcity to excess. Just think of how Skype has revolutionised international telecommunications. What was once expensive and relatively rare is now routine and virtually free. The so-called sharing economy has unleashed latent supply in areas like short-term rentals (Airbnb), cars and transport (Lyft) and Wi-Fi (Fon).

Data is just one example of how the Internet has completely changed the business environment, but the examples are legion and we have already seen it transform sector after sector which had been optimised for conditions of scarcity. It's also worth remembering that the increase in data and information has deep roots dating back to steam presses, which massively increased print volumes, and before that to one of the earliest industrial technologies, Gutenberg's printing press. The web is still growing. The advent of mobile and wearable technology means digital connectivity is, by the year, becoming more ubiquitous and deeply entrenched across more of the world than ever before. That jejune word 'prosumer' – the idea that consumers are now, thanks to the Internet, producers – may be a commonplace, but it's true. Videos, photos, behavioural data – you name it, it's super-abundant. Productivity growth has always relied on general purpose technologies (GPTs) like steam and electricity to unlock new waves. There is a good argument that computation and connectivity are just such a GPT and that we are currently living through its consequences.

Despite talk of 'secular stagnation' (the generalised slowing of advanced economies) the end is not yet in sight. New technologies including artificial intelligence, the Internet of Things, nanotechnology, bioengineering, super materials like graphene and the widespread rollout of 3D printing (poised to do for objects what the Internet did for data) all mean that we could be entering an even more intensive phase of this centuries-long process. Meanwhile the shale gas revolution and advances in renewables are securing energy supplies. New organisational forms like the collaborative commons and the sharing economy are unlocking new areas of economic growth. Each of these has the potential to turbocharge new areas of growth and upend entire industries. It's at once exhilarating and unsettling.

If computer technologies represent a third Industrial Revolution, here are the seeds of a fourth. Indeed some thinkers believe this new infrastructure could unleash a wave of productivity so radical it leads to the near-elimination of the marginal costs of production – and in the process to the eclipse of capitalism itself.[16] Imagine if every human being on earth had an advanced 3D printer and the materials to go in it. What would happen to the economy then?

Every day we are still experiencing the full force of the Long Boom.

But what does it have to do with curation? And isn't it a good thing? Broadly, yes, the Long Boom is a good thing. Abundance, it should be stressed, is generally positive. It has given us a formerly undreamt-of quality of life. It gives us the luxury of #firstworldproblems. It means that Danica May Camacho, growing up in a still poor country like the Philippines, should have a much better quality of life than her immediate predecessors. At the same time the Long Boom doesn't mean everything's just fine. Far from it. Billions still live in poverty without medicine or enough to eat, let alone a new phone or this season's fashions.

As we will see, the Long Boom's downsides are making themselves felt. This is where curation comes in. The Long Boom is the business and social context of the twenty-first century. Whether we are talking data or human beings, new music or plastic trinkets, the Long Boom means that in many areas of our lives, thanks to a combination of economic and technological growth, scarcity has given way to abundance. In short the Long Boom means that many people have too much of one thing or another, not too little. Without the changes described here, I don't believe we would ever have felt the wider need for a term like curation. It's in this context, beyond its home turf of museums and web content, that curation's full impact is felt.

2

Overload

Lisa's problems (sorry Lisa) get to the nub of the kind of issue we see cropping up again and again at this stage of the Long Boom. 'Information, data is the lifeblood of the markets. You can't really get enough. That's the theory.' But in fact, Lisa and others are increasingly overwhelmed by the data on offer. 'Actually it's not just about the volume, it's about having the right data, the stuff that actually matters, and then knowing how to make the best decisions on it. That right there is how you get ahead.' The system generates more and more information about financial markets, whether pricing data, historical data, company reports, news media analyses or write-ups by in-house analysts and all the tantalising and endless information provided by the $24,000-a-year Bloomberg terminal. Simply adding more data isn't necessarily useful. The signal-to-noise ratio for traders is already out of whack; by adding more, you are probably just increasing the level of noise, which will lead to worse outcomes. Instead the trick is to find the right data, that telling piece of actionable information.

Lisa has what I call an overload problem. Overload

problems are when issues occur not because of having too little, but because of having too much.

Even for the simplest financial transaction there is an excess of data – company reports and earnings statements, share and option prices, supplier information, commodities pricing and executive profiles, the macro outlook for the sector and the wider economy. Each contains reams of detail. Simply adding more creates information overload, not enlightenment. In the context of equities trading, information overload is costly. This is why the future of financial information won't simply be about more supply. It will be about building tools that let financial workers sift the data deluge more effectively. Companies that succeed will find willing customers with huge amounts of money on the line.

This is the impact of overload. If businesses exist to solve problems, not only are we now seeing a trend for more companies to solve overload-style problems, but it's a trend that will intensify in the future.

Information overload is the classic case. Lisa swims in a sea not only of financial data, but of information full stop, the great maelstrom of web content from Buzzfeed to the *Wall Street Journal* and the hundreds of TV channels at home, with Netflix piled on top. Like many of us, her attention span is falling to bits. Concentrating on an email let alone a sustained activity is problematic. But overload-style problems are more widespread than that. Despite having everything, I ask Lisa, is she satisfied with her life, is she happy? There is an awkward silence. 'Yes and no,' she answers. 'It feels ungrateful to say no, as I have so much and I've had amazing opportunities. Materially I'm comfortable. But am I happy? Sometimes I don't know. I never feel like I have the time or the space to enjoy anything.'

Statements like this are increasingly a normal part of overload. Adding more isn't going to work.

If we are familiar with information overload, the futurist James Wallman suggests we are also suffering an overload of possessions. He calls it 'stuffocation'.[1] Having more things was always good – hence the demand that powered the Long Boom. And boy, do we have more things. Americans consume more than three times what they did fifty years ago. In 1991 they each bought thirty-four new items of clothing a year; this had risen to sixty-seven new items by 2007. The average British woman meanwhile buys fifty-eight items of clothing a year, having almost doubled her spending on clothes in the fourteen years from 1990 to 2004. In 1995 Americans bought 188 million toasters and similar devices a year; by 2014 that had risen to 279 million. The Energy Saving Trust estimates that British households increased their ownership of electronic consumer gadgets by a factor of eleven in the period 1970–2009.[2]

Now, Wallman argues, having more simply leads to clutter and excess. It neither serves a purpose nor makes us happy. Wallman looks at a study from UCLA's Center on the Everyday Lives of Families. Their report, *Life at Home in the 21st Century*, found a state of 'material saturation' in the lives of the families they worked with. They had, on average, 139 toys, 438 books and magazines and 39 pairs of shoes each.[3] Even the smallest home in the study had over 2,260 items in three rooms. They concluded that Americans are living amidst 'extraordinary clutter'. Stuffocation even manifests itself physiologically – the more clutter people, especially women, had, the higher their stress levels. All that resource and productivity of the Boom and, after a certain point, all it does is stress us out.

Overload isn't just about information, but what has been called 'affluenza', or the challenge of affluence. A growing body of research looks at how what was once a basic truth – that having more money and more things is an intrinsic good – is at second view more complex. The classic statement of this was made by the economist Richard Easterlin, who came up with the eponymous Easterlin Paradox. Easterlin argued that although rich people are happier, they are not happier in proportion to how much richer they have become. The argument is that beyond a certain point money doesn't contribute to happiness. While many have always suspected this was true, Easterlin aimed to give it a foundation in social science. Precisely where that point lies, if indeed it exists at all, is subject to debate. One study funded by the French government suggested that national rates of happiness do not really increase after a per capita GDP of around $20,000.[4] Within richer countries Wallman suggests that the effect kicks in at around $75,000. Figures from the World Database of Happiness show that since 1973 UK real per capita GDP has almost doubled; but 'happiness' levels have flatlined.[5]

Regardless of the more arcane political debates around the Easterlin Paradox, the mechanisms behind it are easily understood. There is, for example, the idea of the 'hedonic treadmill'. We quickly get used to new possessions or circumstances and the initial buzz and boost they give us wears thin. We tend to have a kind of emotional ground state to which we return regardless of positive or negative influences. What was once a shiny new coat from the glossy boutique eventually becomes the worn out old coat languishing in the hall. Novelty and excess become the norm and no longer excite us. Moreover, all this wealth increases pressure to keep up with the Joneses. Your Ford, impressive enough last year, loses its lustre now your neighbour owns a Mercedes.

This is the nature of the positional goods which increasingly dominate the economy – goods not purchased for their utility so much as what they say about us. 'Snob goods', for example, are bought for the claims they make about our taste. This might be a designer coat but it might be, say, education. Parents don't just send their children to Eton for the education, but for what it says about them socially. Veblen goods, named after the economist Thorstein Veblen who coined the phrase 'conspicuous consumption', buck the normal laws of economics and get more desirable as they get more expensive. (Traditional economics argues that as prices go down, demand goes up.) Fine art or wine, rare jewellery, limited edition sports cars – these goods are about showing off how much money you have and so the more they cost, the more effective they are. It's no wonder we don't always feel the benefit of rising wealth when the oligarch on the news is buying cases of Romanée-Conti for fun, or rather, to show off his bank balance.

We also become more impatient. We want things now and in the way we want them. We prioritise immediate and short-term pleasures over long-term goods. As I will discuss in more detail later, we have an excess of choice in almost all areas of our lives and too much choice leaves us feeling overwhelmed and anxious. When survival and subsistence, *pace* Maslow, aren't major problems we find ways of creating new ones. In technical language this is all described as the declining marginal utility of consumption: the more you consume, the more you need to consume to remain happy.

This isn't just a subjective question either. The economist Daniel Alpert argues that the cardinal problem with the global economy today is oversupply. All those consequences of the Long Boom mean supply and demand are out of sync; supply outstrips demand. Supplies of labour, capital and technology are all at unprecedented levels and have led to a situation of oversupply around the world, with worrying consequences. Systemic financial imbalances, for example, can partly be explained by the enormous reserves of foreign currency held by countries like China and Japan (around $4tn and $1.2tn respectively). Money sloshing around world markets without any generative assets to invest in creates bubbles. Bubbles burst. This kind of oversupply has happened before, in the early twentieth century on the back of the innovations of the second Industrial Revolution. The response then was not just to manufacture more goods but also to create the consumer economy we now inhabit. People were encouraged to buy for the sake of buying, not out of necessity. It's clear that (a) this is no longer available in large portions of the developed world and (b) if everyone on earth lived like this it could, to say the least, create difficult environmental conditions.

It's worth reiterating again that in general overload problems are good problems to have, in that they result from solutions to older problems. When we face overload we are doing it from a position of relative strength and understanding. Yet just because they are good problems, doesn't mean they aren't problems. Deciding which coffee shop to go to or which app to download is laughably trivial. Even calling it a problem, in a world of continuing extreme hardship, verges on the unethical. Yet when we compound all the areas in which we are overloaded it adds up to a situation that requires new ways of working. We should start thinking about approaches to life and business that take a different slant, taking away rather than adding more.

In fact, the nature of overload problems demands that we do this. Let's look in a bit more detail at an overloaded area where there is simply no possibility of adding more. Where we have to find better ways of using what we already possess, something far beyond the usual purview of curation: time.

By definition time, for us, is finite. Trouble is, many of

us feel, as it were, that time is becoming *more* finite. The demands of family and work, let alone leisure, feel all-consuming. Digital technology, tempting us with just one last glance at Facebook, asking us to send that last email, exacerbates the problem. Indeed, our brains secrete an excited little hit of dopamine whenever we get a new message, a pleasurable reward that leaves us craving more. All those extra gadgets, manufactured no doubt at Longhua, make demands. We never switch off.

Worries over our jobs and finances mean we have to work harder than ever just to stand still and pay the mortgage. The cost of everything, but especially health and education, carries on rising. The result is what author and journalist Brigid Schulte calls 'The Overwhelm': the point at which our time management completely breaks down. Part of this is known as 'role overload', the idea that we are taking on too many roles at once (mother, boss, employee, co-worker, wife, friend, sibling, chauffeur, etc.). Having a rich and diversified life is one thing, role overload is when that is taken to an extreme.

A growing body of time-use research supports the thesis that we are overloading our lives. A study carried out by the Oxford University Centre for Time Use Research in 2011 found that despite long working hours, the time parents spent with their children trebled between 1975 and 2000. In US the trend was even more extreme. This contradicts a perception that we are sacrificing childcare for careers. In fact, we really are trying to have it all. A further Oxford study of 20,000 people found that educated women were doing four hours more work a week in 2000 than in the 1970s. As well as spending more time with children there was a universal increase in the amount of time spent watching TV. We are working harder than we have for decades and yet also devoting much more time to our children – and to the TV. More than half of our waking time, at work or at home, is spent on tech or media products – more time, that is, than we devote to sleeping.[6] It's hard to see how spending more time on child-care is a bad thing, but given the slack hasn't been taken up elsewhere – apart from sleeping less – something is going to hit breaking point.

Schulte reports, from an International Association for Time Use Research conference, further research backing this up: 60 per cent of working parents were cutting down on sleep just to fit things in, while 46 per cent said they had no spare time at all. In the General Social Survey by the National Science Foundation, none of the mothers with a child aged 0–6 said they had spare time and only 5 per cent of fathers felt they had time for leisure. Forty per cent of college-educated American men work over fifty hours a week. Another study found that mothers and fathers in total worked thirteen hours more per week in 2000 than they did in 1970.[7] Meanwhile work itself is getting more intense. One study in a major company found that one weekly meeting of the firm's executive committee generated an eye-watering 300,000 hours of extra work for people across the company. We've all been there. The stats go on: 15 per cent of company time was spent on meetings, many of them not regarded as useful. In the 1970s senior executives would each receive around 1,000 external communications a year. By 2014 this had ballooned to 30,000.[8]

Part of the productivity boost has been about the acceleration of flows – flows of capital, ideas, data, products, people and media. It all takes its toll on us as human beings, as well as driving the world into an ever faster, more switched on and more productive engine.

At work and at home time is stretched thin like never before. We have to be incredible parents and model workers; we are expected to helicopter around our children and be ready with a quick answer for our boss twenty-four hours a day. Time is one of the most precious resources we have, yet our time is overloaded. The demands of the modern world mean that we keep adding to the load. Almost every aspect of our lives has implications for time management that simply exacerbate the problem. Just as having too much stuff shrinks our brains through the activation of stress hormones (yes, that's right – too much stress shrinks our brains and our ability to think clearly), so does having too little time. The stress of having lots to do is compounded by the stress of never having enough time to do it. Then we spend days sitting in meetings that only create unnecessary work. Unless we make what people regard as unacceptable sacrifices, we are on a one-way street to time overload.

Of course, it's not just time that's pressured. The contemporary world produces all kinds of strains, pressures and imbalances. We use too much water, for example, and now face alarming shortages in some of the world's most significant breadbaskets, like California's Central Valley, the Midwest, and the Punjab region spanning India and Pakistan. Snowpacks are run down, aquifers are depleted and seasonal rains like the monsoon become irregular, all compounding the problem of overuse. We have too many cars for the road system we have inherited, resulting in gridlock in the world's major cities. Drivers in Moscow and Jakarta are used to sitting in their vehicles for well over four hours a day, while both São Paulo and Beijing have seen traffic jams in excess of 100km long. Debt levels – government, bank, corporate, personal, secured and unsecured – accumulate to near-record levels, all to underwrite economies built on a model of increasing production and consumption year in year out.

Our society is a great engine wanting more, more, more. Yet we can't just ramp up. We are already overloaded. New approaches and ways of thinking will, one way or another, have to come into play.

I don't believe 'curation' alone is the answer to macro problems. Curation is clearly not some kind of saviour. Given that many people react badly to seeing curation in contexts outside art galleries, let's give it time! Curation, however, favours an approach that isn't adding to overload, but actively cuts it down. If we started thinking about time as something to be curated, not ransacked, we might approach our lives differently. We can and should make improvements.

If the Long Boom frames our business context, so overload represents the problems that come with it; problems that emerge from the transition from frugality to consumerism that has dominated the last few centuries. For most of us they are still small-scale and relatively harmless – paralysis in the food-store aisle, unable to decide which breakfast cereal to buy; staying up half an hour later than would be ideal just to get everything done. This kind of choice overload is ubiquitous and central to why curation has grown in importance. Then there is the big stuff. We have financial crashes because the debt pile has grown too big and overloads the financial system. We have problems with antibiotic resistance thanks to over-prescription of medicine. A country like Russia has grown much richer over the past twenty-five years, but its happiness levels have not improved and life expectancy, for men, has plummeted.

Overload problems don't mean curation is a magic bullet; curation will be targeted at a subset of those problems. But they do radically change the context in which we conceive and execute business strategy. The Long Boom means there is more of everything, whether data, debt or doughnuts. It doesn't mean life is easier or better. In an overloaded world, the locus of value is shifting. Tech companies have known this for a while. From their position on the frontline of overload, they realised that taking away, curating, is important. When bewildering choice is the norm, as it is on the web, curating is essential. Hence all the talk from investors about the opportunity in curation and hence, as we will see, the great work being done there. Overload means the methods of the Long Boom are not only faltering, but make the situation worse. As with Big Data, the challenges are about dealing with surplus and severe complexity, not making it worse.

Curation strategies work against the trend towards overload. Curation helps cut through overload and navigate this new economic phase. Sure, it won't do this alone. But because value is increasingly being created in areas and services that alleviate overload, it will be profitable and significant, especially at the consumer end. For organisations of all kinds, then, the nature of the problem indicates that curatorial approaches will play a much greater role in their future. Approaches that don't add more. Approaches that cut things down. That take away. That simplify, contextualise, helping us see and live more clearly. Over the past thirty or so years we have already seen a growth in such approaches. But the scale of the challenge means that we will need to be open about where we find new strategies and models for the future. If it comes from the outliers in art and on the web, so be it. We shouldn't dismiss it.

As for the next thirty-plus years, overload will intensify. Overcoming overload, wherever we find it, in our diaries, shops, national balance sheets or taps, is the great challenge and opportunity of the twenty-first century.

3

The Creativity Myth

The meeting between Beethoven and Goethe, two of history's great creators, was always going to be fun. They were giants of their age, each eager to meet and appraise the other. Eventually, in 1812 in the Bohemian spa town of Teplitz (now known as Teplice), the encounter finally happened. It was by all accounts somewhat awkward. Goethe was a polished courtier, a refined man of learning and manners. Beethoven was wild, difficult, lugubrious and obtuse. In town to recover in the spa waters, beset by deafness, Beethoven was introduced to Goethe by a mutual friend, Bettina von Arnim. On paper they had a lot in common – powerhouses of German culture, they shared the highest aesthetic ideals. They had both admired Napoleon. They were famous and talented. Perhaps for all those reasons they didn't click.

One incident stood out to Bettina.[1] As they walked down one of the picturesque Baroque streets of Teplitz, they noticed royalty ahead. Goethe, ever urbane, did as he was trained to do – doffing his cap to the assembled dignitaries, he politely acknowledged them with due deference and stepped out of the way. Older than Beethoven and from a different world, this would have been the default setting for even a great artist and intellectual like Goethe. Know thy betters.

Not so Beethoven. Thrusting his hands in his pockets. he marched on without stopping to acknowledge the royals. Instead he stormed through them and then had to wait, dismissively, for Goethe to catch up. Beethoven saw himself as an artist, a creator. Nothing else mattered. Nothing could match that. It was being a creator that set people apart, not wealth or family. This is the difference between the two artists – one chatting amiably, as he was meant to do, head bowed; the other storming off, refusing to stop for anyone. More remarkable still is that such was Beethoven's reputation that the royals saluted him as he went past. Servant had become master. Goethe was shocked by the man he met, writing to his wife that Beethoven had 'an absolutely uncontrolled personality'. Later in the century the artist Carl Rohling depicted the scene (see Figure 2).

Alas, the story is quite possibly apocryphal, a later invention by Bettina. But it's still instructive. At the time there was no doubt that Beethoven was writing revolutionary music, changing the very idea of what an artist could be. 'There will be many princes and emperors,' he wrote, 'but there will only ever be one Beethoven.' For Beethoven the important thing was that he was creating new, unique and extraordinary art. And he really was – composed in a style all of his own, his music is amongst the greatest ever written. No other composer changed music like Beethoven. Yet he also changed how we see creativity. He was part of the Romantic revolution sweeping Europe at the turn of the nineteenth century that put raw and unfettered creativity on a pedestal.

Before then creators had been seen in terms of religion or the aristocracy. For much of history creativity was subordinated to religious concerns – music was in praise of God,

Figure 2. Carl Rohling, *The Incident in Teplitz*

painting and architecture were in the service of religion. Only thanks to the largesse of institutions like the Catholic Church did we have artistic material of any scale. Alongside that, art was funded by patronage. Aristocrats and royalty provided funds that enabled artists to live. In turn artists dedicated their work to the glorification of their patrons. Both ideas of creativity can be seen in those other giants of classical music, Bach and Mozart. Both wrote much of their music for either the Church or grand patrons in the mittel-European courts. Both subordinated their music and creativity to others.

Beethoven wrote for himself.

This was a new conception of creativity and it soon gained wider currency. Poets like Byron and Shelley or painters like

Delacroix and Friedrich spread the doctrine throughout the arts. Creativity was in. As Beethoven said, 'Only art and science can raise men to the level of gods.' Originality, newness, boldness and awe were to be praised. Today we live with Beethoven's legacy. We have inherited the Romantic view of creativity as something to be striven for under all circumstances. We lionise our great creatives, shower them with awards and media coverage. Creativity is seen as the key to business and success. We are addicted to the 'game-changing'. We admire creative entrepreneurs like Henry Ford or Steve Jobs, people who create new things, more than we do rentiers like J.D. Rockefeller or Carlos Slim. Someone like Jobs is a corporate Beethoven – wilful, impulsive and difficult, but also utterly heroic – someone willing to sacrifice everything in the name of creative perfection. Jobs, like Beethoven, refused to compromise in the search for newness. He wasn't interested in focus groups or market research, just as Beethoven wasn't writing for the tastes of a restrictive patron. They bent the world to their will and changed it in the process. And we love them for it.

In almost every area of our lives creativity is seen as desirable. From our schools to our workplaces, creativity is encouraged, in theory at least. It's noteworthy that this idea of creativity came hot on the heels of the Long Boom. Beethoven was only a few years behind people like Arkwright and Smith. When you think about it, they were all doing something similar. Even though Romanticism is often seen as opposed to the industrial mindset, they both were innovative and put a premium on creativity. Factories were not only creating new technologies, but literally creating new products – and lots of them. Arkwright, like Jobs and Beethoven, was a creator. Adam Smith was trying to formulate ways to create wealth. The nascent discipline of economics was codifying rules for society to become more productive. For Smith and generations of later economists the role of the entrepreneur in the free market, what John Maynard Keynes called 'animal spirits', was a key driver of economic growth. Creativity went hand in hand with prosperity. Economics and industrial technology shared with the Romantics, in a different way, the idea that creativity is a paramount good.

This is the 'creativity myth': the idea that creation and creativity are intrinsic goods. In the present context of overload it may be time to question this assumption – to, as it were, Roll Over Beethoven.

First, let's differentiate between two kinds of creativity. There is the creativity expressed in creative solutions. This entails clever, new and unobvious ways of working. Whatever happens in the future we will always require this kind of creativity. There will always have to be room for the unexpected and brilliant. It would be foolish to jettison this, probably our most vital trait. Then there is the creativity of creating new and more things. This is incremental creativity. Adding more. People like Arkwright, Beethoven and Jobs are, in their differing ways, clearly aligned with the first kind of creativity. The problem is that it's all got bundled into one. Creativity full stop is lauded, when actually creating more, 'being creative', is perhaps not always appropriate.

Nowhere is this more apparent than on the web, the world's largest and most democratic publishing platform. What was once called 'user generated content', initially an exotic idea that anyone could create their own stuff, has become the default. Creativity has gone absolutely mainstream and yet remains lionised, with the result that content has exploded. YouTube tells us that 400 hours of video are uploaded every minute.[2] Adding video to YouTube may indicate mass creativity. But is it always the best thing to do? On the one hand the web gives us all an outlet for self-expression. On the other, is there any value in yet another cat photo? Democratising creative tools brings a huge range of positives. But it would be crazy to deny it also leads to surplus production. In turn, this crowds out good work. Quantity not only doesn't equal quality, but hampers quality. If we are going to have vast amounts of production we need to build – and value – the mechanisms coping with it. As writer Clay Shirky famously put it, there is no information overload, only filter failure. Whether you agree with that or not, it highlights that as circumstances change, as the Long Boom goes on and we experience more overload, we need better filters.

The flipside of the Creativity Myth is that we devalue the 'non-creative'.

Critics, editors, merchandisers, yes, curators, are all seen as subservient to the creator. These roles are increasingly important, but they are regarded as being below creators in the pecking order. Most of us probably feel that is right. But as we experience more overload I think the balance should shift a little. If we live in a world saturated with images, the value of choosing the right image switches vis-à-vis the value of adding an additional image. Creativity can be exercised in analysis and addition. Just as we gained a brave new creativity in the nineteenth century, we need a brave new creativity for our own age – one that prizes 'second order' roles more highly than our existing, still Romantic concept. This is important because, as the example of Steve Jobs shows, these ideas are deeply enmeshed in our economy. The Long Boom was powered by a model that believed more was more. More was lauded and was what made money.

Now is a pivotal moment. For the first time in history, less *is* more and this means our ideas about economics and creativity need to evolve. Businesses will lead this change by unlocking new stores of value.

For the past thirty or so years a shift along these lines has been discernible. In many areas there are already signs that the creativity myth is being undermined and overload being countered. Much of this book will go on to explore examples of where acts of secondary creativity are being prioritised – in nightclubs and art galleries, but also in retail, leisure and even the edifice of contemporary finance.

Evidence is mounting that we want to consume less physical stuff. Although total global consumption has continued to rise on the back of growth in new markets, in developed economies it has been tailing off. It might not be the end of stuffocation, but it could be the beginning of the end. The US, for example, exports far more by value today than it did in the late 1970s. Yet the weight of those exports has not increased. Physical stuff has been replaced by non-physical assets like intellectual property, software and entertainment, and services like the law. Energy usage and physical production peaked in the UK in 2001–2003.[3] And of course, growth has slowed since the post-war years to a lower level across developed countries. Indeed, in places like southern Europe and Japan, a return to so-called normal levels of economic growth is a long way off. Meanwhile countries are looking at introducing alternative measures to GDP growth: the Human Development Index is becoming a widely used alternative, the Australian government launched the Measuring Australian Happiness (MAP) initiative and the UK government charged its Office of National Statistics with measuring national happiness. It reflects a recognition that simple measurements of growth – such as GDP – are not, in an age of overload, the only thing worth looking at. Of course production, growth and energy usage are all still rising in most places. And what was once a physical excess has now only been joined by gains in the intangible world. But it offers an indication that the Long Boom needn't be unidirectional. Growing for ever – in good or in bad ways – is not inevitable.

At the same time we are gaining a better appreciation of how creativity, growth and innovation actually work. Harvard economist Joseph Schumpeter famously character-ised the capitalist economy as one of 'creative destruction'. But what if it was really about clever recombination? The image of the creator as a lone genius, a God-like figure, is dated. It might have worked in a more heroic age, but in the jaded, savvy context of the twenty-first century we can do better. The thinker Arthur Koestler wrote an epic treatise on creativity, arguing it is more a function of arrangement than of originality.[4]

Creation, argued Koestler, comes from syntheses of exist-ing ideas; from looking at things in new and different ways. Think about creativity in art. The Renaissance wasn't about the completely new, it was, as the name implied, a rebirth – it changed the world not through unblemished originality but by reinterpreting the art and learning of the ancients. Likewise Picasso's art, that paragon of modernism, drew inspiration from so-called 'primitive' works. Koestler argued that scien-tific discoveries work in the same way, often using metaphors of ordinary things to make breakthroughs. Think about the water pump which inspired William Harvey's ideas about the circulation of blood, or the strings in string theory. As Newton said: 'if I have seen further it is by standing on the shoulders of giants.'

This also applies to technological innovation. The business thinker Mariana Mazzucato analyses the iPhone in detail.[5] Although we think of it as the classic 'game-changing' device, so new and revolutionary that it has immediately dominated and transformed an entire sector, this story doesn't stack up. In fact there was very little new about the iPhone at all. The crucial technologies deployed in the iPhone – capacitive touch screens, GPS, solid state memory, internet connectivity, microprocessors, even the 'intelligent personal assistant' SIRI – were not invented for the iPhone but long pre-dated it. Apple brought them together in an attractive easy-to-use package. Seen in this light, Jobs looks less like the Romantic artist and more like one of Koestler's creatives, seeing what's out there on new levels, combining things, mixing them, and so introducing newness. W. Brian Arthur concurs. When you look through the history of technology, he argues, you find it's a dynamic system where parts combine and recombine at new levels of complexity. Technology works by adding to existing assemblies – not by wholesale leaps into new territory. All of this doesn't mean Jobs wasn't a creative visionary. It means that we need to rethink our idea of what creative visionaries are.

Unsurprisingly Jobs himself was the first to admit this, telling *Wired* magazine: 'Creativity is just connecting things. When you ask creative people how they did something, they feel a little guilty because they didn't really do it, they just saw something. It seemed obvious to them after a while. That's because they were able to connect experiences they've had and synthesize new things.'[6]

The creativity myth is seductive. We want to believe it's true. It's romantic as well as Romantic. It's humanity at its best. We like to think that humans can be completely original. Beethoven or Jobs did change the world, just perhaps not in the way we would like to believe. Creativity, when looked at closely, is as much about working with what already exists in new and better ways as it is some kind of divine flame. Romanticism and the rise of the entrepreneur were necessary to shrug off the weighty hand of social and religious control. Now that battle has been won, we can start to see that creativity always contained elements of what we now call curation.

By the same token, CEOs are seduced by the lure of top-line growth at all costs. Top-line growth is the Romantic way of doing business. Governments think the answer to almost every problem is to boost growth. We've engineered our companies and societies to encourage it. We still to a great extent believe more is more. Despite widespread overload and a context of abundance, we haven't adapted. This is the underbelly of the creativity myth. The 'growth complex', perhaps. Just as creativity doesn't have to be about quasi-divine newness, so growth can work differently. Growth can come from adding value, not adding more. Paradoxically, as the century wears on, we will realise that creating less, indeed, actively cutting down, leads to more prosperity.

The strains of the Long Boom are showing. We've enjoyed the many upsides but overload isn't apparent only in information. It's everywhere. Choice, media and stuff alike have proliferated and continue to proliferate at an ever faster rate. Swathes of life, like leisure, are commoditised and subject to the diktats of mass production. From our water supply to our free time, from rising and complexifying debt to shortages of metals to a break between happiness and wealth, the problems of having more, the results of the creativity myth and the Long Boom, are being felt.

Yet the traditional way of doing business and growing is getting harder. Growing the old-fashioned way won't be an option for some companies. We need to make less from more; to switch from a creativity mindset to a curation mindset. Now that is becoming a reality.

Curation is part of the emerging discipline of 'post-scarcity economics', a context where the laws of supply and demand are transformed.[7] In the past five hundred years our population has increased fourteen-fold – but our energy consumption has increased by 115 times and the global economy is now 240 times bigger than it was in 1500.[8] In economics, scarcity and value are correlated. Across the global North scarcity no longer holds in media, information and data; for some fortunate individuals it doesn't hold in terms of food or financial products. Consequently, the price of such goods is collapsing. Normal economics breaks down when goods can be infinitely copied and instantly scaled at zero (or very low) marginal cost. You only need to look at a landfill site or visit Freecycle to realise we have a surplus of physical items. The new scarcity is the expertise needed to filter options. The impact of the Long Boom's abundance is creating a new reactive economy. This book should be read with this in mind.

The nature of value is changing. As much as – and often more than – simply adding, value is about taking away. Boosting productivity the old way is insufficient. At the same time we should recognise that some of our beliefs about creativity, innovation and growth also need to change. Curation is not the only or even the main response to these three phenomena. The context of the Long Boom, overload and the creativity myth do however take curation beyond the platitudes, not just culturally but for businesses generally.

I'd been chatting to Lisa for well over an hour. The conversation ranged widely, from the perils of the daily commute to financial technology to the way nobody takes their full vacation allowance. The discussion underlined to me the immense business opportunity available in sorting out overload. People like Lisa at the cutting edge of the modern economy, hardworking and well remunerated, do not feel things function effectively.

As we're leaving I ask one last question. 'Have you ever thought about curation as a business strategy? As something that might help with all of this?' She laughs. 'No! No I haven't.'

Well, here goes.

Part II
THE ANSWER

4

The Origins of Curation

From the Roman senate to a New York urinal

Hans Ulrich Obrist and Stéphanie Moisdon are two of the world's most celebrated curators. Known in the art scene as tastemakers and jetsetters – Obrist alone has made over two thousand trips in the last two decades[1] – they are power curators. The fast-talking and hyperactive Obrist in particular, with his record of 'high impact' shows, series of books and globetrotting agenda, has become the model of a contemporary art curator. Clad in distinctive transparent glasses and scribbling endless notes, Obrist has topped the *ArtReview* Power 100, an influence bellwether. That a curator could top the list is an indication of how far curating has come. No longer niche players, curators are now what the German critic Willi Bongard has called 'Popes of art'.[2]

Obrist and Moisdon co-curated the 2007 Lyon Biennial. Biennials and other international art shows are vast events, with artists, dealers, collectors, curators and perhaps the odd spectator jetting in to see money change hands on an epic scale. Champagne-fuelled parties are alive with gossip – who is the next big thing? Who's lost it? The top events – Basel, Miami, Venice – are etched into the art calendar.

Art Basel Miami Beach is perhaps the biggest such show in the US. Growing out of the original Swiss fair, it was established as the organisers noticed how many collectors hailed from Miami. Now, amidst the Art Deco sunshine of Miami Beach, distributed through enormous halls, with hundreds of galleries and thousands of premier league visitors, Art Basel Miami Beach is the art fair in its purest form. Having spread from the original Convention Centre to a host of satellite venues, it packs elite hotels with famous artists and, increasingly, celebrities keen to show off their avant-garde credentials. Biennials are the perfect breeding ground for curators as they cram everything into one room – different kinds of art from around the world, different media, different-sized works, all jostling for attention.

But back in Lyon Obrist and Moisdon wanted to be a little different. Rather than selecting and organising artists and artworks, they selected a further sixty people to get involved. Many of these were curators in their own right, and had now been designated players in an intricate art world game. Each of these 'players' would select an artist for inclusion in the programme. Each player chosen by Obrist and Moisdon was a mini-curator. So, effectively what you had is – wait for it – curators curating curators curating. And then, given that they also made artists and critics curators, the whole category of curator had been blown wide open. Everyone was a curator. This was hyper-curation, curation cubed. The thinking behind the show was that, as the world becomes more complex, so no artist or curator can individually represent it. Only by increasing the variety of selection can you ever hope to do justice to life. Or was it just another art game? It's an open question.

What it undoubtedly showed was that curation had swamped art. Curation was now at the centre of the art world. How did we get there? And how did curation then leap from this context into so many others?

Although the meaning of curation has radically evolved over the last decade, becoming relevant in many new areas, a brief history of the idea is illuminating.

The word itself comes from the Latin *curare*, meaning to take care of. In addition to caring and nurturing, the word had political overtones. *Curatores* were civil servants with responsibility for infrastructure, amongst other things like public games and river traffic on the Tiber. Procurators were responsible for provincial taxation, administration and estate management. This political sense of the word echoed throughout history. Senior politicians in the Venetian Republic, for example, were called procurators. A more familiar usage is that associated with the Church: curates spiritually tended to their flock, an integral part of the ecclesiastical hierarchy registering that old Latin meaning. From the beginning a curator was somewhere between priest and bureaucrat, combining the practical with the otherworldly. Either way curators had access to and mastery over difficult, concealed knowledge.

That sense of 'looking after' was clear in the origins of museum and gallery curators. In the sixteenth and seventeenth centuries rich collectors assembled 'cabinets of curiosities' or *Wunderkammer*, rooms filled with interesting objects from scientific instruments like astrolabes and chemical samples to fragments from the ancient world and mystical relics. Looking after these collections became a full-time job. Elias Ashmole, for example, founder of the eponymous

Ashmolean Museum in Oxford, was the classic Renaissance all-rounder, a scientist, traveller and soldier who built an incredible collection of objects which still stands at the centre of the museum today. Eventually, as such collections grew, so the difficulty in arranging, storing and caring for them increased.

By the eighteenth century a new approach was needed. The British Museum, now the world's second most visited museum, started as the unruly amalgam of three private collections. There was the manuscript collection of the Cotton family, the library of the Earls of Oxford and the collection, or part of it, of Sir Hans Sloane, who had amassed natural history specimens and ancient sculpture.[3] Put together this was the museum. Entrance protocols were uncertain. Staff guided visitors lucky enough to be admitted around the collections on an ad hoc basis. It was far from professional but, thanks to the scale of the collections and the complexity of what was involved, the museum was taking on new form.

Nowhere was this clearer than in what is today the world's most visited museum: the Louvre in Paris. Opened post-Revolution in 1793, the Louvre was from the beginning a new prospect – conceived as a museum for and of the people, it was symbolically placed in the palace at the centre of the *ancien régime*, now given over to the edification of the masses. Its holdings were buoyed by extensive formerly royal collections. Under Napoleon (it was even named the Musée Napoleon in 1803) they were further boosted by booty snatched from the conquered capitals of Europe. Within a short space of time the Louvre's collection was unmatched.

Around this time the director appointed by Napoleon, a colourful character called Dominique Vivant, Baron Denon, responded to the enormous increase in the amount of art in the collection in a new way. Rather than display work in a great morass, as was normal, Denon organised it. He based displays on chronology and national schools. He looked at art's evolution over time and space. In doing so he not only set the agenda for museum curation throughout the nineteenth century but he changed the Louvre – it was no longer about revolution, but about appreciating and understanding the history of art. Curation, then, wasn't just looking after things. It was selecting with a purpose, then arranging to tell a story.

It might have been rudimentary, but compared with the chaos of most contemporary equivalents it was a step change. By responding to the flood of art and building the modern museum, Denon gestured towards how curators add value amidst excess.

In the nineteenth century a new breed of connoisseur, middle-class and upwardly mobile, found their cultural home in institutions like the British Museum and the Louvre. Both wrestled with the still relevant problem of how to show large collections to broad audiences. At the same time museums became a giant game of imperial one-upmanship; they were an excellent way of proclaiming your national might.

Around the turn of the twentieth century Germany got in on the act. Berlin's great director of museums, and the driving force behind the city's Museum Insel, Wilhelm von Bode, further transformed curating by bringing a new sense of organisational rigour. In the United States, meanwhile, a wave of civic pride saw the foundation of a host of great museums whose immense collections would soon rival and even surpass those of the Old World. Yet curating would spin off at a tangent. While collections kept growing and the challenge of working with them increased – a good case study are the medical collections of pharmaceutical mogul Henry Wellcome, whose mania for collecting saw him accumulate

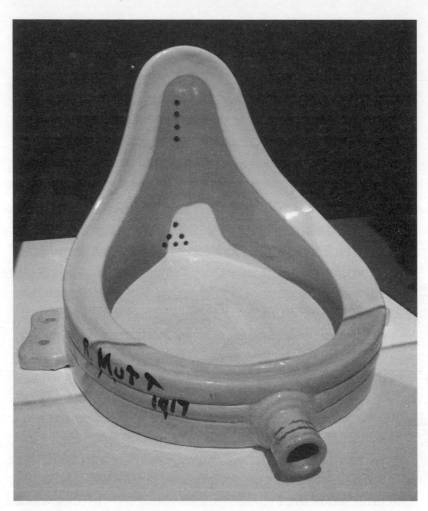

Figure 3. Marcel Duchamp, *Fountain*

warehouse upon warehouse of arcana, all waiting for diligent curators to eventually sift through – it was the art world that bounced curation out of its museum niche.

Just as the Industrial Revolution changed the meaning of productivity, art was about to change the meaning of meaning. That, in turn, needed new roles to make sense of it all.

Marcel Duchamp was a troublemaker. The artwork

shown in Figure 3 is what it appears to be: a urinal laid on its side, signed *R. Mutt 1917*. Safe to say that when it debuted in that year no one had seen its like. As the first 'readymade', a manufactured object Duchamp called art, it immediately challenged assumptions of what art was and could be.

Called *Fountain*, it was originally 'made' for an exhibition of the Society of Independent Artists in New York. The idea was cooked up by Duchamp in a New York restaurant whilst having lunch with two friends.[4] Although the event was planned as a typical exhibition, for a submission fee the society was obliged to accept entries from members. Duchamp, a board member, was going to have some fun and submitted the work, supposedly by one 'R. Mutt', from a fake address in Philadelphia. Shocked at Duchamp's proposal, the selection board rejected the work. Whereupon Duchamp promptly resigned his position in mock anger. The board claimed to accept work from any qualifying artist! Who were they to legislate what was art? What, exactly, made it unworthy? It didn't help that, as a urinal, it was considered indecent. Duchamp was arguing there was nothing timeless or obvious about art. The artist and the reception, not innate features, made something art. Galleries made art art. In perhaps the greatest irony of all, the original urinal was lost, and now all that exist are lovingly handmade replicas spread around some of the world's most famous galleries.

People read much into the urinal. It's sometimes seen as a body, sometimes as a sensuous, clean sculpture. Or it may just be a urinal. Only when we are told that it's art, when it is positioned as art, do we think of it as such. Duchamp marks the point at which art went on a conceptual journey where it needed further elaboration and contextualisation. It needed someone to say what it was and why. As art continued on this journey, proliferating along the way, so the role of the curator grew. In the words of the artist Grayson Perry, suddenly art required 'validation'. Now that anything could be art, roles that said what was art in the first place had new power and influence. As Perry argues, even if curators don't create the art, they create the spectacle of art.

Art became increasingly conceptual during the 1960s and the 1970s. No one knew where the boundaries were any more: performance, installation, video, participatory art, architecture, politics and protest, dance, food and digital technology meant that art could be – and often was – anywhere and anything. Art became about the discussion of art. Appreciating art required new levels of knowledge and sophistication. It barely made sense without reference to a body of theory – if at all. At the same time more and more of it was produced as art schools boomed. Simultaneously, exemplified by what had already become the *grande dame* of modern art institutions, MoMA in New York (under the leadership of another famous curator, Alfred Barr), museums were getting into the swing of modern art. As the 1970s became the 1980s the money started to get serious. By 2013 a total of $66bn was spent in the art market and one painting like Cézanne's *Card Players* was sold for $260m.[5] Big business by any standards. Artists like Jeff Koons even celebrated the fact, his works echoing the shininess of the high end luxury goods they were in fact becoming.

So here were the ingredients behind the curation boom that led to events like the 2007 Lyon Biennial: art could be absolutely anything; there was more and more of this stuff that could be anything; and it was all worth more and more money.

Hence the rise of the curator.

The curator tied it all together. The curator said what was art, explained why it mattered and hinted at its value. Iconic and anarchic curator figures like Harald Szeeman emerged in this period. They saw themselves as a new kind of artist, the exhibition as a canvas, the works of art as a kind of paint. Formerly marginal figures, curators were projected by Szeeman and others into the big time. Duchamp hadn't just invented a new kind of art. He necessitated a new kind of role. The character of exhibitions was also changing. In Paris, just shy of 200 years after Denon, the curator Pontus Hultén would, at the newly opened Centre Pompidou, a museum as radical in its own day as the Louvre after the Revolution, attempt a different kind of exhibition. Bode had already pioneered the mixing and matching of different kinds of works – fine art with furniture, say – to illuminate a historical period. Hultén and others went one step further by breaking the boundaries of time and space. Exhibitions featured work from different places and periods, bouncing off against one another. The curator was telling the story here. For better or for worse, curators were now truly the Popes of art. Gallerists, wealthy collectors and, still hanging in there, artists, all remained big. But if one figure defined the new anything-goes jet-setting big-money overly conceptualised steroidal-production art world of the 1990s and 2000s it was the curator.

Which is where things got really interesting.

Around this time the terms curator, curating, curated and curation started becoming more widespread – and changed their meaning. As a Curator of Fashion and Textiles at the V&A, Oriole Cullen told me: 'Anyone can be a curator now, especially as it has come to be understood as personal choice. Today the word curation means personal choice.'

'It's a word that's drifted,' says the art critic Martin

Gayford. 'It originally meant to take care of and preserve. Museums were originally stable and safe environments to keep things. The stress on selecting, arranging and displaying has become more prominent as museums became geared to temporary exhibitions. The curator goes from looking after things to a quasi-artistic role, becoming an impresario, spotting movements and picking stars.' It's a change Gayford has watched from the frontline. 'Curation has become big in the last twenty or thirty years. Being a freelance curator has become a career. Curators are moving up the scale. There is a power grab. They weren't so important fifty years ago. The artists and the collectors are still the powers, but curators are challenging now. Curate became a verb in the last twenty-five years. To curate, I bet, entered general currency in the 1980s.'

This is significant as it also started to enter wider use beyond art. As Gayford puts it, 'All these other kinds of curation are seeping from that [artistic curation]. It's a useful word, there didn't use to be any word for the activity.'

Somewhere along the line curation went from a narrow museum-based activity to something, as Oriole Cullen hints, that is much more about choice, selection, arrangement – something that responds to wider problems of too much. How?

It all started, like so much else, with the invention of the World Wide Web by Tim Berners-Lee in 1990. Before that the Internet was limited. Without an easy-to-use interface, its enormous potential was unlikely to be realised. The web changed that, putting connectivity within reach of millions. Open and low-cost, the web flicked a switch from scarcity to abundance in a host of fields. Suddenly content was everywhere, virtually free and with few barriers to creation. How people interacted with content had to change. Knowingly or unknowingly, the web was forcing us to act like traditional curators, thinking through the selecting, arrangement, explanation and display of information and other media. Like Denon at the Louvre, ordinary users and companies faced a mass of material which they would have to make sense of – for themselves and for others. If the web made us all creators and publishers, it also made us curators.

Art curation rapidly morphed into 'content curation'.

Take a site which was in its heyday one of the most visited on the web: GeoCities. Today we think of GeoCities, if we think of it all, as emblematic of a certain early era of the web, synonymous with pixel design, bright colours, patterned backgrounds, moving gifs and unfortunate quantities of Comic Sans lettering. Synonymous in other words with awful web design and user experience.

Yet GeoCities was actually an early example of how what would come to be called curation underwrites the new digital age. Users established customisable home pages in areas of interest. GeoCities let people select and display information at will, in an easy-to-use format. Founded in 1994 as Beverly Hills Internet by David Bohnett and John Rezner, the site was divided into 'neighbourhoods' of fan pages or mini-websites. 'Nashville' was about country music, 'Augusta' golf and 'Rodeo Drive' shopping. Users were typically amateur enthusiasts and would filter and carefully curate their pages, collecting links and relevant material from across the web. It was an early example of how the Internet was going to be curated by its users. Even in the earliest days it was clear that a proliferation of information and choice required a behavioural change in Internet users from consumers to curators.

Moreover, a huge business was built on the back of this distributed curating. By the time it was acquired by Yahoo!

at the height of the dotcom bubble, GeoCities was the third most visited site on the web and went for $3.57bn in stock. Personal curation was popular and valuable. The Yahoo! acquisition was when the problems started, however. Formerly loyal users deserted the site. Never regaining traction, it was eventually retired in 2009. If GeoCities' execution was dated, though, its business case was only getting started. Companies from Google to Facebook would supersede anything achieved by GeoCities. The model – allowing users to curate material on the web related to their interests – proved enduring. Even if nobody saw GeoCities as a curatorial proposition at the time, in hindsight we can see it was just that.

It would be a mistake to think of GeoCities as a sudden break with the world of Jeff Koons and Pontus Hultén. Instead it was the mass adoption of such an approach, on a scale that sometimes bewildered and angered those in its original heartlands.

Curators weren't just widely distributed on these highly scaled platforms. In another sense the web replicated the old structure of curators, with some quickly gaining large numbers of followers, big ad spends and worldwide status on the back of their online content curation. As with Hans Ulrich Obrist, professional curation would prove an attractive career. A good example is the blog Boing Boing. Originally a fanzine, arguably itself a classic form of curation, Boing Boing became a website by 1996.[6] To begin with traffic was modest. Things really took off once its founder, Mark Frauenfelder, moved the site to a new platform, Blogger. Boing Boing was now in a position to redefine itself as one of the first blogs with significant traction.

Frauenfelder brought in collaborators, editors and writers who would become famous in their own right, people like

Cory Doctorow, David Pescovitz and Xeni Jardin. With the new team in place traffic grew fast. By the middle of the 2000s Boing Boing was on a roll: one of the most visited websites in the world and the most trafficked blog. It was pulling in millions of readers and making huge amounts from advertising. What started as an amateurish fanzine had become an impressive media outlet setting the online agenda. It did this by linking and sharing. Boing Boing wasn't really in the business of creating content so much as pointing out what was interesting. It maintained a resolutely casual atti-tude. Despite making millions of dollars a year the site had no office, maintained no structure or staff in the manner of a traditional company and kept the anarchic, open web ethos it developed during the 90s. It was still more fanzine than professional media operation. All the editors continued to work on other projects even as Boing Boing became huge – Frauenfelder worked with *MAKE* magazine and the maker movement, Doctorow continued to work with the Electronic Frontier Foundation and wrote science fiction, while Jardin often commentated on television.

Boing Boing's value came from its editors. Their sheer eclecticism and commitment, and Frauenfelder's early spotting of blogging's potential (he signed on to the platform in early 2000; three years later it would be acquired by Google) as a medium for sharing made the site a success. Jardin has spoken of how they never have a content programme. They run on their instincts and interests. That's it. Yet those instincts and interests, in the pure and unadorned form of Boing Boing, turned the editors into superstar curators analogous to Obrist, with the added bonus that they had built a sustainable busi-ness. To this day Boing Boing maintains its commitment to a unique curatorial blend. On a random visit the homepage included a rather horrible jumper based on the computer game Street Fighter 2, a discussion of racist college admission policies, an advert for free encryption classes and a gallery of '3D tattoos'.

Curation had gone mainstream. Taste and whimsy, operated via underlying platforms, made the web useful and enjoyable rather than a cacophonous mess. It was a new model, creating a new breed of job and celebrity – people like Maria Popova and Jason Kottke, who have built flourishing websites around their identity as curators. As Bobbie Johnson, a journalist and founder of online magazine Matter, put it to me: 'I think the Internet has had a lot to do with it: this idea that we have too much information, too much data – too much good stuff – and we need to sift it to find the real gems. Curation here becomes a sort of wayfinding through a swamp of content. In the early days it was often sifting through user-generated material – sites like Metafilter or Slashdot or Reddit – but increasingly, the media landscape has just become a noisy place. As our attention becomes more pulled-apart, so the curator becomes the person who helps you spend it wisely.' Here is curation as antidote to online overload.

Having lost its original political and religious overtones and made the transition first to museums and then to the art world, curation now found its apotheosis on the sprawling web – both in terms of producing celebrity curators and by making curators of us all. Techniques which reacted to the web's content surplus would soon migrate offline. It turned out that those techniques had value amidst the excess of the Long Boom. Not everyone was happy with it, but curation broke its boundaries, becoming not only the buzzword *du jour* but also something more significant.

Data from Google's Ngram Viewer (see Figure 4) bears out this rise. Looking at word usage in indexed books there is a big spike in the appearance of the words 'curation' and

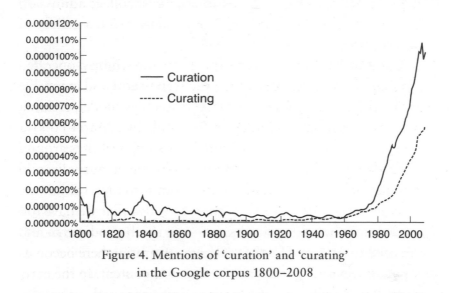

Figure 4. Mentions of 'curation' and 'curating'
in the Google corpus 1800–2008

'curating' in the 1980s, which corresponds to the boom in the art world. Sadly the Viewer only takes us up to 2008; it's likely that in the years since then curation has spiked even more as writers respond to the growth of web content curation and the increasing uses of the word in areas inconceivable even during the 80s or 90s.

Google Trends (Figure 5) records a similar although less extreme rise, which shows how often curation appears in search engine results pages relative to everything else. There is a notable increase in the middle 2000s, in the wake of Boing Boing's epic traffic growth and that of sites like Popova's.

Google can also tell us what people were searching for. In descending order the most searched items are: curation content; digital curation; data curation; definition curation; social curation; curation tools; what is curation; art curation; museum curation; media curation.

No surprise that on the web content curation dominates art or museum curation, supporting the view that it is the Internet,

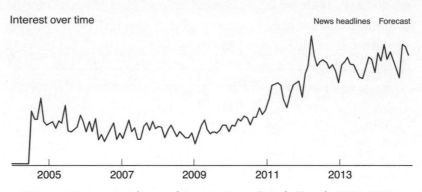

Interest over time   News headlines   Forecast

2005   2007   2009   2011   2013

Figure 5. Interest in the word 'curation' on Google Trends 2004–2014

and Internet-based businesses, not art, that have dominated curation over the past decade and are responsible for its recent popularity. More interesting is that many searches display confusion. People are looking for definitions. Lastly, curation here is not just a concept. It's an activity. People want to know about the tools for curating. The curation of content is not, thanks to platforms from GeoCities on, a spectator sport. It's an activity carried out by millions if not billions. Curators, curation, curating aren't static terms. They have histories and, like many words in English, have continuously evolved and changed. Stasis is the exception not the norm and we should expect this evolution to continue. As contexts have changed – because of Denon's Louvre, Duchamp's *Fountain* or Berners-Lee's web – curation has reacted and expanded.

Despite protests, snobbishness and resistance, curation has come a long way from Rome. Now it is entering an exciting, far-reaching phase. From the white cube to the black box and beyond, it has never had wider relevance or more important ramifications. Whether many of its newer uses constitute curation or not is now irrelevant: while what started on the web may not have been immediately recognisable as traditional curation, the word has now travelled, and will continue to do so. Yet, as those Google searches indicate, a lot of people don't know what it is. Moreover, the examples in this chapter are of what I call explicit curation – but today much curation doesn't go by the name.

So, just what do we mean today by curation?

5

The Principles of Curation

Hidden value

'Trouble with running a business is that whatever you do – whatever targets you hit, however quickly you scale – you always need to do more. There is never a moment when everyone stops and thinks, yup, that's pretty good. It's relentless. That's the deal.'

A friend of mine is the CEO of a large medical information company. He'd flown into London from Massachusetts and we grabbed a beer by the Thames. It was one of those warm summer evenings when the bars are thronged with post-work drinkers. Talk turned to shop, as it inevitably does. My friend's company aggregates research papers, textbooks, clinical reports, reference works, 'how to' guides and interactive materials for healthcare organisations. As the sector has ballooned over the past decade the business has flourished, growing from scrappy start-up to serious player.

My friend was under pressure from the board. Results were impressive – every year registered significant growth, the kind most businesses would kill for. But the board wanted more. He'd delivered a new technology platform that made the service slicker, easier to use and more reliable. He'd rebranded, bringing the corporate image up to date. He'd massively expanded the sales force, which now landed blue-chip customers on a regular basis. And he'd spearheaded an internationalisation programme, taking the service from its home market in the US into Europe and Asia. While he understood that boards have a duty to keep pushing, it was nonetheless frustrating that there wasn't greater recognition at that level of what had been achieved.

Like most boards (and CEOs) they were obsessively focused on more. More top-line growth. More staff. They bought into the creativity myth. One metric, content uploads, was watched especially closely. Having more content was seen as critical. Their position as market leader was thought to rely on having the most comprehensive set of medical information and so they were in a constant battle to add more. I'd mentioned I was working on a book about curation and we got thinking. Having worked with the company on a project, I was familiar with their content-acquisition process. Although they always wanted more, I also knew they were choosy. A well-drilled content team filtered and carefully selected content. They only wanted material which specifically added value in healthcare terms.

I suggested that far from relying on adding more, his business actually relied on curation. Their proposition to hospitals, businesses and universities was that by subscribing they wouldn't waste time. Everything done on the platform was in the interests of healthcare. Value was predicated on the business offering *Gray's Anatomy*, not *Fifty Shades of Grey*. At a fundamental level this was a business whose sales pitch was really about selection. Technology can be replicated, sales teams hired. But building a corpus of expertly selected information, handpicked by specialists to ensure health organisations don't waste time and money, well, that is a harder moat to bridge.

So I put it to him: your business isn't based on more. It's based on less. The value you add isn't just about adding. It's about excluding what isn't important or valuable; it's a business that on the face of it looks like technology platform + medical information, but in fact is saturated in curation. Looking at the content growth metric was, then, precisely the wrong way of working. A better indicator of its value to users was the amount of content it excluded, how easy it was to find that must-have piece of material. The selection process was what made it useful.

It got him thinking. When he mentioned it at the next board meeting it got the board thinking too. Thinking in terms of curation helped to refocus the company strategy on what really mattered. It led them to think about what was core to the company's activities, to avoid getting distracted by the trap of adding more in all areas.

Having that beer showed, once again, how curation was happening in more places than might be supposed. But although curation is becoming integral to many businesses, they don't realise it. There is not, in most companies even directly associated with the activity, a Curation Department. My guess is that if there were, it would be laughed out of the office. There is in company accounts no income line attributable to curation. Explaining it to the accountants would be headache enough but truth is, most of us would be hard pressed to join the dots between curating and hard cash receipts. Curation isn't budgeted for and isn't discussed by management.

Curation is more often an emergent property of organisations. Most companies don't have curators. They don't call what they do curation. Nonetheless they are curating. Curation is integral to their activities. This only becomes a problem when it leads them to miss parts of their value proposition. Given overload, this has immediate force. My friend's medical information company is a perfect example. Much of the information they provide is available online. But has it been peer-reviewed? Is it from a respectable source? On the web you don't always know. Within the platform there is still, as on the web, a great deal of content, but the company spends a huge amount of time organising and presenting it to users, ensuring that despite this profusion they find exactly what they need.

If curation is such a great store of value it makes sense to ask – what do we mean by curation anyway? It's certainly what my friend the CEO asked me. I went to get another beer and explained my thinking.

Curation is where acts of selecting and arranging add value.

Put together, such acts are an extraordinary store of value for an overloaded world. Many curators, especially from the art world, are reluctant to define curation in such bald terms. This allows them nuance. But it means curation gets lost – as another dismissible theoretical construct, an intellectual luxury, a passing fad, not an engaged or practical activity. If we are to take curation seriously, as I believe we should, it needs something more concrete reflecting its widespread use – something to go beyond the much-parodied and obscurantist clichés.

What we have come to call curation is the interface, the necessary intermediary, for the modern consumer economy; a kind of membrane or purposeful filter that balances our needs and wants against great accumulations of stuff. At its broadest curation is a way of managing abundance.

Often it is much more than that. For example, a presentational or performance aspect was long an essential part of curation. It was about putting on a show or display. This is still important, but as I will argue, that element is now often dropped. While curation is still for the most part directed at audiences as a service, to provide entertainment or education, as it percolates out, as more of us start to resemble traditional curators, so this aspect wanes. I don't expect everyone to agree with or accept this definition; but I think it reflects how people have popularly come to understand curation. It offers a useful template for thinking not only about that new usage, but also the wider context we live in. There will never be a correct or final definition, but we shouldn't shy away from helping to clarify understanding, practice and strategy.

Beyond this definition lie supplementary principles often found in curation. I call these 'curation effects' – refining, simplifying, explaining and contextualising, for instance. Each comes with its own history and practice, explaining its power in a world of too much. Curation combines these effects into one overarching practice.

A good example of how curation underpins entire industries is the app economy.

Apple launched the App Store in July 2008 as part of the iOS 2.0 update to the iPhone (released a year earlier). I remember it well – for those in software and content it was a bombshell. At the publisher I then worked for we quickly partnered with an exciting team of developers based in Texas. Together we managed to release books through the App Store in a matter of weeks. It was frantic and involved many late-night Skype sessions, but we felt exhilarated by the challenge of this new platform. Selling content or software of any kind on the Internet was tough. The App Store promised a controlled retail ecosystem with a simple payment mechanism. All in users' pockets 24/7.

It wasn't long before the number of apps started growing. Fast. By opening the floodgates on mobile application development, Apple unleashed a Cambrian explosion of new material.

Developers realised that they could replicate software to release large numbers of apps. It meant that with enough content and one app framework you could easily release almost limitless numbers of apps. Having launched with only 500, in just a few months the App Store was able to offer thousands upon thousands of apps. Many were high-quality, some revelatory; many, though, were filler.

The problem, for Apple, was clear. By opening the development of apps they had initiated a tidal wave of new product. Broadly speaking this was good for users – never before had so much been available so easily. Yet at the same time, the sheer rate at which new apps were produced threatened to bury good products in a sea of rubbish. Unless you knew exactly what you wanted, finding good apps would become impossible. In other words, making the App Store work required finely balanced curation. Indeed, ensuring the market operated, that users had the best service and that, in a competitive space, good apps were not lost was all a matter of curation.

Apple helped themselves by restricting the platform. Before going live every app requires approval from Apple HQ. The App Store has tough gatekeepers. The approvals process and the rules governing it have constantly been adjusted to reflect Apple's priorities. For example, releasing many apps when one app with further in-app purchases (a later development) would work fine was banned. You couldn't just flood the Store. Technical specs, analysis of the content and rule changes were all used to limit and funnel app creation.

Because of this tight control App Store editors were always close to the process. They saw everything in advance and could pick out promising apps. What constituted a promising app was highly subjective, governed less by download or usage figures and more by what editors perceived as offering originality and quality. Apple have consistently made decisions that don't maximise profit or sales in the short term, instead looking at the bigger picture of creating lasting value for users, partners and themselves. The App Store has been no exception.

I've seen this curation at work. One app I worked on was picked as an Editor's Choice, the App Store's premium real estate. The same app was later picked as one of the App Store's Games of the Year and was consistently supported in promotions long after launch. Called 80 Days, it retold Jules Verne's *Around the World in 80 Days* as an interactive adventure. For the most part text-based, it was developed on a modest budget by a small team in Cambridge, England (the incredibly talented inkle studios). Mixing steampunk writing with board-game mechanics, this literary product without any backing from games publishers would struggle in most retail environments. Which would be a shame, as the game is brilliant. One early play showed its promise. Unlike anything I had encountered before, 80 Days was utterly original, stylish and absorbing. The hands-on curation of the App Store recognised that. Having picked the game early, the personal attention of App Store editors helped make it a great success. Despite the extraordinary number of apps being launched every week, this attention to curation keeps the App Store interesting and lets work like 80 Days – different but exceptional – find an audience.

Over time the App Store evolved to curate better. Apple understand how our behaviour gets locked into patterns. We download a few apps, play with them for a while and get stuck in a rut. Tweaking design to ensure the right spread of app icons, tailored collections, regular features (like Editor's Choice or New and Noteworthy) and category pages is meant to ensure this doesn't happen. Certainly, compared with Google's Play platform, which is more open and relies more heavily on algorithms than Apple's, the App Store has a better standard of app. It's still the go-to platform for app launches. And it is still the launch destination for what might be called more artisanal apps – things like 80 Days or Paper or Flipboard or Garageband or The Room or The Elements.

By carefully selecting and arranging apps, Apple ensured that the extraordinary boom in app production didn't lead to overload.

The App Store is a consumer technology, a software and a retail business. But its success is underpinned by an unerring focus on curation. If apps themselves are the explicit value, curation is the implicit addition of value (more on this implicit element later). Take curation away and the app economy would struggle, would not offer the same quality and variety.

Apple's recognition of this is evident in its acquisitions and launches. Despite large capital reserves, Apple notably acquires few businesses. However, it recently bought Booklamp, pitched as Pandora (free, personalised internet radio) for books, for somewhere above $10 million, and Swell, a radio curation service, for around $30 million – not to mention the $3 billion acquisition of Beats Electronics, not just a high-profile consumer brand but a direct rival to music curation sites.[1] Although the sums it paid for Booklamp and Swell weren't huge in terms of Apple's cash pile, the fact they went to the trouble of investing, acquiring and integrating companies in these areas is telling. Subsequently Apple Music and Apple News became key services for the company – and both are built around a large investment in curation. Indeed, when people talk about Apple and curation this is usually what they mean. We should expect many of the lessons from those services to be reverse-engineered into the App Store. Recent adverts for the iPhone have taken to highlighting this feature – that its apps are 'handpicked' is explicitly seen as a sales point.

Yet the battle against app overload isn't over. Many developers and commentators say that Apple isn't doing enough. Once again, the question can be framed in a number of ways but curation is at the heart of it.

The *Financial Times* reports that the top 1.6 per cent of developers make more money than the bottom 98.4 per cent combined.[2] This is a lot of money – in 2015 revenues were up to nearly $2bn a month. Makers of addictive games built around cunningly crafted in-app purchases – Candy Crush or Clash of Clans – reap the rewards. Everyone else sweats it out for meagre sales. Research from Activate suggests that even as the number of apps has continued growing over the last three years or so, the number of downloads has held steady.[3] Apps are, in other words, a highly skewed market, where certain apps claim disproportionately large rewards and the thousands of new apps entering the market are likely to disappear without trace. To some extent this is true of my experience. While I've seen some apps do very well, other excellent products struggle to a surprising degree despite large marketing budgets.

The question for developers is how long is this viable? Yes, one developer in their bedroom can put together a quality app; but more often it needs an expensive team working flat out for months. Thanks to the falling price of apps (free now being the norm), the tech commentator Ben Thompson points out, users benefit from cheap or free services, but the companies behind those services cannot capture that value.[4] He argues that Apple needs to change the App Store, allowing subscriptions and paid updates as part of the mix. Speak to most app developers and they lament that despite all the curation, Apple isn't doing enough to encourage a vibrant ecosystem and stimulate a long tail in app sales. Clearly this isn't happening – once you fall out of the chart's highest echelons, sales drop off a cliff.

Curation helped build the App Store. But its work isn't done.

If Apple want to keep encouraging good apps (and not rely on hype, naivety and expectation) they need to ensure that downloads, usage and revenue accrues to the 98.4 per cent. The bottleneck is the App Store; the solution is good curation.

Apple are curators. My friend and his medical business are curators. Although they don't always talk about curation, that's what they're doing. Curating is about selecting. But also about arranging, refining, simplifying and contextualising. So what does that mean in practice, and why are these activities so important?

Selection

Blockbuster wasn't just a video rental company; it was part of the weekend routine, an iconic part of American culture. Despite its suburban image, there was, in truth, always something exciting about Blockbuster. You'd drive up on a grey Saturday, its strip lights blaring from broad windows, the distinctive blue and yellow livery shining with promise. Inside it smelled like a cinema – of popcorn and sweets. Row upon row of videos were lined up, waiting to be discovered, their loud covers competing for attention. Empty cases – they never actually left the videos in, assuming they'd be immediately stolen – were taken to the counter and filled by bored-looking assistants (see cult film *Clerks*). But this was the weekend! Entertainment! Possibility! Hollywood! In our family, hiring films was part of the Saturday ritual. We'd go for a swim, get a Chinese meal, hire a video and head home to watch it. The movie would inevitably be mainstream, family-friendly, funny and action-packed. It was the week's highlight, and this was a scene replicated in millions of households around the world. Blockbuster was big business, yes. But it was one of those brands that become part of our lives.

Blockbuster specialised in, well, blockbusters. Although there was always a reasonably large selection towards the back, most outlets never had much depth. Instead customers were funnelled towards great front-of-store racks of the latest big-budget releases. Walls of the same film, served straight up. Choices of non-English film, art house cinema or genres outside the mainstream were often hard to find. Blockbuster was about new releases rented en masse in part because this was one of their USPs. You didn't just rent a video because it was cheaper to do so, but because rentals were released earlier than retail versions. It was the next best thing to cinema, smell of popcorn and all. It also heavily promoted those titles because, it was assumed, they were what the audience wanted. And for a long time it appeared they were indeed what the audience wanted. In my family it was the big hits that brought us in. For several years this modus operandi served Blockbuster well: fill stores with the six or seven latest releases, cassette after cassette of the same film dominating prime in-store real estate; leave a short tail of classic fare hidden at the back.

Founded in Dallas in only 1985, Blockbuster grew fast. In the late 1980s it took on games company Nintendo in a battle to hire out video games and won. Through the early 1990s its expansion gathered pace across the US. It bought rivals in a series of ambitious acquisitions before itself being acquired by media giant Viacom for $8.4 billion in 1993. In a display of confidence, its headquarters moved to the showpiece Renaissance Tower in downtown Dallas. Stores were opened abroad. At its height Blockbuster employed over 60,000 people across 9,000 stores; it had achieved high street ubiquity, its name synonymous with media rentals. What could go wrong?

Everything, it turned out. Blockbuster's fall from its 2004 peak was frighteningly fast. By 23 September 2010 it had filed for bankruptcy. Stores started closing. When it filed for Chapter 11 (the first stage of bankruptcy in the US) the company was experiencing considerable losses and was unable to meet a $42.4 million interest payment on its $900 million debt pile.[5] Blockbuster ran out of road. This was despite the fact that by 2010 it was the only nationwide video rental chain in the US. A buyer, satellite TV network Dish Network, was found but the closures continued. This once mighty empire was bought for only $233 million and Dish was still closing hundreds of stores every year. Eventually, by November 2013, the old model for Blockbuster was dead. The retail model of video and DVD hire it represented was finished and the name, the grand cultural institution, was all but retired.

Blockbuster faced many obstacles. But its biggest mistake would remain hidden for some years. In 2000 it passed up the opportunity to buy a then fledgling start-up for $50 million. At the time the deal must have seemed a waste of good money to Blockbuster executives whose indicators were all positive. As it turned out, the failure to buy the start-up – or recognise the change it represented – sowed the seeds for eventual collapse. Blockbuster failed to see where the media and retail market was going. In 2000 the dotcom boom was coming to a close, but the Internet was still changing people's experiences and expectations. Fast-forward ten years and those changes had solidified. That fledgling had driven them forward. Blockbuster, despite its immense head start and everyday household role, did not evolve and crashed.

That start-up was called Netflix.

Founded just twelve years after Blockbuster by entrepreneur Reed Hastings, Netflix is a textbook example of what Professor Clayton Christensen, of Harvard Business School, calls 'disruptive innovation'.[6] At first Netflix's model would be ignored and even derided by the industry establishment;

before long its hockey stick growth curves would render the old guard obsolete.

Starting with mailed-out DVDs before moving to online streaming, Netflix's proposition was supported on several pillars. First, it was convenient. No more driving to the store. Second, it was cheap. Using a subscription model and removing the overhead of extensive bricks and mortar meant that, especially once postage costs had been eliminated by the online offering, the marginal cost of lending a given film was approaching zero. Third, Netflix offered more choice. Whereas Blockbuster would always be constrained by the limitations of what a store could display, and hence always prioritised those films most likely, in its eyes, to be hired, Netflix could radically expand the catalogue available to any given user. Moreover, from the beginning Netflix wasn't just about having a lot of content; it was about giving users the content they wanted. They also applied the same principles to TV shows. In 1990 about 100 new scripted TV shows aired in the US. By 2015 that figure had grown to over 400.[7] As one network executive put it, 'there is simply too much television'.[8] Netflix wasn't just going to be about more content – that would be counterproductive. It would be about better-curated content.

Over the years Netflix had developed an algorithm called Cinematch to predict viewing preferences. They saw finding movies people would enjoy as a major part of their competitive advantage. Nothing too revolutionary for a tech company, you might think. But then they did something different. In 2007, in an attempt to beat their own algorithm, they launched the Netflix Prize. Teams would create an algorithm that performed better at suggesting films, based on Netflix's film grades and a preordained dataset of films and users. The winner would be the first to cross a 10 per cent improvement threshold and would receive $1m. Until an outright winner was found, an annual Progress Prize of $50,000 would be awarded for an improvement above 1 per cent. Netflix was inviting anyone with the skill and determination to beat their curation.

Teams from places like AT&T Labs and the University of Toronto applied sophisticated data science techniques to the problem. A start-up, Kaggle, even grew out of the idea.[9] The competition was tough. Throughout 2007 no prize was awarded, but a Progress Prize was given to BellKor, the team from AT&T. In 2008 the story was similar. No outright winner, but a Progress Prize.

Things were getting serious. A flurry of team mergers took place in 2009. The original AT&T team went through several mergers, demergers and permutations but eventually submitted a new algorithm as BellKor's Pragmatic Chaos. It breached the 10 per cent threshold, triggering a 30-day grace period for other teams to submit entries before the final result was announced. Other merged teams scrambled to submit and after tests were run on their great rival, by then known as The Ensemble, BellKor's Pragmatic Chaos was found to have won the $1m prize on 18 September 2009.

By the end over 5,169 teams had taken part. It was a revolutionary new way of selecting films (and doing business), a million miles from Blockbuster. Netflix harnessed the collective wisdom and hard labour of some of the world's best minds and research institutes, all to better curate their movie catalogue. The most remarkable thing was that after all that effort, all the prize money, all the ferocious intellectual competition, all the publicity, Netflix never implemented the new algorithm. Things had changed. Streaming grew faster than expected, mobile tech altered users' behaviour. Netflix now thought the results weren't good enough. Having gone to great lengths to improve its film selection, creating a new method for data science in the process, Netflix were so committed to the best means of selecting films they abandoned the whole thing.

Another example of how far Netflix has come featured in an investigation by journalist Alexis Madrigal for *The Atlantic*.[10] Like many customers, Madrigal noticed Netflix's baroque film categorisations: Emotional Fight-the-System Documentaries or Foreign Satanic Stories from the 1980s for example. It all seemed weirdly specific. How many categories could there actually be? How the hell did they generate these categories, and what were they doing with them? After some investigation Madrigal found that there were precisely 76,897 discrete categories on Netflix. Suffice to say, this was more categories than anyone had hitherto bothered to contemplate, and explained why Netflix was the destination of choice if you wanted Films With Cool Moustaches or Violent-Nightmare-Vacation Movies. Netflix was using this immense database to build a recommendation engine far superior to the competition, more specific and tailored – eerily so.

Speaking on the record, Netflix's Vice President of Product Innovation, Todd Yellin, confirmed the categories and explained how they worked. In a significant curatorial pattern, Yellin combined cutting-edge algorithmically driven systems with an unmistakable human touch. He called it 'Netflix Quantum Theory'. Every film in Netflix's corpus was watched by a trained viewer (the manual runs to thirty-six pages) and tagged in intricate detail. Moment by moment the film was categorised, often on a five-point scale. Was the ending a happy one? If so, was it a sentimental happy ending? Did such and such character have positive traits by the end (or even, one assumes, a moustache)? The results of this vast tagging process were then computed with reference to every other film to generate categories which could be matched with users – often telling them more about their preferences than they ever would have guessed.

This is a tricky process, combining labour-intensive work – *Wired* claims over 1,000 people work on it at Netflix – with significant investments in R&D and technology.[11] There was no certainty the system would actually work. Yet Netflix persisted and now, according to Madrigal, have one of the most sophisticated media recommendation and categorisation engines ever devised. They can find your filmic doppelganger – the person most similar to you in viewing taste – and suggest things based on their choices. Everything is A/B tested to within an inch of its life. All in the name of helping you choose your next Saturday night movie. They even used all this data when they branched into production – *House of Cards* was made because they knew political thrillers worked well, Kevin Spacey was one of the platform's most popular actors and David Fincher films were watched to the end. *Orange is the New Black* was commissioned because they knew people wanted LGBT content, clever comedy and women-led drama.[12]

The collapse of Blockbuster and the rise of Netflix isn't by a long way just about these two ways of selecting films. But it's part of the story. Standing back from these examples we can see that one way of choosing – Blockbuster's – gave way to a new and more powerful method – Netflix's. If, at most, Blockbuster looked at generic areas or broad demographics, Netflix can respond to and build selections around individuals. It's a pattern we find not only in movies, but across sectors. It's nothing less than a sea change and it responds to the context of overload.

The earlier model is what we might call the Industrial Model of Selection. For most consumers the modern era was dominated by the Industrial Model of Selection. There was choice, but it was circumscribed. Growing up in the 1950s, my parents' generation had, in most consumer decisions, two or three choices of shampoo, televisions or baked beans. Once mass production had been mastered in the second Industrial Revolution it seemed mass production was enough. Henry Ford is the Industrial Model of Selection's patron saint – you can have any colour, so long as it's black. Here was a model optimised for an affluent and productive world – but not too affluent or productive. It worked when a few Western businesses dominated markets or when product categories and consumer lifestyles were new and unfamiliar. When retail and inventory space were scarce, when distribution and logistics were still being perfected, the Industrial Model of Selection – choice, yes, but limited choice, limited curation, from a narrow range of producers – was enough.

Broadly speaking this was Blockbuster's model: fill key slots with the same film, usually produced by the same Hollywood studios. Sure it had more range, but its selection was limited and most of the time it made money from the narrow hits it stocked in bulk. Put another way, the Industrial Model of Selection was the opposite of a long-tail business.

The Industrial Model of Selection looks something like Figure 6.

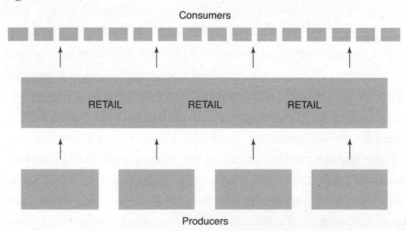

Figure 6. The Industrial Model of Selection

Of course, things changed. The second Industrial Revolution wasn't a one-off, but unleashed waves of development. Productivity and economic growth became the norm. Digital technology supercharged the expansion in choice and consumption. New economies emerged. The result is a consumer landscape offering more choice than was available to our parents in every area of our lives. Movies are only Exhibit A. This explosion in choice leads to what I call the Curated Model of Selection. In essence it means more producers and products, but more expertly matched to consumers. It means Netflix not Blockbuster, and it looks like Figure 7.

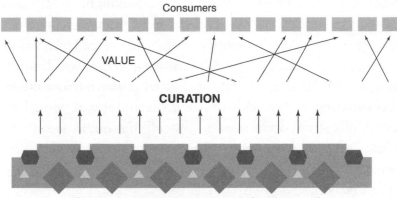

Consumers

VALUE

CURATION

Diverse, complex and productive set of producers

Figure 7. The Curated Model of Selection

Given increased complexity, value accrues not just to retailers, as in the Industrial Model; value also lies in the process of selection for specific consumers. Selection no longer happens wholesale; selection is considered, worked at, constantly improved. Selection isn't just a necessary part of doing business; selection is a primary asset. Selection isn't an afterthought; it's the priority. Selection is no longer a by-product of being a retailer; it is the point of being a retailer.

It means having highly qualified teams of people like Todd Yellin working on ways to match consumer and product.

The Curated Model describes one of the major business transitions of our time. It's not a binary shift but an evolution: usually there is a spectrum, with retail companies lying somewhere between the Industrial and the Curated. If the Industrial Model is exemplified by a Soviet shop, selling one dreary mass-produced product, the perfect Curated Model is the dream of companies like Amazon and Google: you always have the correct product pre-selected from an infinite catalogue. In between is everything else, but companies veer towards one or the other end of the spectrum. What has happened over the past twenty or so years is that technology and growth have rendered the Curated Model not only practically viable but increasingly valued.

This transition has immense consequences for retailers of all kinds. Traditional big box retail is in serious trouble. Blockbuster is only one example of such a retailer going bust as the Industrial Model breaks down. In the US, think of once mighty electronics empires like Circuit City or Radioshack (which filed for bankruptcy in February 2015), brought low by online competition. In the UK this shift has been especially marked. Once familiar names like Woolworth's, Comet, HMV, Borders, Tower Records, MFI, Jessops, Habitat, JJB Sports and Dreams have all either gone bust or drastically shrunk. For years major British supermarket groups like Tesco looked unassailable in their home market. Now they too struggle.[13] These companies are closer to the Industrial than the Curated end of the spectrum.

It would be a stretch to say the Curated Model of Selection finished them – as with Netflix and Blockbuster, convenience and price played a big role. The continued success of Costco and Walmart or European discount grocers like Aldi or Lidl, businesses that epitomise the Industrial Model, their product ranges coming and going according to availability, is predicated on price. Although they all work hard on selection, it's not their USP – ultra-cheap prices are. Whatever happens to selection, it seems, there'll still be room for a bargain.

It is worth re-emphasising, moreover, that the move from the Industrial to the Curated Model is on a sliding scale, not a binary shift. Blockbuster always had some curation. Many of the old video stores were already curated – and these are the niche and boutique places that today stand the best chance of survival. They were the kind of places that apprenticed great film directors like Quentin Tarantino and Kevin Smith working in video stores before they started directing (just as bookstores helped people like George Orwell, Patti Smith and Jonathan Lethem become the artists we know today). Somewhere like Rocket Video on La Brea Avenue in Hollywood was both a storehouse of cult cinema and part of the Hollywood culture, frequented by 'The Industry'. Like many indie video rental outlets, it's now closed despite all its efforts. And users of Netflix will vouch that neither its range nor selection are perfect. There's still a long way to go.

Yet that sliding scale is moving in one direction – towards the curated model. Somewhere like Netflix has been able to scale up with the abundance of film whilst also offering a more personalised selection.

Blockbuster was a part of our culture, but that culture changed. Selection grew in importance. You started to need not only more selection in absolute terms, but also better individual selection to compensate. Retail, media and consumption generally, more than ever before, were about sophisticated ways of selecting, and not just across ranges, but for specific individuals. All of this equated to success for those positioned to ride the wave. When Blockbuster passed on buying it, Netflix was still fighting to attract customers. By the middle years of the 2010s it had over 70 million subscribers from Brazil to Germany, its own in-house studio rivalling the production prowess of much-hailed veterans like HBO and billions of dollars in revenue. If Blockbuster had been synonymous with video renting, Netflix became synonymous with video streaming.

Selection matters.

Decisions, decisions

Consider jam.

Jam was the centre of a classic study of choice by Sheena Iyengar, now of Columbia University, and Mark Lepper of Stanford. The study – 'When Choice Is Demotivating' – challenges the idea that more choice is a good thing. Under the old theory of economics, the more chance of finding what you were after, the better. Hence the more choice was available to them, the more it was assumed people would buy. A body of research connected choice to life satisfaction. Not only did more choice lead to a booming economy, but more options meant we were more satisfied with life. No wonder that for most of the twentieth century choice was lionised; an imperative for governments, businesses and individuals.

Iyengar started to wonder. Might choice sometimes have negative consequences? Were we feeling what the futurist Alvin Toffler, at the beginning of the 1970s, had already named 'overchoice' – choice overload? Despite going against the conventional Long Boom wisdom, Iyengar believed our understanding of choice was wrong. The jam experiment came out of her doctoral research studying children and choice. She'd found, contrary to expectations, that children told to play with one toy appeared to have more engagement and fun than children given freedom to choose their toys.

Enter jam.

For the first part of the study she went to a branch of high-end San Francisco Bay Area supermarket Draeger's. Founded by Prussian immigrants, Draeger's prides itself on choice: they offer 250 kinds of mustard, 75 types of olive oil, no less than 300 varieties of jam and, at Menlo Park, over 3,000 cook-books and 20,000 kinds of wine. It's the kind of place where customers are willing to spend money trying new, interesting foods. In offering this excess of choice Draeger's is not alone. The average supermarket contained 3,750 items in 1949, twenty-four years after Draeger's first opened. By 2010 this was 45,000 items, while large supermarkets like out-of-town Walmarts had over 100,000.[14] Over consecutive weekends Iyengar used different selections of jam, all from high-end brand Wilkin & Sons (Purveyors to Her Majesty the Queen, no less), to investigate different selections.

As you entered the store there were always tables with goods for customers to try, showcasing the diversity of food on offer. Iyengar set up two tables in that front area to test the idea that excess choice might be 'demotivating'. Customers were used to the idea of sampling new products; it would not be unusual for the open-minded and well-heeled residents of Menlo Park to stop by a table and try something new. On one table six jams were displayed to taste. Another table had twenty-four. In both instances the full range of twenty-four jams was for sale in the shops.

The wider range of jams attracted more people – 60 per cent of passers-by stopped to look at that table, against 40 per cent who looked at the limited selection. But it didn't lead to people trying more jam. Those sampling both the large and the small selections tried about the same number. However, subsequent purchasing behaviour was seriously altered. Whereas 30 per cent of customers who viewed six jams went on to buy jam, the figure plunged to 3 per cent of those looking at twenty-four jams. In other words, four times the selection resulted in only one-tenth of the eventual sales. The result was that 'consumers initially exposed to limited choices proved considerably more likely to purchase the produce than consumers who had initially encountered a much larger set of options.'[15] Despite the shop priding itself on range, the more focused selection resulted in better sales. Draeger's customers might be offered 300 types of jam, but in fact, that sheer range put them off.

These results were replicated elsewhere. Students wrote more elective essays when offered six topics than when offered thirty – and they were judged to be of better quality. Participants in a study of chocolates (undergraduates at Columbia) were more likely to purchase based on a small set of choices. It was further 'compelling empirical evidence that the provision of extensive choices, though initially appealing to choice makers, may nonetheless undermine choosers' subsequent satisfaction and motivation'. Since the paper was published in 2000 others have come to the same conclusion.

An example cited by academic Barry Schwartz replaced jam with pens.[16] After completing a questionnaire, participants were offered a $1.50 reward or a pen worth $2. Seventy-five per cent duly chose the pen. More choice changed the calculation. A new set of participants were offered either $1.50, the $2 pen or two felt-tip pens worth about $2 between them. After being offered a further choice only 50 per cent of people went for pens, even though they were clearly more valuable. Introducing more choice made people not want to choose. Rather than allowing people to maximise their gains, as traditional economics suggests, choice had the opposite effect.

Astoundingly Schwartz also cites studies of this same effect occurring in healthcare. Faced with more medical options, doctors would abrogate the choice. Iyengar's research has subsequently looked at how her conclusions can be applied to areas like pensions and health insurance.

So what's going on? Why would more jam attract more interest but result in less jam being bought?

It's what Schwartz calls the 'tyranny of choice'. Understanding this tyranny takes us further into psychology and the behavioural economics challenging the view of *Homo economicus* as a rational being.

For a start, thanks to the complexity engendered by the Long Boom, many of us don't have the expertise to make choices. Moreover, our ability to know is complicated by advertising, which activates our 'availability heuristic': the more we encounter something, the more it is 'available' or easily remembered.[17] The more available something is, the more significance we ascribe to it. The more we see mobile phone x, the more we are likely to choose mobile phone x regardless of whether it makes sense to do so.

Too much choice overwhelms us. The responsibility of making the 'right' choice quickly becomes a burden. It creates conflict and indecision. Plurality of choice leads to one choice only – the decision not to choose! We have, no doubt, all experienced this in the supermarket aisles, staring at hot sauce or soft drinks rooted to the spot, overcome with trivial indecision. One principle behind this feeling is known as loss aversion. We feel losses more acutely than gains. Choosing immediately opens the possibility of loss – the possibility that we could have chosen better, and so have missed out. We'd rather not choose than make the wrong choice.

Choice forces us to trade off. Every choice comes with an opportunity cost, the idea that every choice we make closes off the possibility of all the others. Knowledge of those opportunity costs impacts on our ability to choose and our satisfaction with the choices we make. For example, say I choose mobile phone x and it repeatedly goes wrong. I immediately think back to other choices and how much less frustration I would be experiencing had I made one of them. The more options you have, the more opportunity costs you have incurred, psychologically speaking. We don't just experience regret after the event either – we anticipate regret. We ruin our own pleasure anticipating regret we might feel about other choices we could make! Which again impedes our ability to choose, inhibiting our desire to make a choice in the first place. This spills over into our work and our everyday lives – the tens, hundreds, thousands of unanswered emails we have to parse and prioritise; the impossible to-do list; the endless choices about not just jam but our insurance, electricity, Internet providers, our children's education.

Returning to jam, if we think we'll regret buying Jam A because of the opportunity costs of not buying Jam B, we are more likely to buy no jam than Jam A. Given the confluence of this effect with the sheer rise in choice and a market system, the prevalence of a Curated Model of Selection is predictable and understandable.

A further consideration is that the existence of an excessive range of parameters for decision making again impairs our ability to decide.[18] Say you are purchasing a car. There are any number of possible parameters to consider – colour, brand, top speed, safety record in side impact collisions, in-car stereo quality and so on. When spending significant sums most of us believe the availability of more parameters leads to better decisions. More information, we assume, means we're better prepared. Yet this isn't true. After considering about ten parameters our ability to make decisions is impaired. We get confused and lose sight of our priorities. Even ten is a stretch and many psychologists argue anything beyond five is suboptimal. Saturated not just in choices but in information about choices – from the fuel efficiency of an engine to the size of the boot – we struggle to grasp what we want and why we want it. When buying a car we shouldn't take in every factor – we should choose five and focus on them.

Our choices define us. Likewise businesses and organisations are defined by their choices, which speak more clearly than any advertising campaign. The long-running Whitehall Study by Professor Michael Marmot of University College London indicates that it is the feeling of choice, rather than anything else, that promotes wellbeing.[19] Our wellbeing is dependent on the ability to exercise choice, but too much choice backfires. The feeling of choice, rather than its reality, is what we want.

Curation's role should be clear. In Western markets we have choice saturation – whether it's dating options or mobile phones or jam. The old theory said this was virtuous: good for us, good for everybody. But evidence suggests that there comes an all too familiar point when choice flips from positive to negative. Presenting the six best or most interesting jams leads to more sales than a table that's overflowing with variety. Pre-selecting which information is important about a given product helps us make better decisions. To put it bluntly, having jam today means curated jam.

Schwartz's solution to what he calls the paradox of choice is that we 'learn to love constraints'. Although we think of constraints as negative they can be helpful, even liberating. Curation produces such constraints. It limits us, but productively. Arbitrary and unthinking constraint, or the kind of constraints that come from scarcity, are unproductive. Curation, in contrast, frees us from the tyranny of small – and large – choices. Curation allows us to focus on what matters. It takes the chore away but leaves us with the benefits; curated selection leaves us with choice, but better choice. In a time-scarce world it saves time. In tough markets where 80 or 90 per cent of products fail, curation helps focus on what works. It's why, for example, companies like Proctor and Gamble are rolling back the long-term strategy of product creation to focus on a smaller number of better-defined products and why Tesco, the world's fifth-largest retailer, is slashing its product range by a third.

When it comes to selection, curation is how we can have our cake and eat it. How we can have unprecedented production and multiplying choice without the associated anxiety, confusion and tax on our cognitive resources. Prior selections – curated selections – are needed. If we carry on expanding choice, the conclusion Iyengar suggests is that we will only grow more demotivated, whether in our desire to see masterworks in a gallery or buy breakfast condiments.

Yes, selection matters.

Platform says this

During my conversations with curators, one topic came up again and again. It's not just that curators are selectors; they're expert selectors. They have studied or practised for years to build a body of knowledge. Their curation is based on judgements and instincts honed by tens of thousands of hours of learning and immersion. Good taste, one diffuse but central idea behind curated selections, is carefully cultivated.

The value of curation is never *just* about selection. It's about knowledgeable selection, knowledge you can't fake. It's this mastery which makes curation so significant. Typically a museum curator will have both undergraduate and postgraduate degrees, supplemented by globe-trotting museum placements. But the blues fan running an amateur blog and collecting old records has probably spent similar amounts of time immersing themselves in the sound of the Delta. Either way, their choices are worth following because of that deep expertise.

Comparisons are easier when in-depth knowledge is available. Curators automatically know which features are important, what fundamentals are at play and why. They parse irrelevant information faster. Experts cut options down to manageable levels without breaking sweat. Without expertise, one has to evaluate in detail, on a case-by-case basis, rather than zeroing in with an instantaneous glance. When buying that car, an expert can, choosing from thousands of criteria, instantly home in on the right model, saving you months of stress.

Yet expertise is never static. In an age of technological transformation, what it means to be an expert, and how that impacts selection, changes. This doesn't mean old-fashioned virtues of learning are becoming irrelevant. As we will see, curation straddles the new and the old, each complementing the other. But the issue is this: on the Internet, machine-driven curation, based on sophisticated algorithms and data mining, has increasingly replaced human curation. Is the expertise behind curated selection becoming more about coding and designing software than a rich understanding?

The answer is yes – and no.

Amazon is in some ways the bookish analogue of Netflix. While bookselling was always closer to the Curated Model of Selection than, say, Blockbuster, Amazon had at least a ten-fold advantage in total product stock: while the biggest bricks-and-mortar bookstore could support around 100,000 titles, from the beginning Amazon had no effective cap on range. Choice was unlimited. As always, this created problems as well as opportunities.

Two early Amazon employees illustrate the shifting fortunes of machine and human curation. Back in 1997 Greg Linden was a 24-year-old artificial intelligence expert living in Seattle. He got a job working for the local book retail start-up. James Marcus was a cultural critic for the *Village Voice* – someone steeped in the world of bookish culture.[20] Like Linden, he took a job with Amazon, working as a site editor. In those days Amazon employed people to post reviews and provide recommendations. They were, like Marcus, from literary backgrounds. Marcus wrote hundreds of reviews and edited the home page, which reached millions of people a day. He had a column called 'Book Favourites' which built audiences for worthwhile books. His job was to slot Amazon into the book world, to give it the feel of a local indie. The editors had real power. Their curation could make or break books. 'The very early history is that Amazon,' Linden tells me, 'had a very strong human editorial voice back in early 1997. It was a bookstore only at this time and had editors and reviewers crafting the front page, much like the reviews you see if you go into a good small bookstore today.'

But Amazon's founder, Jeff Bezos, was a hedge-fund analyst and engineer: a numbers man. He felt more at home with hard metrics than the luvvie atmosphere of Manhattan publishing. Written material, Marcus told the *New Yorker*, was dismissed as 'verbiage'.[21] Bezos wanted to change the messy, subjective, Old World curation of the site – the curation that first attracted editors like Marcus. The mood was frenetic: 'The company was chaotic and growing fast, we could barely keep the wheels on,' says Linden. 'Our work was mostly trying to keep up and scale with the rapid growth, with some big projects to expand into new product lines (music, movies) or internationally.' Despite Amazon's focus on data, he tells me, 'Any breakthroughs or innovation on things like personalisation happened as side projects, totally unplanned and unsanctioned by management.' It was becoming obvious to those on the engineering side that the site was growing too fast to maintain the hands-on, boutique approach. 'With millions of books in the catalogue, millions of customers with widely different tastes, and soon expanding into music, movies and many other product categories, a handcrafted approach couldn't keep up.'

Amazon knew what products people were buying – couldn't it also automatically recommend products based on this dataset? Their dream, and that of engineers like Linden, was to offer the customer only one book – the next book they wanted to buy.

At first the systems were crude and couldn't match human curation. If you bought a book about cooking, you then only got more of the same. It wasn't subtle.

In 1998 Linden saw a way to use the data more effectively. It was called 'item to item collaborative filtering'. It looked only at the relationships amongst products. Linden's insight was that if you just compared product correlations (ignoring a customer's individual buying history) – noticing that product a was often bought with product b – and if you had a large enough dataset, the system could suggest goods with uncanny accuracy. Enough correlations and you could safely assume that almost anyone buying product a would also want product b. It meant that all products could be included. Relationships were already in place. It noticed hidden nuances without getting distracted by odd juxtapositions. Linden had hit on a new way of auto-curating retail. Within Amazon the process was known as 'personalisation' and soon had its own dedicated team, P13N.

They tested the system against human recommendations. It won decisively.

Editors couldn't compete with the algorithms. Unlike editors, the system couldn't understand *why* a book was desirable. But the aggregated data didn't lie; correlations between products were clearly useful to consumers. Some estimates claim that a third of Amazon purchases now arise from the recommendation system. The MBA suits triumphed over old-fashioned curators like Marcus. As the dotcom boom ended, most of the site's editors were let go.

Today it's a constant process of refineement. Amazon can't just rely on its stock of data – data ages. Just because products were correlated in 2001, doesn't mean they will be correlated fifteen or twenty years later. If recommendations are wrong, the system is undermined. So there is a constant balancing act between harnessing historical data and discarding what isn't useful. Amazon has built sophisticated techniques for guessing the 'depreciation' of its data. It has systems that analyse whether consumers' tastes have changed, and whether recommendations are likely to be inaccurate.

Linden, who as much as anyone pioneered machine-driven curation, changed retail for ever. Marcus was out of a job. Linden himself places recommendations as part of a wider change at Amazon, but all of these changes were built on automation and the empirical evidence of traffic: 'Experiments showed that the editorial content could be outperformed by machine-generated content – personalised recommendations, top N lists, crowdsourced reviews – and quickly the front page and other pages on the website became automated.'

Since the late 90s machine-driven curation, fed by the enormous datasets that have sprung up in the interim, has grown. Companies like Amazon and Netflix that mastered this shift flourished. Meanwhile researchers at McKinsey estimated that such personalisation had a return on investment of five to eight times.[22] It became clear that the Curated Model of Selection would at least in part be the domain of algorithms.

Yet that isn't the whole story. On the App Store, as well as in iBooks, iTunes, News and Music, Apple hadn't abandoned human curators. In fact, it was doubling down on them. Indeed, even as the big platforms powered onwards, the rise of curation was happening on a micro scale. Sites like Boing Boing weren't growing fast on the back of machine learning, but on editor taste. In millions of niches individual curators were carving audiences. Even Amazon eventually changed course and started to rehire human editors.

What's more, others saw an opportunity to reverse engineer human selection back into the former poster child for automated selection. Amazon's range is so vast that while recommendation systems are essential, they far from exhaust the potential for curation on the site. Canopy.co is built around Amazon. Everything for sale on Canopy is supplied via Amazon. In effect, Canopy exists on top of Amazon – a version where designers and creatives spend hours deliberating over each item. On Amazon you can buy any item of furniture you want. On Canopy you will find only that perfect piece, otherwise buried deep in the system.

'We all liked shopping on Amazon,' says co-founder Brian Armstrong when I ask him about how they got started. 'But we didn't really discover new products there. We often learned about great products from our friends, through word of mouth.' Working in a design studio at the time, Brian and his co-founders decided to do something about it. They set up Canopy to curate Amazon using their design expertise. 'As product designers, we know the importance of maintaining a high level of quality on our storefront,' he tells me. 'Amazon

sells practically everything, but not everything in their catalogue is worth buying.'

I ask Brian about the place of hands-on curation in a world
of machines and Big Data. His response is worth quoting at
length: 'We've only seen the very beginning of machine-driven
curation – it's still super-early in the game. People have been
hand-picking things for thousands of years in their homes
and shops, so human curation has a huge head start. Even
though it's becoming more and more pervasive, algorithmic
curation is not yet a solved problem. Algorithmic curation will
definitely get better, but it won't ever have discerning taste or
a unique point of view. People can perceive and appreciate the
human thought that goes into manual curation. They pick up
on the time and effort that's been invested, in the same way
that with a well-designed object you can see the fingerprints
of a designer who thought deeply about the problem and came
up with a unique solution. This human quality is also behind
the appeal of "artisanal" goods and services.'

Canopy has gone back to the Amazon of James Marcus.
Armstrong's answer tells us why. Part of curation's appeal
is an unmistakable personal touch. A qualitative dimension stemming from an individual's style, taste, learning or
opinion, interesting and useful precisely because of quirks
and insights deriving from what makes that person unique.
Curation is, in part, about what machines cannot do. Think
back to Netflix. While they use data-processing systems,
every film is watched, tagged and reviewed by a film buff.
Why? Because they are grading things like a film's sentiment,
humour and any number of subjective factors beyond the
modelling capacity of software. If machine-driven curation
was the pinnacle of selection, there would be no room for
a site like Canopy or Boing Boing or Wanelo or countless
other human-curated concerns. We would fire all the visual

merchandisers. Get rid of the magazine editors. Gallery exhibitions could be fed into an app.

But that doesn't happen. People still enjoy the experience of bricks-and-mortar bookstores, in part because of their curation by booksellers. Selection is about finding the right things. Defining what is 'right' in any given context can't be boiled down to the information analysed by a machine. Which is not to say machines aren't valuable – they are, and will be a massive part of curatorial business over the next century.

But we will see a balance.

Human and algorithmic curation working together, complementing each other. Linden, the original architect of retail selection by personalisation algorithms, agrees: 'On the balance of algorithmic versus human selection, the short answer is that, with millions of items in the catalogue and millions of customers, you can't do anything but algorithmic. Nothing else can get coverage over enough of it. Nothing else scales. The longer answer is that the algorithms entirely depend on human selection – it's human actions of buying, looking, searching and reviewing that the algorithms are surfacing to other humans to help them – so the reality is that the algorithms are helping humans help other humans, not replacing humans at all.'

Search indexing means we have become very good at finding things we know we want. It's usually just a brief enquiry away. But faced with abundance – millions of books, say – we often don't know what we want in the first place. In the words of the technology analyst Benedict Evans, 'Google is very good at giving you what you're looking for, but no good at all at telling you what you want to find, let alone things you didn't know you wanted.'[23] If search algorithms fixed the problem of finding things on the Internet, curation, in its myriad forms, is what helps address the latter – what is it you want to find in the first place? It's altogether a subtler and more nuanced question and plays on the uncertainties we experience when faced with enormous choice.

Whether it's driven by machines or humans, curation goes beyond 'I want/need this' to ask more fundamental questions. If you want to find something, search is the key; if you want to *discover*, then it's about curation. This distinction rests at the heart of all web curation and goes a long way to explaining its power in a world where consumers are overloaded with options.

While algorithms are very good at analysing some things, they are terrible at others. For example, algorithms may be able to tell us we might like to watch a particular film, or even whether a film is likely to succeed at the box office (there is in fact a company that specialises in this) – but they can't tell us whether a film is any good.[24] Beyond statistical correlations, they can't explain why we might like it. They can't create random, dimly felt linkages. The Netflix Prize offered no marks for judgement on quality; no criteria for aesthetics or taste. Whether it's books, films or anything at all, to an algorithm it's just data. No one can deny their power – not just to sort our media, but, for example, to find directions, fly drones or even predict terror attacks and outbreaks of disease – but at the same time we often want more. We don't yet have an algorithm that truly understands meaning beyond a set of heuristics; that sees beyond data. Google's Deepmind division are said to be developing artificial intelligence software capable of (something like) this, but for the time being algorithms don't have the meaning-rich quality of subjective judgement.

Expertise, then, is not a matter of old learning giving way to new; they reinforce one another. In an age of web-based platforms like Amazon, the process of selection can be depicted as in Figure 8.

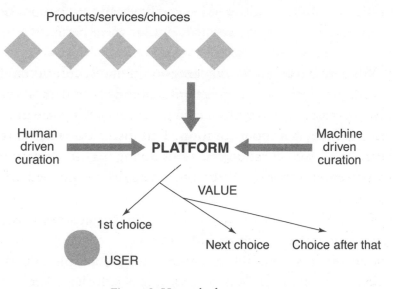

Figure 8. How platforms curate

The best selection makes the most of both human and machine curation to offer bespoke choices. This is how the Curated Model of Selection will develop. It's how we will manage the enormous proliferation of choices available to us and cut them down to a manageable number. The arts of connoisseurship aren't dead in the age of algorithmic selection – they're augmented.

Expert selection is a core principle of curation. The examples I've given here are mainly from retail and illustrate how central selection has become to overloaded consumers. But they need not be retail. Going back to that earlier use of curation, in museums, centuries of collecting have resulted in unmanageable collections which need sifting by curators.

If you were in London for the weekend I'd suggest you visit the British Museum in Bloomsbury and the Natural History Museum in South Kensington, two of the city's – and the world's – most visited and impressive tourist attractions. At the British Museum you could spend hours behind its neoclassical facade looking at ancient treasures from the Parthenon frieze to the Rosetta Stone. In total the British Museum displays an awesome 80,000 objects. Far more than is viewable in a single afternoon. Yet this represents only 1 per cent of the museum's holdings. Its eight million strong collection, much of it kept in 194 storerooms beneath the main site, would take lifetimes to truly appreciate. Like our industrial production, it is the accumulated heritage of centuries of work (and plunder). Curators, experts in their field, take that eight million down to 80,000 – and then to direct us to the eighty objects they believe we really should view.

Arriving beneath the neo-gothic towers of the Natural History Museum you witness, aside from the dinosaurs, an even more extraordinary process of selection. The Natural History Museum's life and earth science collections amount to over eighty million items, including a giant squid, extinct species of insect, records from Darwin's voyage on the *Beagle* and over 5,000 meteorites. There are seven million fossils alone, some of them dating back 3,500 million years. Most importantly the museum holds over 850,000 'type' specimens – the first identified instance of a species and its benchmark thereafter. While some specimens choose themselves, it takes an enormous process of selection, underpinned by world-leading knowledge, to curate this immense collection. You can glean at least a sense of its scale and mission from just a day in its galleries.

Both the Natural History Museum and the British Museum, of course, do far more than merely select objects to display, just as Amazon doesn't only help select your next book. But without serious selection, Netflix and the Natural History Museum alike would long ago have been overloaded by their sheer quantity of material. They are both curating, selecting, choosing. As institutions they derive enormous value from their vast holdings. But they wouldn't if there wasn't a knowledgeable, extensive process of selection at work. The chance of finding that one must-see piece, or that extraordinary specimen, would be vanishingly small.

The displays, in contrast, are curated and because they are curated, selected, they help us navigate the collections. They take over-abundance and make it work. As the nineteenth-century mathematician Augustus de Morgan put it: 'Take the library of the British Museum ... what chance has a work of being known there merely because it is there? If it be wanted, it can be asked for; but to be wanted it must be known.' Selection is the difference between known and unknown, overload and balance, chaos and value. Put simply, the more we have in any given area, the more we need selection to make it manageable.

Given the growth in productivity and hence in choice, the Industrial Model of Selection is, in many instances, struggling. Selection is no longer an unexciting business necessity but an important USP in its own right. When that happens you move towards the Curated Model of Selection, offering both a wider and a more tailored choice, now a major part not just of museums, but of the wider retail and business environment. If too much choice overwhelms us, curated selection reins it back in.

Selection might be the central principle of curation. But as any curator will tell you, selection is still only the beginning.

Arrangement

Mass mourning broke out on the MIT campus as the demolition squad rolled in. It was the end of an era. Starchitect Frank Gehry had designed the new $300m Stata Center – a state-of-the-art research facility designed to project MIT's path into the twenty-first century. Limned in the trademark Gehry style – with protruding windows and a mash of collapsing angles and jagged planes – the building was described by its architect as looking like a party of drunken robots gathered to celebrate. The Stata Center was meant to change the way people worked. By combining different disciplines and labs, the idea was that new forms of knowledge would be created. Arranging the offices, departments and research spaces in an open and fluid way would itself generate new thinking. It would be 'hackable', 'post-disciplinary'; innovative inside and out.

The ironic thing, and the reason for mass mourning, was that the building the Stata Center replaced had already done these things. Building 20, the long, hulking block that previously occupied the site, had a reputation as the most innovative space on earth. Nicknamed the 'magic incubator,' it showed that a different arrangement was, sometimes, all that is needed.

Building 20, or 18 Vassar Road, was never given a formal name because it was never meant to last. Hastily thrown up in 1943 at the height of the Second World War, it was designed, allegedly in one afternoon, to house the Rad Lab – a radar laboratory helping the Allies identify Nazi planes. A sprawling 25,000 square metre structure, it was three storeys of rickety wood (which was why it was temporary – Cambridge fire regulations wouldn't allow wooden buildings on that scale). At its peak it housed some 4,000 radar researchers. The Rad Lab developed radar not just for planes but also for navigation, understanding the weather and spotting submarines. In 1945 the Department of Defense claimed its work would have taken twenty-five years in peacetime. As with other Second World War research centres like Oak Ridge or Los Alamos it held a curious mix of characters and disciplines from maths, science and technology, experimentalists and theoreticians thrown together in the deep end. It's fair to say that if radar wasn't invented in Building 20 it was perfected there.

After the war Building 20 was scheduled for demolition. Yet despite – or because – of its jerry-built structure it became one of the most iconic structures not just on the MIT campus but in research. Post-war it became a home for random departments of MIT. Before long this assortment of misfits would change the world.

The first interdisciplinary research lab at MIT, the Research Laboratory of Electronics, was founded in Building 20. Noam Chomsky began his research into the structure of linguistics there, drawing on fields as diverse as biology and computer science. The MIT machine shop was moved there, along with a particle accelerator. Harold Edgerton created underwater photography there. The first computer hackers, members of the Tech Model Railroad club, based in E Wing, found a home there. Companies like the Digital Equipment Corporation, once one of the world's leading computer producers, were formed there. Nuclear science, systems control, new electronics, advanced acoustics technology (Amar Bose, founder of audio equipment manufacturer the Bose Corporation, was playing with speakers), the first atomic clock and microwave physics were all incubated in the space. In C Wing walls were painted with lurid murals to test the effects of LSD. There was even a room for repairing pianos.

Building 20 was, in many ways, inadequate. Ugly, featureless and cold, it lacked the creature comforts of modern buildings. Its humidity gave it a musty smell. The inside was dark. It didn't have a disciplinary identity. But it all worked. Why?

Because it was jerry-built and always supposed to go,

Building 20 was, unlike a permanent brick structure, endlessly and easily reconfigurable. If you wanted to take down a wall, you did. If you wanted more height, you'd knock through the ceiling. If you wanted to chat to someone down the hall – as often as not there was no hall. People met in new ways. There was no real sequence to the numbering of rooms and wings, which meant everyone got lost. As it was a horizontal space, getting lost took you past potential new colleagues. Groups could form and share information in ways impossible in the segregated offices and labs that characterised most research buildings of the time. Departments, research groups and oddballs from across campus came to Building 20 because there was nowhere else to go. Once there they started talking and thinking together, knocked through walls, embarked on joint projects from backgrounds no one had ever thought of combining. In Building 20 they were free – free to change the building and free to work differently.

Most buildings and offices limit rearrangement. They set patterns of work literally in stone. Some buildings like old warehouses and factories do the opposite. They allow constant rearrangement. It makes them more durable and adaptable and explains why, in cities around the world, these once derelict spaces have become so desirable. Their inherent capacity for the productive reconfiguring of space means that, unlike most offices from the 1950s with their walls and elevators, they leapt from industrial to digital revolution without breaking sweat.

A 1978 press release from the MIT museum puts it well:

Unusual flexibility made the building ideal for laboratory and experimental space. Made to support heavy loads and of wood construction, it allowed a use of space which accommodated the enlargement of the working environment either horizontally or vertically. Even the roof was used for short-term structures to house equipment and test instruments. Although Building 20 was built with the intention to tear it down after the end of World War II, it has remained these thirty-five years providing a special function and acquiring its own history and anecdotes. Not assigned to any one school, department or center, it seems to have always have had space for the beginning project, the graduate student's experiment, the interdisciplinary research center.[25]

Building 20 bucked the dominance of planned, top-down research programmes. Want to research something? Build a building, hire a team, do the work. It was an additive, linear process. Instead Building 20 took existing university assets and allowed them to flexibly rearrange themselves. It wasn't a process of addition so much as recombination. By arranging work spaces differently, MIT harnessed more overall value than virtually any research programme in history. By making a space that rearranged both itself and the disciplines and research groups within it, the Stata Center only aped the old building.

Informed by these lessons, architects and office designers are approaching layout anew. When Pixar needed a new office Steve Jobs was insistent that it had to bring people together.[26] As a blend of creatives, artists and technologists, this intermixing of minds, not just hiring more people, would make Pixar a success. The same principles are found in new laboratories like the Crick Institute in London, a $1bn medical research facility. Both Pixar and the Crick are built around large, open atria designed to facilitate chance meetings and foster internal relationships. They have open stairways and bridges, numerous casual meeting places that allow serendipitous conversations, 'breakout spaces', entrances used by everyone, openness to the main space from surrounding galleries. At Pixar the mailboxes, the cafeteria, a gift shop and, most importantly of all, the bathrooms were all placed in the atrium, necessitating visits there. You couldn't avoid running into your colleagues even if you wanted to. Tech companies from Airbnb to Facebook now design their offices like this as standard.

Physical connections still matter. Our interaction with space is a function of its arrangement. After crunching the data on peer-reviewed papers, Isaac Kohane, a Harvard Medical School researcher, found that the co-authors of the most cited papers usually worked within ten metres of each other. The authors of the least cited were usually over a kilometre apart.[27] The buildings that really work, like Building 20, are those that blend people and ideas in the best ways. A simple matter of arrangement can, in short, change everything. MIT didn't need the Stata Center to change the world. All it needed was the freedom and self-arrangement of Building 20.

If a central part of curation is selecting, what you do with those selections – how you arrange, organise, display, juxtapose and order them – is utterly crucial. As Building 20 suggests, some forms of arrangement or organisation are more generative than others – sometimes by an order of magnitude. In an overloaded world, rather than incrementally adding, perhaps we should re-examine what we already have and use it better. Understand that recombining can be recreating. That seeing and drawing out existing patterns, amplifying and altering them, is often a wiser and more valuable approach than creating more. Perhaps you don't need a new building – you just need to use the one you have more intelligently.

As online curator Maria Popova puts it: 'The art of curation isn't about the individual pieces of content, but about how these pieces fit together, what story they tell by being placed next to each other, and what statement the context they create makes about culture and the world at large.'[28] This is, she argues, a process of 'pattern recognition'. Seeing how things fit together, understanding connections (which multiply in a networked environment), but then also, crucially, creating new ones by recombining them, is a massive part of curation.

Building 20's success was about relationships between people and ideas. By arranging and allowing them to combine in new, previously unthought-of ways it produced more than the sum of its parts – albeit, unlike curation, at random. We even see this at the level of individual relationships. Building 20 was full of people sparking off each other in what are known as 'creative pairs'.[29] Relationships like that between Noam Chomsky and Morris Halle fundamentally changed at least one aspect of knowledge and probably many more. This is the power of the creative pair, whether in music (Lennon and McCartney), science (Marie and Pierre Curie), business (Charlie Munger and Warren Buffett) or technology (Larry Page and Sergey Brin), a species of relationship with outsized impact.

Life throws these things into place. Curation cultivates them into being. Arrangement, and by extension curation, is about the transforming impact of relationships – not just amongst people but images, words, ideas, groceries, historical curios, anything at all. Curators find and establish relationships. They are matchmakers, contrasters, minglers, pattern spotters and pattern producers – people who can see, understand and interpret the *gestalt* and in doing so create a new one.

After selecting, the question becomes – what do you do with those selections? How do you arrange them? How do you make sure you have Building 20? How can you make the most of what you already have? What you do alongside selecting makes all the difference.

Sum of parts

If supermarkets teach us about selection, they also tell us about the power of arrangement. Cornell University's Brian Wansink spent years studying consumer behaviour and the way we eat. His investigations show how simple matters of arrangement influence it to an extraordinary degree. In one experiment he wanted to encourage students to eat more healthily at a college canteen.[30] Changing ingrained habits is difficult. Students knew what they wanted and it didn't involve vegetables. Rather than go about this the traditional way – by changing the menu – he wanted to achieve the same effect simply by rearranging the canteen.

Wansink moved broccoli to the beginning of the line. The first thing hungry students now saw wasn't fast food. Fruit was taken out of functional containers and put in an attractive wooden bowl. The salad bar went in front of the tills, making it more prominent, something you couldn't avoid. The ice cream freezer went from invitingly transparent to opaque. Buying sugar-rich desserts was made more complex, requiring additional calculations. Wansink hadn't actually added anything, the food on offer was the same, but he rearranged the process. The results were clear.

Broccoli consumption increased by 10–15 per cent. Fruit sales from the wooden bowl doubled. Sales of salad tripled. The percentage of students buying ice cream fell from 30 per cent to 14 per cent. In general the composition of meals was far healthier.[31] Arrangement, not any other inducement, led to healthy eating. Wansink studied other instances of how food's presentation and arrangement affects our relationship with it. We get full faster from eating off small plates, for example, because the smaller plate frames our expectations to make us feel we have eaten enough. Even a plate's colour changes how we eat.

Just as behavioural sciences are teaching us about choice and selection, so they are teaching us that arrangement shapes how we behave and how business works. Simple cues or ordering have marked consequences. Supermarkets have known this for some time. It's why they put chocolates at the till and their own brands at eye level. It's why fruit and vegetables are usually near the entrance. They realised that changing in-store arrangement was more valuable than building more outlets. Lower risk and higher return, patterning and merchandising became a central strategy.

Old business models were about crude expansion. This was based on making existing assets work more intelligently. Just as at MIT, supermarkets understood that what you had was potentially a rich source of value. Which isn't to say they didn't pursue linear growth – most of them did and now they're running into headwinds. They went for both, but now, in more difficult circumstances, once again working the arrangement to the maximum will be key to their future prospects. Virtually all placements in supermarkets are based on these insights.

Noticing that British consumers drank far fewer cocktails than Americans, Sainsbury's, the UK's second- or third-largest supermarket chain, partnered with Diageo, the drinks giant. In British supermarkets accoutrements like limes were at the opposite ends of the store to spirits. Consumers weren't thinking cocktails because the ingredients were so dispersed. Once people reached spirits they no longer wanted to trek back for limes. By putting a new space in the spirits section selling ice, fruits and mixers they increased sales of spirits by 9 per cent.[32] Complementary goods were allowed to complement one another.

Unilever found sales of its Peperami brand disappointing. Having secured space next to the checkout, they were confident it would sell. No luck. Instead Unilever found that sales of Peperami increased when it was put in the chilled snack section. That it didn't need to be chilled was supposed to be a benefit; but consumers expected meat-based snacks to be chilled and weren't buying Peperami, or noticing it, out of context. Everyone in FMCG (fast-moving consumer goods) businesses has a similar story.

Where things come in a sequence and how they are framed influences our decisions. If we're hungry and see broccoli before anything else, we want it. If apples look better in a bowl, we want apples.

Decision science is often based on arrangement – and it is a key tool to guide people in overloaded contexts. The principle here is known as framing. We don't approach things neutrally. Everything we encounter and experience is, in one way or another, framed by its surroundings. Our behaviour and how we understand the world is a result of how the world is framed to us. When plates are smaller they frame portion size to make us eat less. When fruit sits in a nice bowl, its framing, its context and situation, makes us want to eat it.

Figure 9 illustrates how simple yet forceful this can be.

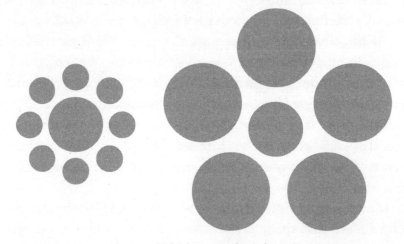

Figure 9. Which centre dot is bigger?

Looking at the two centre dots, most of us would immediately claim the central dot on the left is bigger than the one on the right. But of course it isn't. They're the same size. Our brains process the size of the centre circles only in contrast to the surrounding circles. It's that contrast, that framing, that makes us judge size. It's also true of properties like colour – colours appear to change depending on which colours are shown around them.

It's why we spend good money on bottles of mineral water with a funky-shaped bottle. And it's why we spend even more money on a glass bottle of mineral water with grand lettering on the front. The product is the same, but the framing – the packaging in this case – shapes our expectations. Illusionists Penn and Teller once put on a show called *Bullshit!* In one feature they went around New York City testing bottled waters, discovering in the process that in a water 'taste test' 75 per cent of people preferred the refined taste of . . . regular tap water. They pulled the same trick in a high end restaurant, complete with fancy names, notional health benefits and an on-hand 'water steward'. It was, again, from a tap. We're all suckers. If a product is framed in the right way, we are willing to pay thousands of times more for it.

As the circles demonstrate, framing is far from limited to commercial transactions – everything from our day-to-day relationships to our most difficult life challenges is framed, and that framing shapes how we engage with them.

One aspect of framing, again discussed by behavioural scientists and economists (Kahneman and Tversky foremost amongst them), is anchoring. If you walk into a budget supermarket and see a loaf of bread for sale at £2 you might think that's expensive compared with the surrounding loaves, which cost £1. All that cheap bread frames the £2 and, by being half the price, 'anchors' your expectations about the cost of bread at a lower level. Similarly, if you walk into your local 'arti-sanal' bakery that £2 loaf starts looking cheap next to a £5 rustic sourdough. Your expectations have been anchored up. It's why in negotiations first movers have the advantage – they anchor expectations about the final settlement.

Price, as much as any rational process or idea of 'real value', is a function of context. Value accrues through contrast, immediate comparison; it's implicit in given contexts and frames, not out there as a fact. Change the frame and you change the value proposition.

Curation uses all these techniques. Twentieth-century works from an artist like Matisse can look radical, daring and unconventional when placed in a gallery full of Renaissance masterpieces. They stand out and break the rules. Yet put those same Matisses in a room full of Damien Hirst vitrines or next to a Marina Abramović performance and they start to look quite traditional. They're still paintings, still depicting the human form. Curators play on these effects, contrasting works, shaping and upsetting our expectations. Just as price and value are produced through framing and anchoring, so the avant-garde is an expression of arrangement. No art *is* avant-garde, in the same way that no bottle of mineral water *is* worth $20; in both cases context imparts the property.

From Denon at the Louvre through Bode and Hultén, curators haven't just selected which works to display; they've hung them as well, helping to explain and appreciate the art or challenge and provoke the viewer. If the neuroscience and behavioural economics are by now well known, the con-nection to curatorial practice is less widely discussed. The same techniques are present in the work of Wansink and Hans Ulrich Obrist. We just don't really talk about curating supermarkets because it sounds ridiculous. But both use arrangement to achieve precise goals. Whereas an art curator might, say, change our opinion on an aspect of visual culture, a shop might guide us to buy more baked beans; both achieve this through framing.

Frames are so powerful because we aren't generally aware of them. When going to the college canteen most of those students weren't thinking about how their food was presented. They were hungry, loading up on what seemed easy. Unless we are serious connoisseurs we tend not to think about the hanging of paintings in an exhibition – we just take it in. And we don't think about how companies steer us in their shops, or about the increasingly sophisticated marketing techniques which play off these insights.

One study conducted by the University of Newcastle shows how this works.[33] Taking a random sample of students, the researchers wanted to see what would affect whether they paid into an honesty box when taking tea or coffee. Students received emails reminding them to pay and a notice was put up reminding them to do so. On alternate weeks the researchers put another image in the room – either a control image or a pair of eyes. This was very subtle, simply a photocopied picture in both cases. No one really looked at it. Yet on those weeks when the eyes were present they collected on average 2.76 times what they did when the control image was on display. The study concluded that 'the images exerted an automatic and unconscious effect on the participants' perception they were being watched.' In other words, even if students weren't consciously aware of eyes in the room, the poster nonetheless changed behaviour by reframing a private activity as public. Whether it's in a clothing store, on a cruise ship or in a school textbook, our experience is conditioned by carefully constructed frames we don't realise are there. The more we understand how this works, the better we can understand our interactions with the world.

Arrangements are never *just* background. Or rather, background creates foreground. How things are arranged changes our actions. It makes us eat differently, spend more money or see art anew. At MIT a new approach to the arrangement of research kick-started revolutions in science and technology.

Just as selection is the obvious counterbalance to overwhelming choice, arrangement, patterning, makes the most of what we already have. Curators arrange; they frame, creating context through contrast. Selecting and arranging between them are, thanks to the results of the Long Boom, in an overloaded world and because of some deep properties of our minds, a way of recreating our culture, media and business for the twenty-first century.

So arrangement isn't only for florists and composers. Arrangement is one of the most powerful tools we have.

Artful arrangements

For most of human history recorded information was scarce. In ancient Mesopotamia this changed with the advent of a breakthrough technology used to record debts: writing. The increasing availability of information is one of the Long Boom's central planks and key to the overload we now experience. From the beginning of textual abundance in the wake of Gutenberg's press to its full realisation with the print factories and mass media of the twentieth century, culminating in the unprecedented inflation of the digital era, information has become more widespread and available in almost every one of the last 500 years. In recent times, thanks to the mass adoption of digital media like smartphones, this has been true on an eye-popping scale.

Information overload is commonly accepted. The question is not whether it exists (given that our conscious brain can process something like sixty bits at a time and the amount of information now available is such that each American consumed the equivalent of 175 newspapers per day in 2011[34]) but rather, what is the best way of handling it? Information is a good thing; how we ensure it remains a good thing in an era of overload is the real issue. Selection will, of course, have a huge part to play. Selecting the right piece of information, the critical piece of the puzzle that makes the difference between profit and loss, victory and defeat, has enormous significance. But selection alone is not enough. How you arrange information matters as well. As it has become abundant, the need for arranging information has become pressing.

Today a whole industry is devoted to the presentation, visualisation and organisation of data. Information designers create new ways for us to see information. Data scientists help process swathes of data into manageable insights. How we arrange and consume information has become big business. But this is an industry that dates back further than we might suppose.

Charles Joseph Minard (1781–1870), from Dijon, France, was one of the first to perfect data visualisation: the art of representing the world in abstract. A civil engineer, he changed how we see information – and hence how we understand the world. Having spent a long career building bridges and dams he approached information in the same way, as flows that could be visually represented. His image, the *Carte figurative des pertes successives en hommes de l'Armée Française dans la campagne de Russie 1812–1813* (see Figure 10), has been called the best statistical graphic of all time by modern information designers.[35]

Minard's map depicts Napoleon's disastrous Russian campaign of 1812. The Grande Armée set out for Moscow as one of the largest and most successful forces ever assembled – 442,000 men with a string of famous victories behind them.

Nations lay at Napoleon's feet as his attention turned to the vast power on Europe's eastern flank. It was to be his crowning glory. But then history intervened: the Russian winter, the immense size of the country itself, the huge Russian army and their scorched-earth policy ensured the invasion became a rout of epic proportions.

Minard's map immediately makes clear the scale of Napoleon's catastrophe. The lighter band represents the army, numerically, heading east. As it gets thinner it shows the force being whittled down. The black band is the retreat from Moscow through the Russian winter. In all the map condenses into a simple two-dimensional image six metrics: the numerical size of the army; the distance and course they travelled; the temperature; latitude and longitude; and the location by date, including cities and geographical features. By the time they had taken the abandoned, still smouldering ruins of Moscow, Napoleon's force was reduced to 100,000 men. When they finally left Russia it was with just 10,000. At one stage the black line abruptly halves as the Armée crosses the Berezina river under attack. Over 20,000 troops are lost.

Understanding the scale of what happened to the Grande Armée is difficult. Many in France were shocked, struggling for years to comprehend the historic calamity of this seemingly invincible force. It involves huge numbers and distances, played out over a long timescale. There are numerous data points, difficult to entertain all at once. The complexity of warfare, then as now, was challenging. Arranging information graphically – and really it is an arrangement – Minard revealed the disaster with extraordinary clarity. At a glance we understand. Tables of data would be information overload; one well-executed image is information perfection. Arranging information changes how we look at the world; it shapes our understanding, deepens our experience, reveals trends and

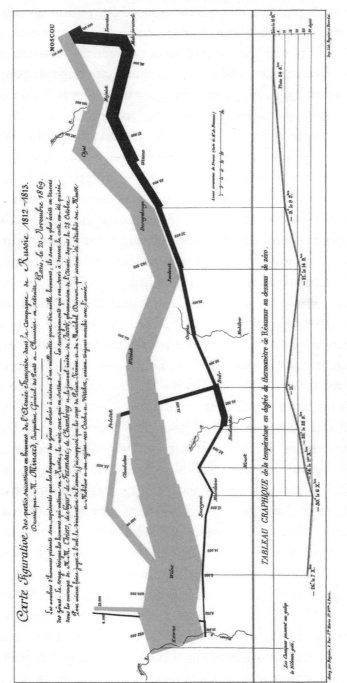

Figure 10. Minard's map of Napoleon's 1812 Russian campaign

tendencies we would otherwise miss. Minard wasn't an artist in the traditional sense. Instead he arranged data.

What Minard (and others) pioneered in the nineteenth century is now becoming routine. Newspapers have whole departments whose role is to produce such diagrams. Information companies work with corporate clients to produce graphs, animations and videos designed to help them understand themselves, boiling down the confusion of modern business into digestible packages. I've worked with animators who specialise in internal coms for big companies – so complex are these multinational, many-layered organisations that they need to be graphically reinterpreted for their own executives. Anyone who has worked in an organisation of some size can testify to the bewildering nature of corporate structures. Project managers create Gantt charts or use tools like Trello to map and arrange workflows. Intricate projects employing diverse workers, dependencies and processes are made possible through clear visual arrangement. Visualising (and organising) data in every sense is a huge part of our world, from the Dewey Decimal System to computer programming ontologies.

If one company exemplifies this trend it's Google, the information business *par excellence*. With its mission to sort the world's information, Google's obvious pitch is selection: we'll give you the best possible search results. We'll whittle down the information maelstrom into manageable and accurate answers. The fabled Google algorithm, with its hundreds of variables and ever-changing parameters, is above all the world's most valuable selection engine. But Google is more than just a selector. Eric Schmidt himself acknowledges as much in his co-written book *How Google Works*, saying that Google 'curates' the Internet.[36] If curation is where selection and arrangement add value, then how Google arranges information must play a big part in its user proposition.

When Google was founded in 1998, search engines like AltaVista and Excite were already popular. Google was the scrappy start-up. It won the search battle for two reasons. First, other search engines used basic Bayesian analysis to deliver results; they looked at the frequency of search terms. Google went one better with its PageRank system (named after co-founder Larry Page). Google looked beyond the density of words to the inbound links coming to a website. Not only would it analyse the number of such links, but it would rank their importance. A link from a website which itself was heavily linked to was worth more than a link from websites with few inbound links of their own. Each inbound link was seen as a kind of vote for the significance of a page's content. PageRank was an immediate success. While there is no 'right' way to shuffle the Internet, Google's results felt relevant and intelligent. With PageRank Google nailed selection.

Second, Google changed the design of search-engine interfaces. The competition had cluttered search and results pages, stuffed with information and news. GeoCities-style design might be fine for your website; not for a search engine. Google went minimal – a search bar, the logo and a list of links. The number of words on the home screen was and is rigorously policed. This design was user-friendly, an attempt to deliver well-chosen information and nothing more. When Google first launched they made the copyright notice at the bottom of the screen more prominent to let users know the page had finished loading. People were so used to overstuffed pages that they couldn't believe the simplicity of the Google homepage. It is basically a bar, or part of the URL field – simpler than virtually any other interface. Arranging the requested information efficiently and cleanly has always been the design priority.

So it continues. Knowledge Graph, for example, was launched in May 2012. Again this is not just about selection but also arrangement. A wholesale redesign of the basic search concept, display boxes differentiate Knowledge Graph from the body of search. They cluster information including pictures, links and excerpts in a tightly bundled hierarchy. The boxes act as a search page within a search page. With just a single glance they convey rich information. If I'm looking for a product they have links to buy, reviews and information on related products. If I'm looking for a person they have a biography and birth dates. If I look for a company they have a snapshot of the business and their current market cap. It's only designed as an introduction, but it complements the main results, acting as a gateway. The box itself separates and highlights the digested information.

Moreover, Figure 11 shows how Google has evolved. Knowing Oxford is a place, it breaks out both news and longer-form articles ('In the news' and 'In-depth articles' respectively). These are inserted into the search engine results page (or SERP), briskly showing the variety of information available, breaking it down according to relevance and, in those sections, how new it is. In general it shows how Google has constantly tweaked the arrangement of its pages. Selection is Google's USP. But how selections are then arranged on screen is the hidden source of Google's success and the reason it invests in new programs and design concepts like Knowledge Graph. All this information is in

Figure 11. An early 2015 Google SERP for Oxford

the system, but its arrangement makes it doubly useful. With its interface design, Google nailed arrangement.

As Schmidt himself says, PageRank and clean design are about curating the Internet. What Minard did for the Russian campaign, Google does on a macro scale for the web. Both take large volumes of information and, by appropriate arrangement, overcome overload. Just as supermarkets understand that selection and arrangement are key in crowded markets, so Google understood they would be decisive advantages in the digital world.

Selection works by taking away. Arrangement is a subtler shift; it makes the most of what you have. Outside Qatar most art galleries can't simply buy any painting they need to fill gaps in their collection. They must tell the stories using what they already have. Hanging makes the most of existing holdings. In the digital world, where we are not limited by inconvenient atoms, we can go even further. What David Weinberger calls miscellaneous organisation (things like tagging) allows – unlike paintings in a gallery, which can only have one arrangement at a time – near-infinite and productive recombination. We can arrange and catalogue things in multiple ways simultaneously. The scope and force of arrangements is duly increased.

The new value is, as often as not, latent – it's already there, waiting to be unlocked. Arranging requires us to shift our view. To understand the hidden frames that structure our world. To go from the specific to the general. To become pattern spotters and pattern creators.

There isn't a best way of arranging. What works for Google won't work for Walmart or Minard or MoMA. The challenge of curation isn't just about building expertise in order to choose well, it's also about building the understanding to arrange for the task at hand. There isn't a rule book.

Instead curation demands hard work. Not everyone will be able to curate properly in any given area. Supermarkets and Google are both investing in insight teams to ensure arrangements are based on sound principles and have the required impact.

Search results are based on decisions in systems design. Select information the user wants and arrange it legibly. In other words, curate. And what about the value? As of 2015 Google's parent company, Alphabet, had a market capitalisation of above $525bn, not to mention the value, financial or otherwise, created through its free services.

Here's a small example of how arrangement changes everything. It's a classic from the field of user experience (UX). Jared Spool, a UX specialist, was working for an ecommerce client whose business was struggling.[37] After researching the problem, watching how users interacted with the site in his lab, Spool thought he had identified the answer.

It all rested on a web form. All it wanted were two fields – an email address and a password – and it had two buttons – Login and Register. There was a link to Forgot password. That was it. Fairly standard.

Users went to the site and shopped as usual, filling up a basket with goods. When they were done, having spent time choosing what they wanted, they hit Checkout. Then the form came up. In theory this was good for customers. By creating accounts, repeat purchases would be easier. For first-timers it was a tiny inconvenience that, in future, would make life better. It seemed like a great idea and was at the time standard procedure.

Spool's analysis showed, however, that the form was a big issue. Some customers couldn't remember if it was their first time on the store. Others typed the wrong password and gave up in frustration. Registration was almost universally seen as an unnecessary chore. Some customers didn't want to share personal data. Indeed, Spool's analysis showed that 45 per cent of customers had multiple registrations and some had up to ten different accounts. Of those requesting password reminders, 75 per cent would never go on to purchase.

The solution was simple – they removed the Register button. In its place was Continue, with the message 'You do not need to create an account to make purchases on our site. Simply click Continue to proceed to checkout. To make future purchases even faster, you can create an account during checkout.' Customer purchasing leapt 45 per cent. In the first week this meant $6m in extra revenue. In the first year the company made an additional $300m. All they had done was rearrange the process. That Continue is now called the $300m button. One small change in the arrangement of our interaction with a single site was worth $300m.

How we arrange things – experiences, merchandise in shops, forms, gallery exhibitions, web pages, information, food on a plate – makes a big difference. This is true at the deepest level. In the words of the information theorist César Hidalgo, 'Our world is different from that of early hominids only in the way in which atoms are arranged.'[38] Or think about the innumerable forms that result from recombining strands of DNA. Good arrangement or organisation is also in the spirit of *curare* – it means making the absolute best of what you have.

Curation is the best umbrella term we have for how we select and then arrange. It's no surprise that the art of arrangement as a professional discipline started in museums and galleries, where things required arrangement according to complex schemas. But now arrangement is needed everywhere. We have so much stuff that just as we must select, we must arrange it more effectively and more efficiently.

Selection and arrangement are the two central principles of curation. They have spread to new sectors in myriad ways and found millions of new outlets. But they are still only the beginning.

6

Curation Effects

Curation can be hard to grasp because its borders are diffuse and shifting. What is or isn't curation, or curated, is never quite clear. It might be just a bunch of stuff thrown together; it might be painstakingly arranged. In the middle is a grey area, where isolating curated elements, and finding the added value, aren't always obvious. It's one of the reasons curation is easy to dismiss. It's just too wishy-washy, too vague for organisations that need quick and tangible results.

But this is also a strength.

Putting selection and arrangement at the centre of curation gives us an easily identifiable basis for curatorial activity. Around that is a loose but powerful penumbra of what I call curation effects – both principles and side effects of curation whose impact, when properly understood and seen within the wider framework of curation and overload, can be immense. They reach into sectors and problems usually considered far from curation, liberally borrowing ideas and techniques. They add value, whether we are choosing our pensions or organising our homes. Curation effects are where curation overlaps with other techniques, strategies and disciplines from product design to text editing, biological taxonomy to good old-fashioned storytelling. The dividing lines between such phenomena and curation are never clear. But it's precisely this chameleon quality that makes curation so useful.

Curation effects are the positive externalities or beneficial side effects that arise when we curate. But they are also principles to apply to our curation. Saying that we should select and arrange is one thing – saying *how* and *why* we should select and arrange is another. Curation effects are the results that we want to get, the goals of curation, but also the motivation, the route, and the crossover into other areas. Both why you select and what happens when you do.

These curation effects are by no means exhaustive. To some extent each curator will find and chase their own specific subset of curation effects. What follow are some examples of curation effects and why they matter more than ever.

Reducing and refining

Recall that in the British Museum's collection are some eight million objects, of which roughly 80,000 are on display at any one time. Clearly, seeing eight million objects is out of the question, even during a lifetime of looking. But for the average visitor to the museum, appreciating even 80,000 objects is a remote possibility indeed. On your London city break, if you spent just ten seconds looking at each item on display, that would take you 222 hours. Even the most enthusiastic museum-goer would, one imagines, get rather jaded. So even the selection process that arrives at 80,000 objects is incomplete. In fact the average visitor probably wants to seriously engage with something like eighty exhibits per visit. But they don't want to see just any eighty objects – they often want to see the best, most important, most famous, most exemplary and rarefied eighty objects in the collection (agreeing what these are and why is the difficult bit).

Herein lies a key principle and effect of selection. By selecting you automatically reduce. You cut things down, you exclude and say no. Crucially, this isn't a directionless process. By cutting things down you are making them better. Curated selections are never just about reducing – they are about refining as well.

We've all got used to the mantra that less is more. Business books, articles, conferences and symposia tell us that a vital principle of the modern world is that we should be doing less. This book agrees. But less on its own is not necessarily better. Only a process like curation, involved with refinement through selection, can ensure that. It's no good exhorting the world to less, if you don't consider what that less should consist of. There is little point reducing if you aren't also refining. Because curation is built around expert selection with concrete goals, curation ensures that reduction and refinement happen in lockstep.

Less isn't just more. Curation *makes* less more.

Curators at the British Museum use their expertise to say, if you're only going to look at eighty, or even eight, items, look at these, the exhibits found nowhere else: displays that take your breath away or spark your imagination. Here are the greatest examples of their kind. Don't worry about those common shards of pottery found all over Europe – look instead at the Easter Island statue or the Lewis Chessmen. The curators aren't just selecting to make the collection manageable. They aren't reducers pure and simple. The process is one of enormous distillation, a hard, fine-grained process of filtering which makes the visitor experience.

It's not just museum curators who now operate on these principles. When the team behind the Flip camera or the iPhone designed those devices, they spent months removing buttons. What, they asked, was the minimum number a device could support? Reducing the number of buttons made devices easier to use. This isn't just about getting rid of buttons for its own sake. Both devices made revolutionary refinements to the user experience in product categories whose interfaces were often difficult to navigate, and traditionally put off many potential customers. Taking away was market-making – it created demand for the products.

Curation fits into a wider economic pattern of reduction and refinement. Over the past few decades we have begun to appreciate and build businesses around what isn't there. In California, for example, the energy market has been redesigned to calculate unused energy – 'negawatts' – as an incentive. Negawatts accumulate when every household installs energy-saving light bulbs, for example. Most energy companies generate profits from increased consumption and so encourage greater energy usage. Negawatts flip the standard equation, rewarding those companies for the energy they save. Using an elegant solution, the Californian energy market, along with markets in Texas, Connecticut and Georgia, rewards both consumers and energy companies for their restraint. We have started to measure energy by what isn't there in order to make our energy use better.

The owners of luxury goods brands have become ever more conscious of how those brands' value is predicated on exclusivity. Chasing top-line growth is a constant temptation. Sell more handbags and shoes, make more money. But pushed a little too far, this model becomes toxic. Brands flip from desirable to ubiquitous. Suddenly they aren't desirable any more. For the most elite brands, every product that isn't made has value in shoring up the brand image. It's why, for instance, a company like Ferrari would actively scale back production. When the chairman, Luca di Montezemolo, announced in 2013 that they would reduce production from 7,318 units per year to less than 7,000, he did the opposite to every other motor executive. He made his reasoning clear: 'The exclusivity of Ferrari is fundamental for the value of our products,' he told journalists. 'We don't sell a normal product. We sell a dream.'[1] And that dream is based on cars that will never exist.

One of my favourite examples of this principle comes from dishwasher tablets. We used to buy big cardboard packs of dishwasher powder. Then product designers hit on a cunning wheeze. Instead of selling the powder they put it into small tablets, separated into two differently coloured layers, each of which did a different job. Going to town, they put a little red ball on top of the tablet. The net result was that for more money they were selling far less product. But by repackaging that reduced amount of raw material, they made it more expensive. Selling less was worth more even in something as functional and un-aspirational as washing dishes. These tactics and innovations are instructive.

Curation is part of this economy of less. Refinement through reduction often sees some form of curation at work. Whether it's motivated by the drive to sustainability, the desire for exclusivity, simple efficiencies or the restless quest to improve, reducing and refining is a feature of modern business that's impossible to ignore.

As a publisher, I see the value of reducing and refining every day. We call it editing. Countless books come in with incredible potential. But they can be baggy, overlong, over-written and stuffed with unnecessary asides (at this stage apologies are offered to the editor . . .). Editors' value lies in what they take away from books. Books usually don't require rewriting or even major reworking – they just need whittling down to the good bits. It's almost impossible for authors themselves to have the objectivity to see what needs to be done. Which is where editors step in. Moreover editing is a skill that takes time to perfect. There is no shortcut – editors have to get stuck in close to the text, read it many times, think it through, and have a facility for the wider structural questions as well the detailed mechanics of a sentence or phrase.

Today the publishing industry faces the huge challenge of self-publishing and the Internet. In effect the Internet means that publishers can be circumvented by channels like Amazon's Kindle Direct Publishing – as early as 2013 a quarter of bestsellers on the platform were apparently self-published. Even if they no longer control market access, though, publishers have an ace up their sleeve: experienced and expert editors. To date no one has found a way of replicating that relationship. Trusted editors kill your darlings like no one else. They know which cuts will improve, which will impair. If publishing as a whole is about curating a list, making the catalogue into a statement, then editing is a kind of micro-curation, selecting passages to cut, refining the book, and arranging the remaining pieces for maximum impact. Editing is perhaps a cousin to curation, but one who often stops by for a chat.

Editing is an industry in its own right. Beyond freelancers and professional editorial businesses, a new breed of company like GetAbstract or Blinkist is based on reducing books (and other media) to their essence. Blinkist parses books to fifteen minutes' reading. Take Thomas Piketty's *Capital in the 21st Century*: according to data released by Amazon, more readers have failed to finish this groundbreaking work of economics than almost any other book. Although Piketty's book has changed perceptions of inequality and wealth, the data suggests most readers stop around page 26 of 700.[2] Only 2.4 per cent get to the end. Blinkist's team of trained readers digest the information into a short burst, a fifteen-minute reading experience that reduces those 700 pages to its main messages. Cheating, maybe, but to Blinkist's time-pressured readers invaluable. They produce hundreds of summaries a year which are then bundled as a subscription service on the web or in mobile apps. They claim millions of summaries have been downloaded since launch and have ambitious plans to grow. Revision series like CliffsNotes have long understood this model.

Beyond the book industry, new kinds of editing are being industrialised. Outside Manila in the Philippines, banks of anonymous offices house thousands of workers staring at insalubrious images for hours on end. They see the worst of humanity. Not just a bit of pornography, but truly disturbing images of extreme violence and gore which they can never know are real or fake. They scan content which is racist, inflammatory and abusive, working long hours for derisory pay by Western standards – \$300–\$500 a month. These workers are editors. Employed, according to *Wired*, by the major social networks – including Facebook, YouTube, Twitter and Instagram – they ensure the content of uploads remains within service guidelines.[3]

Scrolling through one image after another, fed to them in real time, the office workers, English speakers with Westernised sensibilities, identify and remove images deemed inappropriate. Anything from stray nudity to public executions and snuff movies can be flagged as offensive by users around the world. The results are then fed to Filipino 'content moderators' on long shifts who have to make difficult judgements about what does and doesn't breach the guide-lines. Quite often it's not clear. But equally it can be all too clear and beyond shocking. It's relentless and desensitising. They think through the context and intention of marginal cases to see whether they comply with the guidelines. Facebook has, for example, attracted trouble for removing images of breastfeeding mothers (it has a much discussed 'no nipples' rule). In spite of the toll, the jobs are still considered desirable.

For the social networks this policing, which despite the low wages paid incurs a huge cost given the volume of material involved, is essential. Websites aren't just defined by their content, but also by what is edited out. Parents have to trust that their children won't find disturbing or lewd images on Facebook. If this happened on a regular basis Facebook would lose trust, children would be taken off the site, the user base damaged. Taking away, reducing and refining, is as important to YouTube as it is to a book publisher. Just as Western busi-nesses send offshore unpleasant work from rubbish disposal to mass manufacturing of garments, so they do with this indus-trialised and harrowing editing. Although those tropical office parks might seem a world away from the book-lined study of an editor, their value proposition is remarkably similar. Nimble hyper-growth businesses like Instagram are usually contrasted with sclerotic 'old media' firms like publishers, but both still need to be curators and editors. In both cases value is created by taking away.

People like to know that their selection has been worked on. That the millions have been whittled to the few dozen; that the few dozen has been narrowed to this one selection; that effort and knowledge has gone into what is presented. What's more, this isn't just a pleasant side effect; for those who do it well, it's a major competitive advantage. Selecting and arranging also means reducing and refining. Doing less is meaningless unless it also means doing better. That happens because of good curation.

Simplifying

One way of describing the Long Boom, and the development of civilisation itself, would be to do so in terms of increasing complexity. Complexity is a good indicator of development. To make big, new and difficult things happen, complexity is often a prerequisite. You can't have cars, or microwave meals, or holidays in the Maldives, or nuclear submarines, or contemporary art without a huge dollop of complexity on the side. Inasmuch as it gives us things we want, complexity is necessary and good.

Over recent decades, though, we've started to understand the costs as well as the benefits of complexity. We've begun to see how complexity drives overload. Complexity theory tells us that complexity overload is not just disadvantageous, but potentially catastrophic. Take the Mayans, a society studied by one of the pioneers of complexity theory, the anthropologist Joseph Tainter.

Leaving their monuments and cities still standing in the jungles of the Yucatan peninsula and the Petén of northern Guatemala, the Classic Maya of the Southern Lowlands are one of the most famous civilisations to have collapsed – other examples include ancient Mesopotamia, the Minoans, the Hittites, the Chou Empire in China and, of course, the Romans.

Having started in hamlets, they began to form larger groupings like city states and regional powers. For nearly a millennium up to 800 CE the Mayan population grew. Their cities expanded and they built great temples and palaces.

Their learning increased – agriculture and the arts grew more sophisticated and intensive, which boosted the population, in turn necessitating a further intensification of agriculture. Some evidence suggests the Southern Lowlands was one of the most densely populated regions of the preindustrial world.[4] They created a system of astronomy and science and developed an advanced logographic script, to date the only Mesoamerican script to be deciphered (which was done as recently as the 1970s and 80s). Elaborate ceremonies were conducted according to an intricate calendar. Mighty pyramids were constructed, along with canals, raised fields, crop terraces, military fortifications and reservoirs. Archaeological evidence shows a society becoming more status-driven and hierarchical: ruling elites and priests were supported by bureaucrats and artisans. Within each class there were many further gradations. A tiered system of cities emerged whereby major administrative centres were surrounded by second-tier sites in evenly spaced clusters.

Yet within a short time, a period so quick Tainter calls it 'shocking', Mayan civilisation fell apart. The population collapsed from around three million to 450,000 in seventy-five years. At one major city, Tikal, it is estimated the population declined by 90 per cent or more. Writing and calendrical systems were lost. New building of temples and monuments abruptly ceased. What happened?

The Mayans didn't have enough energy to sustain the complexity they had created. Maintaining complex societies uses energy. That dense population and intensive agriculture, those costly ceremonies and bureaucracy, that building work – it all created complexity that sucked up scarce resources without contributing in return. If that energy use can't be sustained it makes a society vulnerable to external shocks like invaders, disease or natural disasters:

More complex societies are more costly to maintain than simpler ones, requiring greater support levels per capita. As societies increase in complexity, more networks are created among individuals, more hierarchical controls are created to regulate these networks, more information is processed, there is more centralization of information flow, there is increasing need to support specialists not directly involved in resource production, and the like. All of this complexity is dependent on energy flow.[5]

The key point about collapse is that 'investment in socio-political complexity as a problem-solving response often reaches a point of declining marginal returns'.[6] This is true of information processing in most societies – the more information there is, the more diminishing marginal returns can be seen in the processing and use of that information, all of which requires energy, all of which adds to the complexity, so requiring more energy in turn.

There comes a point when the costs of complexity out-weigh the benefits, and this is what happened to the Maya. Their rainforest environment meant any dip in productivity could not be easily alleviated – instead it led to vicious competition for resources. This created a feedback loop between productivity, competition and complexity, with each needing to increase to maintain some kind of balance. Sculptures, monuments and standing armies were symptoms of the battle for prestige and dominance, deterring warring neighbours and attracting allies and securing servants. Building work and cultural sophistication didn't provide more nutrition, but boy did it use it up. The population wasn't large enough nor the resources plentiful enough to support the social structure that had arisen to secure resources in the first place. Wars and disasters that the society would normally shrug off became critical. All that late investment had shown a declining marginal return.

Complexity theory is the branch of science and social science that tries to understand the impact of complexity on any system or situation. It could be the weather or the financial markets, but we all experience complex systems in our day-to-day interactions with the world. The Long Boom and overload can be seen in this light.

Two questions spring to mind. Haven't we got over this sort of thing by now? And what the hell have the Mayans got to do with curation? The financial crash and Great Recession of 2008 show how it fits together.

If we thought we'd mastered complexity, the financial crash was a wake-up call. In the years leading up to it, the global financial system was on a bull run, yielding massive returns for those close to the action on the trading floors of London and New York. Much of it was based on the burgeoning field of credit derivatives – financial instruments existing at a level of remove from primary economic activity. Even in the most benign conditions the world economy is an extraordinarily complex system, far beyond the modelling power of any computer. The sheer range of possible inputs and causal factors at any given stage encompasses, pretty much, the sum of possibilities on earth. Derivatives took this complexity and supercharged it. They came as a blizzard of acronyms: collateralised debt obligations (CDOs), mortgage-backed securities (MBS), credit default swaps (CDS), in China 'wealth management products' (WMPs). Debt was recycled and repackaged, 'securitised', to produce derivatives, which in turn produced more opacity and complexity in the financial system. Despite the crash they remain a vast industry – the derivatives currently in circulation are worth $650 trillion, or nine times global GDP.[7]

All that complexity and opacity meant that, in an echo of the Mayans, the whole system was vulnerable when a shock came. Shocks that would usually be tough – like a dip in demand for Sunbelt real estate, the initial US trigger for the 2008 crisis – became critical. The system was too complex for the 'quants' and economics PhDs to predict or manage. As with the Mayans, a complex superstructure teetered on a base that couldn't support it. Complexity, which had driven such outsized rewards for bankers and hedge-fund managers, turned into the enemy. Thanks to a poorly regulated system, coupled with the opacity of financial instruments and the offshore system of shadow banking, financial contagion spread to the real economy of wages, jobs and tax receipts. In the end complexity and overleveraging did for Lehman Brothers what it did for the Mayans. However smart we think we are, we haven't beaten complexity. Quite the opposite.

There was another way. Canada was the only G7 nation to avoid a government bailout of the financial sector. As an Ottawa official told the *Financial Times*, Canadian bankers are 'boring, but in a good way'[8] (no snickering please). The bankers on Toronto's Bay Street stuck to tried and tested models. The management of risk, not the manufacturing of complexity, was adhered to. Compare Wall Street or City banks with Canada's largest by market capitalisation, TD Bank. While TD Bank emerged without a meltdown, many of its Anglo-American counterparts went bust. While the Royal Bank of Scotland required an unprecedented bailout from the UK government, the Royal Bank of Canada simply carried on.

The straight-talking head of TD, Ed Clark (who publicly said bank bosses earned too much), had a rule for selling financial products: Would you sell it to your mother-in-law?

The mother-in-law test harked back to a different era. But it helped his bank remain solvent. Anything dodgy or difficult to understand was out. Unlike US banks, Canadian banks were tightly regulated. They had tough capital requirements (7 per cent of tier one capital in common stock) and leverage ratios (1 to 20, whereas those of Bear Stearns and Morgan Stanley were both above 1 to 30). It meant they couldn't indulge in the casino tactics of other financial centres. Moreover the mortgage market was well regulated. Those mortgages were not securitised as much as in the US – in 2007 only 27 per cent of Canadian mortgages were securitised, as against 67 per cent in the US. There was less complexity in the system.

In all, it meant Canadian banks were forced to have simpler – but more robust – business models. They had to choose what they did more carefully. Moreover the regulatory environment was itself simple and transparent for those involved in financial activity to understand. It's clear that solving the riddle of complexity is one of the most important challenges we face today, but how does curation come in?

First, let's be honest. Curation alone isn't going to save the world from the perils of complexity. Frankly, complexity needs everything we've got. The point is not that curation would have saved the Mayans – of course it wouldn't. The point is that we need multiple ways of managing complexity; curation is another weapon in the arsenal of simplicity, an element of the antidote to complexity. The more complexity we encounter, the more simplification matters. By selecting and arranging, curation takes what is complex and while keeping the essential elements, makes the whole simpler. This is the balancing act of curation – to keep what is important and valuable about complexity, without the overwhelming, overleveraged and overloaded aspects of it.

If banking before the crash is an excellent example of an overloaded complex system, Canadian banking was a better-curated version. It kept many of the key elements, but dispensed with many of the bad. The Canadian approach to money was curatorial in that it was selecting investments better, and arranging them better (all those capital rules). Its custodial element stayed true to the spirit of *curare*. And the way it approached customers was better curated as well. A rigorous process of selection decided which products the bank would sell (the mother-in-law test). Safe to say, not many on Wall Street filtered their offerings with a mother-in-law test. Curated banking? It's not a phrase we ever hear and not one I am suggesting. The point is that we need organisations and business models that work towards simplicity, not the reverse. That, for example, select only appropriate investments and arrange them in a stable manner. Iyengar, Schwartz and others have studied how choice affects our attitude to banking. As we saw, the more choice – the more investment options, say – the less able we are to make wise decisions or even decide at all.

This kind of thinking can be scaled up and out. Complexity causes problems across the board and a new wave of businesses are figuring out how to combat it. Global just-in-time supply chains collapse if one element goes wrong. Now a new generation of process experts are re-localising and onshoring production in order to take complexity out of the supply chain. Individual products from pharmaceuticals to machine tools get more complex in operation and production by the year. Yet it also means that when they go wrong, it's a nightmare. That added complexity piles on cost. In response, the new movement of frugal innovation – applied to everything from cars to medical tech – retains the benefits of advanced technology but, by going back to first principles, strips out

complexity, making the products more robust, easier to operate and cheaper.

Over the years the cockpits of planes grew encrusted with
gadgetry. Eventually the sheer operational complexity became
a hazard even for experienced pilots. The response was the
'glass cockpit', an overhaul of the in-flight interface to make
it simple – choosing the most important parts of the display
and arranging them intuitively. As data has become a more
everyday part of the corporate environment, so management dashboards have proliferated. Procter and Gamble, for
example, have a 'cockpit' analogous to the glass cockpit of
aeroplanes designed to streamline decision making. Similarly,
over the years legal documents get longer and more difficult
to understand. Alan Siegel, a pioneer of simpler business,
has redrafted many of them, selecting only the most salient
points, rewriting the copy in a straightforward manner and
redesigning the layout.[9] Complex legal agreements are boiled
down to a single, readily comprehensible page. Arguably
WhatsApp became so valuable so fast because it took out anything extraneous. It went back to the simplest fundamentals
of communication.

Just as we are building an economy out of what isn't
there, so the increase in complexity means we are building
an economy to make things simpler. Selection removes the
number of elements in play. There are fewer actors and fewer
relationships. Arranging makes things more transparent
and easy to use. Expert sets of selecting and arranging, even
in areas as large as financial products, help us retain the
benefits of complexity while mitigating the risks. Most of
the time, curation helps simplify on a micro scale – in our
day-to-day transactions and encounters. Given the growth
in complexity, anything that helps, however small, should
be given a space.

As the eighteenth-century English painter Joshua Reynolds put it, 'Simplicity is an exact medium between too little and too much.' Curation helps ensure that exact medium.

Categorisation

Carl Linnaeus (1707–78) is one of the greatest scientists in history. He didn't discover a new law. He didn't make new theories. He is not known for a breakthrough experiment or as the builder of new technologies. Yet as much as anyone Linnaeus changed science. How did he do it?

By labelling, naming and, above all, categorising. Modern biology is built on categorisation.

The son of a botanist and church minister in Sweden, the young Linnaeus showed an early interest in the diversity of species. At the time there was no real means of cataloguing them. Biology was a mess. During his studies Linnaeus realised that without a common understanding of species and their distinctions, those discussing the study of life would always talk at cross purposes. There would be no disciplinary foundation. Deciding to change this, he wrote the *Systema Naturae* (first published in 1735 and revised many times). In doing so he created the system of 'binomial nomenclature' that still governs how we name species in biology.

Linnaeus' scheme divided the world into three kingdoms (animal, vegetable, mineral). These were then further subdivided into classes, followed by orders, families, genera and finally species. Even if the system has since been revised, for example to encompass an understanding of evolution and genetics or the inclusion of new kingdoms like fungi (and the exclusion of minerals), it created the framework that made understanding possible. So for example humans are categorised in binomial nomenclature as *Homo sapiens*, their unique binomial identifier. *Homo* is the genus, *sapiens* the species. Neanderthals are called *Homo neanderthalensis* as they share the genus of human beings, but are a different species.

Not only did Linnaeus' work give each species a unique name but, because it worked, it was stable and made the exchange of information easy. Categorisation meant everyone talking about the same flower was on the same page. Before Linnaeus, learning to remember the names of species, especially plants, was a long and difficult process. At school Linnaeus made a point of memorising as many as he could, but later Linnaean categories made it easier. Such classification wasn't invented by Linnaeus, and nor has it stood still. But he was the first to make sense of biodiversity – Linnaeus alone categorised 12,000 species of plants and animals.[10] A clear, hierarchical classification made biology intelligible, bringing order to the chaos of nature. Biology rests on a process of categorisation – which is in turn about selecting and arranging based on sets of features. In his own lifetime Linnaeus was feted by the intellectuals of Europe as heralding a revolution; in our own, *Time* hailed him as the fifth most influential scientist in history. Not bad for a categoriser.

Linnaeus reminds us how important categorisation actually is. Without categories, we struggle. When we select, we select for. We select into. In the early days of curation, much of what a curator did was categorising. Categories were still being created and understood. What kind of painting was this? What kind of fossil? By using their expertise to place objects in categories still being finalised, curators helped build our understanding of the world. Just as biology needed categories, so every area of knowledge and activity – from art history to film subscriptions to selling medical insurance – requires a prior process of categorisation. Imagine trying to navigate a library without the Dewey Decimal System or equivalent. It would be impossible.

Curators create, manage and sift categories. Facets and features lost on you or me are clear to a curator familiar with the field. Those categories tell us what experts think are important, relevant or useful characteristics.

Categorisation augments our minds. It's expertise out-sourced and stored. Linnaeus' classification is his biological knowledge crystallised and made shareable. But it also works on a more local level. We sort our kitchens and our computer files into categories so we don't have to remember where everything is – just the categories. We don't search all over the place for knives and forks – we have a category, cutlery, and a cutlery drawer embodying that category, externalising our mental organisation. The more there is to remember, the more we need to externalise. To do so, we must create categories. Even arranging spaces like our homes is based on a series of implicit categories without which we'd struggle to get by (things to bake with, clothes for special occasions). Making our house a place of physical categories is what psychologist and neuroscientist Daniel Levitin calls 'cognitive prosthetics'.[11]

Categories simplify the world into meaningful and useful chunks – we don't see individual blades of grass, just the generalised category we call grass.

As we have seen, how stores are arranged, and what they select, is a huge and often critical part of their success. US DIY retailer Ace Hardware specialises in categorisation that makes life easier and more manageable for consumers. CEO John Venhuizen studies how our brains make categories in order to perfect both selection and arrangement. The chain has a stockholding of 83,000 items and any given store has between 20,000 and 30,000 items available. This is a huge amount for both the chain and the customer to process. A dedicated category-management department steps in. Their job is to rationalise the range of products in such a way that the categories will be logical and natural for most consumers.

Part of this entails creating normal hierarchical systems. Starting with Gardening, you then go to Fertilisers, then to different brands of Fertilisers. But it also extends to thinking through how people interact with products. If you're building, say, a cupboard, you might want drills, nails, wood and handles to be located together. Or if you want fertiliser, you might want gardening tools nearby as well. It's not just about having electronics as a category – it's thinking about the use of the items within it. So you don't just find drills – you find a section for putting up shelves. When you have so many products, they can and should exist in multiple categories to help you shift through them. The department curates both the categories and the things included within them to make our navigation of those 30,000 items seamless.

We tend to take categories as natural – for example, in clothing stores clothes are for the most part sorted by clothing type rather than size. But they could be the other way round. I could walk into a section that had all the items already there in my size. It might save time and make comparing things easier. Curators create new categories that make sense of the world – things that make us smile, people we call friends, novels that end wistfully, tools for putting up shelves, types of fungi. New categories create new angles on the world. Understanding, building and using them requires creativity and imagination.

Curators, then, don't just select. They select for and into. Netflix don't just select films for you – they first categorise them with those lengthy names. Melvil (*sic*) Dewey knew that for libraries to work, librarians needed a standardised system to put books in. Linnaeus didn't arbitrarily select species. He selected them within a framework of knowledge which was not only produced by selection, but also aided that selection down the line.

Reducing, refining, simplifying and categorising are all curation effects: principles and by-products of curation. They all have growing value. But we needn't stop there – we could have explored:

- **Displaying and presenting:** a visual or performative element was always at the heart of curation. It put on a show. Curation then has a long-running history with the visual. This continues today, not least because of the prevalence of visual culture. 'Design thinking' has, moreover, leapt from the explicitly visual to all areas of our lives. Experience designers, for example, think through how we interact with anything from a theme park to our office. Having a sense of presentation, and an understanding of the nuances within it, is important not just for gallerists, but anyone organising a conference or show, delivering a presentation (let alone a TED talk) or building a customer-focused environment. The visual matters.
- **Explaining and storytelling:** everyone from great religions and nation states to individuals feels the need for a defining story. Selecting and arranging always creates an implicit or explicit story, context or explanation. In virtually all of my conversations with curators, some variant on this theme has been acknowledged. Curators have a highly developed sense of pattern

recognition, and it's that ability to not just see the patterns but pull them out, make them comprehensible, accentuating important aspects, that they work on. In putting together an exhibition, a curator is generally telling a story about a period, a culture, an artist, as much as presenting their works.

- Businesses realise this power. It's no surprise, for example, that companies like Budweiser or the British retailer John Lewis abandoned traditional advertisements in favour of miniature narratives – generally involving animals like Clydesdale horses, bears, hares and penguins. In order to counteract media saturation, advertisers have become purist storytellers. We are overloaded with adverts. We don't remember them, we don't care. Let's face it, they're annoying. Budweiser, John Lewis and their agencies use storytelling to go beyond the ennui, connecting with audiences above the media haze. Stories capture and retain attention otherwise lost in the deluge. As Peter Guber, former CEO of Sony Motion Pictures and one of America's best-connected executives, says: 'For too long the business world has ignored or belittled narrative, preferring soulless PowerPoint slides, facts, figures, and data. But as the noise level of modern life has become a cacophony, the ability to tell a purposeful story that can truly be *heard* is increasingly in demand.'[12]

- **Preserving and nurturing:** in museums curators are charged with caring for their exhibits, whether they're Cretaceous fossils, fragile reams of papyrus or Tracey Emin's bed. They must safely store, preserve and document their collections. This element of stewardship is often lost in the quick-fire world of online curation, but it shouldn't be; as I will later argue, having some idea of preserving or nurturing is what will stop curation disappearing down its own self-indulgence. When I asked Oriole Cullen, the V&A curator, what she did, her answer was clear: 'In museums we take care of the collections. It's about cataloguing, databasing, physical care of the collection, adding to the collection, access to the collection and putting on exhibitions.' Taking care was still at the top. This sense of caring, not just choosing, helps explain why curation has such an important role today – but it's often glossed over in the newer sense of the word.

We could have continued with distilling, juxtaposing, clarifying, narrating, contextualising, filtering, connecting, elevating ... Curation effects are widespread and powerful. They connect with us at a deep level – we like order, narrative, care, clarity and ease. If Buzzfeed has taught us anything, it's that we have a predisposition for lists. The more we understand how curation coheres with a network of new skills, strategies and capabilities, the better prepared we will be for thriving in the age of excess that is changing forever how we live and work. There isn't one way of curating, or one set of effects than can be mechanically applied. Instead curation is a basket of approaches we can select from, as illustrated in Figure 12.

Businesses solve problems. By solving problems they make money. Businesses make mistakes when they misunderstand the nature of the problem they are trying to solve.

At this juncture in history, with overload spreading and the creativity myth running out of fuel, we are starting to see a grand shift in the problem set. If business used to address problems of scarcity with the solution of production, or services that enabled production, the principles outlined in this

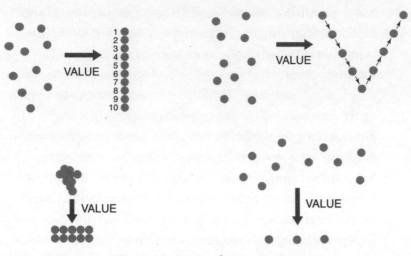

Figure 12. Approaches to curation

chapter – primarily selecting, but also arranging and all those secondary curation effects – address what happens when the problems are of abundance. When the problems change, the answers have to change as well. Business and organisational assumptions fit for the twentieth century are becoming redundant. The answer is to adapt.

Curation helps solve the problems of today and tomorrow. It's the mass sourcing of the expertise needed to navigate and comprehend the saturated, complex markets of the twenty-first century.

There isn't a cookie-cutter approach. You can't take a business or sector and say it requires curation in this, this and that way. Instead, we need to get to grips with the principles and think them through in each particular scenario. How can selecting solve problems? Might a change of arrangement be better? In the next chapter we will see how curators are already reacting to this change, improving lives and altering business and transforming assumptions. They do it by realising that the principles of curation help with (for example):

- **Saving time.** Recall the Oxford study of time pressure. Selecting and arranging can free up time to focus on what we want.
- **Freeing cognitive resources.** Excess choice and research about such choice saps mental energy. The more we have to decide, the less we are able to decide. By outsourcing these processes, curation lets us get back to what matters.
- **Sparing us anxiety.** The more there is to do, and the more chaotic our lives, the more stressed we get. Curation can provide an antidote, from making a trip to the supermarket more pleasant to creating a more stable banking system.
- **Maximising utility.** Think about water crises in places like California. This is never framed in the language of curation. But solving the problem will depend on making better selections about where water is used and managing the existing supplies of that water better. The water crisis has a familial resemblance to a host of problems we think of as closer to curation. In both cases maximising the utility of what is already there and allocating resources wisely is enabled by curation.
- **Cutting down complexity.** On both the macro and micro levels complexity is a problem. Having fewer elements in play makes a critical difference.
- **Finding quality.** Separating the wheat from the chaff has never been more important because there has never been more chaff.
- **Overcoming information overload.** Selection goes beyond filtering. It's a proactive, intelligent, expert filtering – the essential ingredient to beating the cardinal problem of the information age.

- **Creating contrast.** Homogeneity is a by-product of excess; curation can make the world interesting again.
- **Redefining creativity.** The more we appreciate the skills and personality behind good curation, the better we can move beyond the dated Romantic idea of what creativity can be.
- **Channelling attention.** Media and goods are ubiquitous; human attention is finite. Power has already shifted to those who can broker attention (look at tech company valuations). Curators do this – they say, look at this, not that.
- **Providing context.** Exhibitions let us understand a painting by putting it in the context of the painter's life, the period in which it was made or even the trans-historical theme the painting addresses. A playlist lets us understand a song. Curators, through intelligent arrangement, help us make sense of things when making sense of things gets harder.
- **Beating overproduction.** Not only does curation make the most of existing resources, but it provides a new paradigm for generating wealth beyond simply having more of everything (whether more mobile phones or more debt).

Curation is part of the answer to the question: how will we live and work today?

Back on the banks of the Thames, discussing curation and my friend's company, I ordered another round and settled in. Business was indeed relentless, the emails were still coming in, content needed wrangling but, for a few hours, that could wait. For my friend, selecting the most important medical information, and arranging it in the most efficient and clear manner, underpinned a business that was now worth hundreds of millions of dollars. They'd never thought about this as curation; they'd thought about it as a service, as being the best company they could be. In future, rather than only looking at the metrics of more, they could also look at the metrics of less – this as much as any growth figure was a sign the service was working.

'So if we're curators, does that mean basically everyone is a curator?' he asked.

Well, I replied, you might be surprised.

Part III
THE REALITY

7

Curate the World

Building the curation economy

Off the coast of Abu Dhabi a new city is rising. Even by the grandiose standards of Middle Eastern megaprojects, it's ambitious. Saadiyat Island covers 27 square kilometres. The bridge from the mainland, the Sheikh Khalifa Bridge, is in its own right one of the world's largest infrastructure projects: 1.4 kilometres long, ten lanes wide, built using 15,500 tons of reinforced steel.[1] Eventually Saadiyat Island will be home to at least 150,000 new residents, living in a green, oasis-like environment minutes from one of the world's most punishing deserts. Divided into 'districts' – a beach district, a marina district and so on – the island comes richly appointed with the amenities of modern life, from five-star hotels to a fully fledged campus of New York University. There will be schools and parks, music and science centres, a theatre, shopping malls. Unlike many such projects, these will be built on a human scale – the goal is to create genuine neighbourhoods of reasonably sized flats and villas rather than the ranks of skyscrapers so often found in the boomtowns of the new global economy.

Abu Dhabi is going for the big league; it wants to become, in the words of its promotional literature, 'a nucleus of global culture'. It's partnered with some of the world's most famous museums to build a vast new Saadiyat Cultural District, 'a new urban landscape made of *archi-sculptures*, characteristic of the dialogue between architecture and sculpture'. There will be, for example, the Sheikh Zayed Museum designed by Norman Foster. Over 66,000 square metres in area and partnered with the British Museum, it will focus on themes including the Environment, Heritage and Education. Then there will be the Guggenheim Abu Dhabi. Again a huge project, again from a serious player, the Guggenheim Abu Dhabi will focus on twentieth-century and contemporary art, with a special focus on visual arts from the Middle East. Bigger still than the Sheikh Zayed Museum, it is hoped that it will bridge Western and Islamic artistic practice.

Perhaps the biggest coup is that Abu Dhabi will open the first foreign Louvre, the world's most visited and perhaps most richly endowed museum. Designed as a vast dome by the Pritzker Prize-winning architect Jean Nouvel, this is a partnership not just with the Musée du Louvre but with Agence France-Muséums, the government agency responsible for museums across France including the Musée d'Orsay, the Centre Pompidou and the Bibliothèque Nationale. In its first year the Louvre will loan its Emirati cousin 300 works, many amongst its most precious – shown in the Middle East, or for that matter beyond Europe, for the first time. For the most part, though, Louvre Abu Dhabi will display works it has itself acquired. For years Abu Dhabi has, like its neighbour Qatar, acquired a lavish permanent collection, which will form the centrepiece of the museum: a glittering display of world culture, it will be the linchpin of this grand infrastructural theatre the *Wall Street Journal* has called, even before its completion, one of the top ten sights of the world. For once the press release doesn't overplay its hand when it claims Saadiyat Cultural District is 'unprecedented in size or scope'.

Welcome to the curation economy.

At one level this is a superficial change: a classic case of curation as a light dusting on top of the real economy; a plaything for billionaires and trend-chasers, while the hard work goes on elsewhere. This is partly true. Much curation isn't integral to the economy and has only limited impact, usually amongst cultural elites in areas of questionable significance. This is why curation is so easily mocked; sure, curate this or that, but really it doesn't matter. Curation, though, actually goes much deeper. Patterns of selection and arrangement are having a more fundamental impact on the world's businesses, and curation can change the way we work right down the value chain. We tend to think that curation is only happening in a few isolated places like the Louvre Abu Dhabi, where money is no object and culture is a toy of state. This is wrong. And it also misunderstands exactly what is happening in the Arabian Gulf.

Saadiyat Cultural District can only properly be understood in the wider regional context. Abu Dhabi is part of the United Arab Emirates, a group of states collectively about the size of Maine or Ireland. Until recently, it was a hard place. Abu Dhabi's neighbouring emirate, Dubai, only got its first electricity and paved street in 1961. This former British protectorate was a backwater of desert wastes. Bedouin tribes lived lives of timeless austerity. Then Abu Dhabi discovered oil. Beneath the dunes are 9 per cent of the world's proven oil reserves, some ninety-eight billion barrels, worth trillions of dollars.[2] With a tiny population of native Emiratis it means every citizen in Abu Dhabi is a paper millionaire many times over. Yet for many years the Nahyan Sheikhs of Abu Dhabi remained conservative. The trappings of modern life came late. Sheikh Zayed, the long-time ruler, was a beloved figure, charismatic and generous, but traditional – riding a white stallion, he followed traditional Bedouin pursuits like falconry and roving the deserts. While things carried on and revenue continued rising comfortably, it was his neighbours, the Maktoums of Dubai, that hogged global attention.

Soon after the discovery of oil, Sheikh Rashid of Dubai realised his supplies would run dry far sooner than those of Abu Dhabi. He and his sons consciously pursued a different strategy to Zayed – aggressive growth and development. They built ports at breakneck pace, even when everyone thought they were mad. They constructed giant luxury hotels, opening their country to Western tourists and business people, Iranian émigrés and merchants and labourers from the Indian subcontinent. They made Dubai the most cosmopolitan place in the Gulf and the region's air, distribution, finance and trade entrepôt. But above all the Maktoums, with their desert ski slopes, floating skyscrapers, record-breaking builds, district making and fake archipelagos, put Dubai on the map.

A classic example of their pharaonic attitude was the region's first skyscraper, the Dubai World Trade Center, built on an empty stretch of land in 1978. It was speculative, daring and assumed to be a folly – until it worked. Even more ambitious was Jebel Ali port; with sixty-six berths, the largest dry dock in the world and, now, the world's largest man-made harbour, it was originally dismissed as a barmy vanity project. Dubai's strategy was to build big and gamble. It has worked, more or less – at least if you forget the autocratic rule, the environment, the terrible working conditions for builders and some bumpy credit conditions. Dubai moved itself up the value chain. Whereas Abu Dhabi or Saudi Arabia were reliant on crude oil exports, Dubai built a modern economy which included strengths in aviation, banking and (increasingly) the creative industries.

The Maktoums gambled their dirhams on an epic scale; the Nahyans doubled down on drilling. Dubai, with limited natural resources, turned itself into a sophisticated player. Abu Dhabi pumped the barrels. Like other resource-rich countries it was a one-dimensional economy. So Sheikh Khalifa, Abu Dhabi's ruler, decided to emulate Dubai. This has now happened with waves of investment in hotels like the $6bn Emirates Palace, a tie-up with NYU, a Formula One circuit and Ferrari theme park, the Masdar environmental project in the desert and, above all, Saadiyat Island. And Saadiyat Island shows that Abu Dhabi is setting its sights even higher up the value chain than Dubai. If Dubai does glitz, it says, Abu Dhabi does class. The context of the Cultural District is then twofold – at one level it is, as the press officer told me, about building 'a universal museum in the Middle East translating the spirit of openness and dialogue of cultures'. But, again according to the press officer, they also hint at a greater ambition:

> Abu Dhabi's Saadiyat Island creates the perfect location as a natural crossroad for history, art, tourism, development and a diverse population. Building a cultural ecosystem is key to Abu Dhabi's cultural ambitions: with a rich cultural programme including exhibitions, workshops, talking platforms, an international annual art fair, as well as tailored initiatives for students, collectors and tourists. These draw a range of visitors of all ages and backgrounds from all over the world.

In other words the Cultural District spearheads Abu Dhabi's move into higher value sectors; curation reorients

Abu Dhabi. Building museums and curating unprecedented displays, collected on the back of immense wealth, is, in fact, part of a wider programme of building a diversified, post-oil economy. Curation isn't just a facile display of pomp; it's more considered and formidable. Yes, this is an old ruse. The Bilbao effect, whereby a sparkling museum drives urban regeneration, is well known. But rarely has it been tried on this scale, and rarely has curation been so central. In the marketing material emphasis is placed on specific curatorial points – what has been acquired and why, how, where and when it will be displayed, what those displays, galleries and exhibitions are trying to achieve.

Abu Dhabi, one of the world's richest states, is diving wholesale into curation. It's doing this as part of a local race to develop and curatorial practice is at the heart of it.

Gold collar workers

Economists traditionally divide activity into fundamental sectors. At the bottom are primary activities, based on natural resources, like agriculture. Before anything else you must eat. For most of history the primary sector dominated; most people worked in the fields and most wealth was tied to the ownership of arable lands. It extended to the harnessing of raw materials like minerals. But it could also be seen to encompass hunting and gathering, fishing, forestry and mining.

Then came secondary activities, principally manufacturing: classic blue collar jobs. Raw materials extracted and produced by primary activity were transformed, augmented, packaged, assembled and processed. Anyone from BMW to a blacksmith was part of the secondary economy.

Beyond that was the tertiary sector, better known as the service sector: white collar jobs. Facilitating exchange or communication are tertiary activities, as are transport, tourism, clerical work and legal services. Neither plumbers nor hairdressers nor accountants produce anything material; they produce a service. From this outline the general direction of travel is clear: technology-driven productivity gains mean the primary and secondary sectors become more efficient and shrink in terms of their overall proportion of the economy. In tandem the tertiary sector balloons. Policy makers saw this as a good thing – tertiary sector jobs are often more highly paid, higher-status and regarded as 'better' by governments, business and employees alike.

Such is the size and differentiation of the tertiary sector, however, that economists have added two refinements taking us further up the value chain: the quaternary and quinary sectors. It's here we find curation. Quaternary sectors relate to knowledge work, or intellectual services. The staff of universities, for example, would be a good example, as would management consultants or many technology and IT firms. When a pharmaceutical company invests in researching a new drug, in creating the engines of future revenue, this is quaternary work.

Beyond quaternary lies the quinary level; so-called 'gold collar workers', 'rainmakers', knowledge superstars, economic power brokers. In the words of one article this is about 'the creation, re-arrangement and interpretation of new and existing ideas'.[3] Quinary workers are decision makers in the command centres of global trade; equivalent to what Italian economist Vilfredo Pareto called 'the vital few'. They work across disciplines in transnational fields, connecting disparate areas of activity as the nodal points of our networked system. From government to media, they are taste makers, key influencers, paladins of knowledge work or 'info-capitalism', the most advanced forms of added value available.

Curation straddles the quaternary and quinary fields, where learning and expertise drive decisions, selections and arrangements of goods, ideas and capital. It's far removed from primary and secondary work, which in part explains why we don't always have the tangible sense that it's making a contribution. Management consultants will be familiar with the problem. But shifts at the quinary level have ramifications all the way down to major alterations in the primary sector (which still dominates large parts of the world).

As nations recalibrate their economies, they are looking at expanding to higher levels. Primary economies, like raw materials exporters in Africa, want to build a secondary base; secondary economies like China want knowledge-intensive industry. And developed economies like the USA are trying to find ways of supporting the premium sectors and enabling them to grow. Regional associations like ASEAN, Mercosur or the EU, for instance, are largely based around trying to collectively push their regions up the chain. Everyone is trying to turbocharge the drift of history by moving up through the economic gears.

In Russia the government is building a huge research and development area called Skolkovo, in partnership with companies including Microsoft, Siemens and EADS. Divided into major clusters, featuring grand architecture, visa waivers for key workers and an eye-watering budget from the federal government, Skolkovo is part of the Kremlin's strategy to move the Russian economy forward. Largely dependent on raw materials, notably energy, Russia wants to become more knowledge-intensive. In South Korea the government supported the development of industry, helping build manufacturing giants like Daewoo, Hyundai and Samsung – the *chaebols*. But faced with awesome competition from China the government started backing cultural products, switching its successful industrial policy from the secondary to the tertiary sector. Today Korean soaps are watched by hundreds of millions and the musical phenomenon that is K-pop has gone supernova.

Abu Dhabi's strategy can be seen in this context. By installing a Cultural District as their flagship project, rather than say, an entertainment complex, as might be built in Dubai, Abu Dhabi is setting its sights on the quaternary and quinary sectors. If Dubai achieved the unusual feat of leapfrogging from a primary to a tertiary economy, Abu Dhabi, as usual, wants to go one better.

Economic and industrial policy are substantially directed at moving industrial activity towards areas where curation-style activities play a significant role. They probably don't know it and are unlikely to admit it, but governments love curation!

The slow collapse of the Industrial Model of Selection and the rise of a Curated Model is also part of this picture. Consumer preferences, the mechanics of retail, the macro picture of value generation – all are moving, and all are moving in a direction that means we have to better select and arrange.

One way of thinking about this change, well demonstrated by the case of Saadiyat Island, is to see curation as twofold. We have both *explicit* and *implicit* curation:

- **Explicit curation:** the curation of art galleries, biennials and museums. It's thick black glasses and white cubes; it's the mushrooming numbers of curation postgrads. Its roots are in the great museums of the eighteenth, nineteenth and twentieth centuries. But it's also curation centred on the world's fashion and tech capitals: of celebrities curating Instagram feeds and music festivals; boutique pop-ups and fashion blogs. It's when a friend curates his playlist. It's a buzzword, a prominent phenomenon; but it's also a bit of a joke, a touch glib, applying the po-faced seriousness of contemporary art to some of our least pressing and apparently superficial problems. Explicit curation makes the web more interesting and makes our nights out more fun – but it is also open to the kind of Daily Mash spoof we saw in the Introduction. Explicit curation walks the tightrope between creating new forms of value and descending into, well, silliness. Saadiyat Island is clearly a case of explicit curation, inasmuch as Abu Dhabi is investing in classic curatorial practice.

- **Implicit curation:** where patterns of selection and arrangement are quietly reordering industries. We've already seen this at work in the last chapter. It's about new high-end services. It's intensive knowledge work requiring deep expertise. It responds to plurality, excess choice. It's about a post-manufacturing economy and a new kind of retail model, where asset bases consist of knowledge, taste and expertise rather than tangible goods; it's about repositioning to higher-margin activities as underlying productivity increases. It's the macro to the micro of explicit curation. By building Saadiyat Island, Abu Dhabi ultimately wants to encourage this kind of curation. Having great museums is obviously a worthy goal and a good way of attracting tourists. But shifting the economy upwards is the great prize.

Explicit and implicit curation can often be found in similar areas. But it's easy for us to miss the implicit curation because we are too busy sniggering at the antics of moustachioed 'explicit' curators. Design blogs distract us from how retail buyers, investors and property managers, for example, must all now be curators. As we will see in the next chapter, explicit curation is transforming culture. But the rise of implicit curation, that underlying trend exemplified in Abu Dhabi's moves, means we aren't just curating galleries – we're curating the world. This lasts. In the language of economic policy, the change is structural, not cyclical.

As discussed in Part I, since the 1970s and 80s, the value of US exports has greatly increased according to the US Department of Commerce, growing from $364bn in 1989 to $1,579bn in 2013.[4] The physical weight of those exports, meanwhile, hasn't grown at all. As early as 1973 the legendary sociologist Daniel Bell was talking about the 'post-industrial' society or what has been dubbed 'cognitive capitalism'. For economies like the US and the UK it's now taken for granted that knowledge drives growth – advanced technology, intellectual property and imaginative, expert services provide the value. Curation is part of this change, one which some thinkers regard as being on a par with the transition from an agrarian to an industrial model. More importantly it's part of the next evolution of post-industrial work, where the next thirty years of growth will come from. As commodities undergo a downturn, it's a reminder that sources of value change and move. The message for both small and big business is clear: follow value, find curation.

Even at the most basic level curation is transforming the world with those most necessary of goods: food and drink.

The food chain of the future

It was the last straw for Carlo Petrini: a McDonald's had just opened next to Rome's iconic Spanish Steps. A seasoned campaigner and revolutionary, Petrini saw the triumph of fast food and didn't like it one bit. Tired of watching as his beloved gastronomic heritage was sidelined, he decided to do something – and set up Slow Food. As the name suggests, Slow Food was conceived as everything fast food was not. Local, artisanal, natural, rooted in tradition, Slow Food was against monoculture, homogeneity and the extensive use of chemicals. Petrini's fellow Piedmontese, Oscar Farinetti, would, nearly twenty years after Slow Food began, take the concept to the masses.

Farinetti wasn't the obvious candidate. Having inherited his father's supermarket he built it into a consumer electronics chain, UniEuro. It was successful, if dull. Farinetti himself is anything but – charismatic, far-sighted, he always knew that he wanted to go beyond selling electrics. His father, after all, hadn't just been an entrepreneur – he was also a partisan fighting the Nazis in the Second World War. Surely, Farinetti thought, I should have a mission as well? Could this be it?

Eventually selling UniEuro for around half a billion euros, Farinetti found his mission in Slow Food. He saw an opportunity to remake what a supermarket could be; to radically shorten the time spent by produce in transit between farm and store; to build links with the best producers, working hard to find them; to provide an outlet that blended food markets like Barcelona's La Boqueria with a restaurant complex, a wine cellar and educational institution, all built around the best produce sold at reasonable prices. Localism and environmentalism would – at last – get exciting. Eataly, which he founded in 2004, was to be that place, and its first store opened in 2007.

If you want to see where the supermarket of the future began, go to Turin. Taking the Linea 1 to Lingotto I went to the first Eataly on a day of thunderstorms and torrential rain. Nestled beneath Alpine massifs, Turin was once home to the Italian automotive industry. Eataly itself resides in an old vermouth factory, directly opposite the hulking mass of the former Fiat plant, once the largest on earth. A walk around its famous rooftop track is one of the unforgettable experiences of twentieth-century manufacturing. Now, in a neat illustration of the often painful transition from secondary to tertiary industries, the factory has been converted into a shopping, leisure and exhibition complex. Like its American twin, Detroit, Turin is having to build a new post-industrial identity, and it's epitomised by Eataly.

For a gourmand Eataly is thrilling. These shops are big, bazaar-like spaces – the Turin shop is 118,000 square feet. Rome, in an abandoned air terminal, is a whopping 170,000 square feet and includes a coffee roastery, a brewery, eighteen restaurants and even a travel agency for booking gastronomic holidays. Everything is light, spacious, carefully designed, neither kitsch historical pastiche nor *echt* modernity. Above all everything is meticulously selected and arranged.

In the Salumeria (the cured meats section), racks of Parma ham hang overhead, while downstairs rows of them mature. Next to them, ageing, are great wheels of Parmigiano Reggiano. Beneath the hams sit piles of *salumi*, cut and aged on site. There is Salumi Nostrano Lodigiano, the finest Gran Bresaola at €43.90 per kilo, San Daniele prosciutto from the *prosciuttificio* Dok Dall'ava in Friuli and fiery *nduja di spilinga* from producer Luigi Caccamo in Monte Poro, Calabria. The cheese section has thick, melting wedges of Gorgonzola Dolce DOP, fat cuts of Cremonese Gran Padano, Parmigiano Reggiano aged for a minimum of fifteen months, most for more than thirty (anything else is infanticide, says the blurb), and tubs of bobbing *burattina* from producer Domenico Romagnuolo of the Campania, made from pure buffalo milk in the traditional manner. If you want tomatoes you can have Piccadilly, *grappolo*, *allungato* and *marinda* tomatoes – each of which looks stunning. Eataly knows all the producers of this food. Every one is artisanal, examined in detail to be the best examples of that product.

Farinetti's devotion to finding the best ingredients (along with his deep pockets) means he even buys some favoured producers. At Eataly you can buy plenty of Pasta Artigianale Gragnano (Gragnano in the Campania, with its perfect microclimate of sea and mountain air, centuries of experience, and the finest flour, is the area known for producing Italy's best dried pasta). You can specifically buy from the Pastificio Afeltra, a pasta maker dating from 1848. Farinetti liked it so much he bought the company. Their stately building, on the street that has always been the centre of pasta making, combines the best of that traditional craftsmanship with up-to-date technology. Made from the finest fully organic durum wheat semolina, all Afeltra pasta is slowly extruded through bronze, giving the correct porosity and roughness, then dried in wooden cells, regularly checked for everything from humidity to microbiological quality. In total Eataly stocks over 200 shapes of pasta including paccheri, vesuvio, bucatini, casarecce and calamari as well as the more familiar pennes and spaghettis – each one exhaustively, expertly selected.

Eataly is also full of restaurants. The arrangement of these and of all the goods is well thought through, never overwhelming despite the profusion. Antipasti are near each other, and at the opposite end of the store to the gelato counter and espresso bar. There is a natural order bringing out the classical rhythms of *cucina Italiana*. A large bookshop can be found on the right when you enter. Information about slow food, seasonal foods, ingredients and techniques is cleverly integrated into the space.

Eataly stocks thousands of items and serves a large menu across its restaurants. But the care with which they are selected is extraordinary. All the suppliers have rigorous standards. Everything is chosen to be the best possible example. It's all about curating the rich, locally complex heritage of Italian cuisine and ingredients. Eataly contains a lot – but it's a tiny fraction of the possible produce and it's militantly filtered. Even the hand washes in the bathrooms are specially selected. Water, given free at the restaurants, Lurisia, is again controlled by Farinetti. The bottles are glass because Farinetti believes it makes the water taste better.

Eataly is curated through and through. There are no corporate brands, no industrially processed products, no complex supply chains. Food is highlighted as coming from individual farms, co-operatives and even fields. Eataly represents choice – but all those tomato sauces have already been through a vast process of pre-selection. They represent only the pinnacle, the best possible choice. Inasmuch as it represents the future of food retail – and it's hard not to hope that there might be an element of truth in that – Eataly's attention to selection and arrangement is key. As one of the principal investors in the NYC branch, Mario Batali, told the *New York Times*: 'Customers believe they are getting something highly edited.'[5]

Batali argues that Eataly is not an everything store. It's part supermarket, part food court; but, he added, 'it all works together'. It's not a restaurant or set of restaurants; it's not a shop or set of shops. It's not a market, an institute, a cookery school, a philosophy of producing, selling and eating: it's all of them at once, underpinned by an unerring focus on selection that makes a new way of growing, Slow Food, possible. Eataly is the curated antidote to agribusiness; it's where curation changes aspects of primary production. Eataly shows how not only is the future of food retail likely to be one of more curation, but how that future impacts right through the supply chain to the growers.

None of it came cheap. The Turin store was underwritten by at least €20m of investment from Farinetti. In New York it may have been even more. But the results are stunning.

New York's opening was attended by then Mayor Michael Bloomberg and had queues for weeks. Two years later it was taking $1,700 per square foot per year compared with $350 to $500 at even the most lucrative malls. With eight to thirteen thousand visitors a day, by some measures it's the third most popular attraction in New York after the Statue of Liberty and the Empire State Building.[6] Eataly expanded to places like Chicago, Istanbul and Tokyo without sacrificing its values, vision, and curatorial proposition. Now plans are afoot for the next wave of expansion in cities like Boston, Moscow, Munich and Sydney.

Agriculture is the most fundamental industry. Food production, like almost everything else, has continued increasing. Today 40 per cent of the world's land surface is given over to agriculture. The 'Green Revolution' of the 1950s and 1960s ensured that even as the global population swelled, so did our food supply. Pesticides, herbicides, nitrates, fertilisers and breeding kept productivity ticking up, although many experts now fear we will start to suffer adverse consequences. A combination of climate change, soil degradation and water stress will mean growing food becomes harder, but for now the problem is managed. According to conservative estimates from Oxfam research, the world produces 17 per cent more food per head of the population than it did thirty years ago.[7] We have enough food, if anything we have too much – it's just not equally distributed. Food is no more separate from the abundance of our era than most goods.

Foods are also complex. Eataly manages to condense the bewildering complexity of Italian food, where every village has a different culinary tradition with different ingredients and recipes, into one shop, which gives you the full breadth of produce and cooking from the mountains of Lombardy to the coast of Sicily.

Wine is a good example. Burgundy alone has 4,300 growers, most of them with less than ten hectares under vine. While it accounts for only 3 per cent of French production, it has nearly a fifth of the *Appellations d'Origine Contrôlée* which govern the tight regional identity of French wine. Even seasoned wine experts find mastering the intricacies of Burgundy a challenge. Over centuries viticulture has encompassed a bewildering span of grape varietals and growing conditions. It explains why wine has long been curated – why there have always been sommeliers in restaurants, and local wine merchants who would help navigate for casual drinkers.

So we curate wine. I am a member of a not-for-profit wine organisation called The Wine Society which is built around a team of expert buyers, many of whom have the rare Master of Wine status – the organisation's pitch is one of exceptional selection for everyday drinkers. In London I drink at a bar called Sager + Wilde, whose choice of wine is always impeccable. Now they have taken to curating the wine lists for other restaurants. If we didn't curate wine, there is no way we would have the differentiated global marketplace for wine we currently enjoy, a market supporting a dizzying array of tiny producers from the Napa Valley to the Western Cape.

Curation isn't just a nice addition to the global wine market; curation is a structural necessity. The more wine we have, the more countries, chateaux and winemakers that produce it, the more innovation, the longer and richer the heritage of the old world classics, the more complex is the business and the higher the value of curation vis-à-vis the value of producing another bottle.

You might think this is all very agreeable but without serious economic consequences (although in fact the wine industry is worth billions, The Wine Society is growing faster than at any time in its 141-year history and Sager + Wilde are expanding into new bars). But it has enormous ramifications. Wine may be big, but coffee is bigger. Every day over 2.1bn cups of coffee are drunk.[8] After oil, coffee is the world's most traded commodity, meaning that for major producers like Brazil, Colombia, Vietnam and Indonesia it is a critically important export. So any significant trends have serious reper-cussions for millions of producers. And of the many trends in coffee, none is more significant than the 'third wave'.

In the US the first wave of coffee dates back to the nine-teenth century. Major brands like Folgers, founded in 1850, brought it to the masses. From the 1960s to the 1980s there was a change in coffee culture – coffee bars, epitomised by the classic second-wave brand, Starbucks, changed the way people drank coffee. Then in the 1990s and early 2000s came the third wave. Outlets like Stumptown Coffee Roasters from Portland, Oregon, and Counter Culture Coffee from Durham, North Carolina, set about making coffee with a new sense of mission. Coffee was to be treated more reverentially, like wine, with correct methods of preparation, growing and sourcing. In the UK, traditionally a tea-drinking nation, the waves came later. Coffee became popular in the 1960s with the wider adoption of instant coffee. Then came the second wave in the 1990s – Starbucks sprang up in town centres alongside British brands like Costa and Nero. By the late 2000s, starting in London but rippling out around the country, came the third wave.

Third-wave coffee is much more carefully selected than what came before. Roasters and baristas genuinely spend hours looking at, testing and thinking about beans. Third-wave is about plantations. It is about elevation and soil, national and local traditions of coffee growing. Beyond selection, it focuses on improving roasting techniques and places a premium on coffee art.

A big part of third-wave coffee is not only the scientific

approach to production and the connoisseur selection but that connection, like Slow Food, between supplier and end retailer. Often the best coffee comes from micro-holdings, places with, dare one say it, *terroir*. These coffees are incredibly labour-intensive, often needing quadruple picking, by hand, because the beans ripen at different times. It's only by focusing on the details of selection that this is possible, however; bulk and careless purchasers will never make that link. Curating the product brings primary and quinary closer together.

James Simmons of Stumptown Coffee's Greenwich Village outlet tells me about the process of buying: 'It's a considerable amount of curatorial work. All of the coffee our Green Buyers [so called because the beans are bought green, direct from the plantations] secure for us comes through close relationships to producers which take years and a great deal of energy to grow.' He talks about the attention paid to quality – 'Our quality plays an inextricable role in how we grow our business and we wouldn't have high-quality coffee if our Green Buyers didn't have direct relationships with producers.' One example he cites is Stumptown's continuing relationship with the Aguirre family of Guatemala, who not only grow some of the world's best coffee, but actively support their local community.[9] In Simmons' words it takes buyers with 'the highest level of expertise in the coffee industry' to identify and build these relationships.

In London I visited a third-wave coffee shop called, aptly, Curators Coffee. A refined modern space, part coffee shop, part demure fashion boutique, part laboratory, it's one of many third-wave outlets thriving amidst the city's new coffee culture. Over a cup of delicate, almost floral coffee, Catherine Seay, the co-founder, spoke to me about their approach.

'In terms of food and coffee shops,' she said, 'you can walk into the big high street stores, ask for anything and they will just produce it. People don't even want to know or look at the menu at those places. They'll ask for an Earl Grey tea and they get it. But we might only have one single estate Darjeeling on our tea menu. For me, I want someone to sort out the stuff that isn't interesting, to present a few options that are really appealing.' It's an approach where every single thing in the shop is exhaustively selected. They ensure that of the few items they sell, they only have the best, produced to the highest standard. At Curators Coffee the drink is closer to fine wine than the sludgy work-fuel we all know (yes, OK, and love).

But this is a business strategy. According to the *Financial Times* sales of specialist coffee are up 300% since 2002.[10] Seay knows that Curators Coffee, which is expanding, builds customer loyalty through its curation: 'When it comes to new coffees we get customers to trust us – we complement coffees with flavours on a month-by-month basis and customers come in and follow that. They will come specifically to try that one combination.' Sometimes customers just want a cup of coffee without fuss – which is fine by Seay, that's what they'll get, no questions. Because of the selection, they know it will be good. But if they want to spend half an hour discussing origins, permaculture, shade-grown beans, brewing temperatures and all the rest of it, great.

Thinking about the dangers of explicit curation, I ask Seay if this could go too far. Are we making things too complicated, too silly? Her answer gets to the heart of good curation: 'There might be some wild curated food businesses in the future. But I hope it doesn't go too far to the ridiculous side. It should be about mastery of the craft. That's what a curator brings: knowledge. The more I can find out about coffee, the better I can choose it.'

At the explicit level third-wave coffee involves scenesters talking about blueberry and vanilla notes in their single-grower flat white. But it changes the way coffee is grown, distributed, made and consumed. For that single grower, such coffee rather than bulk buys is the difference between good prices and bad; it's the difference, for them as for the drinker, between a mass product and a crafted item. Aesthetically as well as economically it's a different world. And here's the kicker: the curated version makes more money, for the grower, the distributor and upstream for the shop. People will pay for curated experience. Without curation – that new focus on selection – they'd just have another boring, bland coffee.

Instead, entrepreneurs like Seay grow by offering curated choices. Their suppliers then double down on making the best possible product. New businesses like Pact Coffee are scaling the model up to deliver curated coffee to your home. Starbucks is starting to realise they need better options. Even going back to the first wave, something like Nespresso is more select than a jar of generic instant coffee. Third-wave may be elitist and faddish – but it's spearheading a wider change in how we drink *and* produce those 2.1bn cups a day. If enough people choose third-wave, as they have been, the ramifications spread throughout the entire supply chain.

This is the pattern across the food and drink sector. At the explicit level there is a new approach. Menus shrink – it's now perfectly normal, indeed fashionable, for restaurants to have three starters and three mains. Indeed, many restaurants now specialise in one thing only. This was always the norm in Tokyo, where a restaurateur would choose one dish to cook exceptionally well, but is increasingly common in the West. When going out for dinner we don't want excessive choice; we want a curated experience.

Then at the implicit level we see a new approach to the whole business. The network of Slow Food and its retailers is about taking care in choosing what food goes where. The rise of farmers' markets is a related phenomenon. In the UK a service like Abel & Cole and in the US Community Supported Agriculture deliver pre-selected, seasonal, local food to your door. A litany of new food services do the same – not just vegetables, but beers, wines, coffees, even bacon (really), are selected and delivered. Blue Apron not only sends you the food weekly, but also the recipes to go with it. The pitch for such companies isn't about price; they tend to be expensive. Instead it's about choosing the best from a complex field. If I want generic beer it's cheap from a supermarket; if I want hand-selected craft beer then I go to DeskBeers. Beneath these are changes to how the major suppliers and retailers do business. They are forced to react, to more proactively curate their offering. Sainsbury's for example, the UK's third-largest supermarket, has trialled an Eataly-style market store. Whole Foods, a more curated experience than Walmart, has boomed.

Our attitude to food has changed. Where once we stuck within the boundaries of national cuisines, now we pick and choose. And it's not just Chinese one day Mexican the next; it's more specific, Sichuan hot pot and Oaxacan mole. Where once we were limited by local ingredients, now the world's produce comes to our door. Hence the need for a curated approach. Companies like Eataly and Curators Coffee are the thin end of a wedge in our relationship with the most primary of economic activities. I'm not arguing that Eataly will replace Walmart – it won't. But I am saying that in future Walmart is likely to look a little more like Eataly. Well-heeled customers aren't paying because of a food shortage; they pay to have their choices pre-selected so that they are offered only the very best.

Curating our food, our wine, our coffee might sound like (might indeed be) the height of pretentiousness. But when it transforms the most fundamental economic sector and perhaps the most basic activity of them all, we should pay attention. Yes, these examples are cosseted and middle-class. It's rich and often Western consumers who feel the benefit the most. But the world is adding middle-class consumers faster than ever before: 500m in China by 2020 according to Jack Ma.[11] Indonesia alone will add 68m people to its middle class in the next five years – more than the population of France or the UK.[12] Above 2bn will be middle-class at the end of the decade. If curation remains centred on smallish elites, it is rippling out. So it's not just preposterous indulgence, it's the most significant consumer trend; and while there is a fine line between market trend and pointless fad it can't be ignored.

We curate the world. We do it because there is too much stuff but also because there is opportunity in doing so. Curation is a response to overload, but as Abu Dhabi and Oscar Farinetti realised, it's the kind of knowledge-intensive work that's driving the next waves of growth. Curation effects have strayed far from the old heartlands. We are seeing them in:

- **Data.** Such is the supply spike that data management is everywhere – even in places like medicine.[13] As health data becomes more prevalent the conclusions it's possible to draw from it are less obvious. Information about conditions and their associated symptoms is growing more complex and ambiguous. Clinicians find that increasingly there is no 'right' treatment; instead they are required to pick and choose from a menu of options. As the data available from medical and wearable technology grows, so the field becomes ever more about the management of information.
- **Homes.** Marie Kondo has sold millions of books with a straightforward piece of advice: choose your possessions carefully.[14] Be ruthless, and get rid of

most of what you own. Kondo believes in decluttering everything that doesn't 'spark joy'. It's part zero-tolerance approach to tidying up, part Zen philosophy of domestic space; either way, her advice has been taken up on a mass scale. It reflects a more curated attitude to our homes, one that has been developing over many years. Arguably, our homes are both the earliest curated spaces and the most curated spaces. The emphasis on clearing out the crap should not come as a surprise.

- **Reputation.** As *The Chronicle of Higher Education* argues, academics have to curate their online identity.[15] Getting tenure is a matter of curating your work and reputation. Beyond this, again, the prevalence of data means that meta-studies, the choosing and organisation of existing research, is becoming more important than ever. This applies to all of us. We are judged by what we share and post. The Internet is a reputational minefield where we have to edit and construct our image.

- **Nations.** Several years ago Sweden set up Curators of Sweden. Every week it lets different Swedish citizens control the @sweden Twitter account. It recognises that national identity isn't fixed; that to some extent we all pick and choose and curate from the mass of traditions, stories, beliefs, customs, laws, cultures, languages, places and histories that make up every country's identity. Each Swede has their own curated version of what Sweden is, and the national identity emerges from that multiplicity of versions. It's a branding exercise but it hints at a deeper truth about nationhood. So on the explicit level this is about curating a Twitter feed and marketing; at the implicit level it points to the ways in which we all have to select and arrange elements of our national identity.

Curation is relevant to us all. For sheikhs in the Gulf and coffee growers on the Central American isthmus, it changes patterns of work, creation, consumption, strategy and experience. Selecting and arranging are fundamental activities. They've always been with us. What's changed is their relative position in the value chain. They're more significant now than ever.

Our cultural life is not immune from the Long Boom and overload.

8

Curate Culture

Musical mixology

1970s, the South Bronx

Kool Herc was a Jamaican living in New York in the early 1970s. At 1520 Sedgwick Avenue, amidst urban poverty and gang violence, he invented hip hop.

Kool Herc's innovation was to take the beats in hard funk records, and using two turntables to mix them so songs would consist exclusively of beats. He'd noticed the 'break', the beats that set up a song, were the most popular parts of songs on club dancefloors. Splicing two copies of the same record extended the break, forming a new sound called breakbeat. By looping old tracks Kool Herc was making a new kind of music. It was a sound *sui generis* – but it wasn't about creating new music in the sense of writing and recording new songs. It was about mixing.

At first Kool Herc was known mainly on the rough streets of the Bronx. Before long others were getting in on the scene, adding rapping to the beats. By the late 1970s names like

Afrika Bambaataa and Grandmaster Flash were taking the sound to a new level. Hip hop would go on to conquer the world, becoming the signature sound for a generation, the planet's best-selling music genre. But Kool Herc hadn't just invented hip hop – he'd helped redefine the terms of musical creativity; selecting tracks and combining them in original ways to produce new experiences. The age of hip hop also gave birth to superstar DJs bigger than the artists they worked with: first Pete Tong, Carl Cox, Judge Jules and Fatboy Slim and then the EDM superstars of the present like Calvin Harris, David Guetta, Avicii and Armin van Buuren came to dominate music.

1990s, London

One of those DJs was Richard Russell. Russell wanted to do more than just DJ; he'd realised record labels held the power. He joined the A&R department of a fledgling label, XL Recordings, in 1991. Within three years he was running the show. Over the following decades, as the music industry descended into crisis and consolidated into the Big Three majors, he would transform XL into the most iconic and successful indie label of its time.

As everyone went for scale, Russell tacked in the opposite direction: signing new artists wasn't his priority. Russell and XL developed a model built around an unerring selection of brilliant music. Every year they would only sign one or two new artists. Moreover these wouldn't be from one genre – unlike other famous labels, XL never specialised in a particular sound. As he told *The Guardian*: 'We get offered 200,000 unsolicited demos a year and yet only sign about one artist a year. We're basically saying no to everything, lots of big artists as well. You need an element of fearlessness to do that.'[1]

In the process they signed acts including The Prodigy, Radiohead, The xx, Dizzee Rascal, Basement Jaxx, Jack White, Vampire Weekend, Devendra Banhart and Adele, becoming one of the most profitable labels around. It was all based on a relentless focus on the artist. Russell looked at the integrity and vision of artists and let this guide him. Selection, not scale, would create the defining label of the past ten years.

2000s, Berlin

Perhaps the most iconic nightclub of the early twenty-first century is Berghain in Berlin, named after its location between the districts of Kreuzberg and Friedrichshain. Set in a vast Soviet-era power plant, the club features reputedly the world's best sound system, a huge Funktion One rig, and has developed a signature sound of brooding techno. Just as legendary as the darkrooms and beats, however, is the notorious door policy.

Getting into Berghain is a rite of passage in itself. Early into the morning long queues snake around the building. Hopeful entrants wait hours only to be told *nein* by the club bouncer, a pierced and tattooed legend of German nightlife called Sven Marquardt. It's become something of a journalistic trope to attempt entry. Entry tactics form a Berghainology of what to wear (black) and what to say (not a lot, and not in English). There's even an app to help. Marquardt for the most part remains inscrutable. Releasing his memoirs, however, he gave an insight into the reasoning behind the entry policy. It was, he said, about selecting the 'right mix' of people on any one night.[2] Sometimes a rash of designer labels will get you turned away; on another night it might be part of the vibe.

Berghain's atmosphere and mystique rests not just on the music, the DJs, the goings on – it rests on this infamous implicit curation of the audience. It's the same principle behind the Soho House group's 'no bankers' policy. If anyone got into Berghain whenever they wanted there would be no *Rolling Stone* profiles, no underground myth. Nightclubs select and mix the 'right' people as well as the right music.

In different ways these examples show how the drift of musical culture has gone from primary production to various forms of secondary activity. At its height, DJing is a new form of creativity altogether, a claim few would make about night-club door policy. But at another level the direction of travel across musical culture puts a premium on curation of one kind or another, explicit and implicit.

Both the production and the experience of culture is ever more curated.

But what should I listen to next?

If you want an excellent illustration of the Long Boom, you can do a lot worse than music. Music used to come in two forms: the music that was performed live and the music stored in people's heads. While some music was written down, mostly it consisted of folk songs and memorised performances. With the invention of the printing press there came a step change. Printers in places like Venice started printing written music on a scale impossible in the scribal age. In the nineteenth century industrial printing and instrument making meant that the middle classes could own and learn instruments. On New York's Tin Pan Alley songwriters made fortunes penning dit-ties that were instantly rushed into print. Music was breaking its bonds, being stored and performed more widely.

Thomas Edison's invention of the phonograph in 1877 changed everything. Recorded music meant that physical performance and the experience of music were separated. Sound itself was now copiable and replayable. No longer an upper-class luxury, music became a ubiquitous presence in homes, bars and shops. Music wasn't just noise, it had become a locus of culture, a centre of personal identity and a vast global industry. The high water mark of physically stored musical data was the CD. They were cheaply mass-produced, and music fans couldn't get enough. The industry peak was epitomised by the $10.8bn acquisition of Polydor by Seagram in 1998 to form what would become Universal Music.

Then, from an industry perspective, things tanked, thanks to MP3s, Napster, the digitisation and mass piracy of music. Seagram's acquisition now appeared the height of hubris. But consumer abundance reached a whole new level: if music had seemed plentiful in the era of records and CDs, it was nothing to the new digital reality. Music's copiability was no longer predicated on a complex and resource-intensive industrial process – it was instantaneous and free. Once again, digital technology supercharged the long-term tilt towards abundance.

Now, with Spotify, the Swedish music subscription and streaming service, I have access to thirty million songs, with 20,000 new ones added every day. Users of Spotify have created over 1.5 billion playlists.[3] Then there are the radio stations, music videos, rival services and podcasts competing for our ears. YouTube and Soundcloud let anyone upload their songs and have tens, if not hundreds, of millions of unique records. The problem for connected listeners isn't scarcity. The problem is knowing what to listen to. Even before the change we'd spend hours choosing songs or putting together mixtapes. In a relatively short space of time the entire customer proposition around music has been transformed. The music industry has started to make the shift from technologies of production to technologies of curation. If music today has a problem it is about discoverability: how in the endless sea of available music will people ever find what they want, or discover something new?

Thanks to this aural overload we are in the midst of a curation arms race. Spotify started as a response to piracy. Their pitch to record labels and users was simple: you will have the best of both worlds. Listeners could access all the music they wanted, the signature shift of the digital age; record companies would monetise those ears. The problem for Spotify was that, despite its fast growth, users found the service difficult to navigate. As on the App Store, as in the supermarket, they would get into grooves – they'd get stuck in a rut. Literally millions of songs and artists had never once been listened to on the service.

Spotify piled resources into curation. It redesigned the site to make browsing more prominent. It hired experts to produce playlists in genres, for different moods, contexts and times of day, from morning commute to teenage house party. It became more social, allowing users to share and build playlists more easily – everyone could help curate music. Then in 2014 it acquired a company called The Echo Nest for a reported $100m. Spun out from the MIT Media Lab, The Echo Nest had pioneered a technique called audio fingerprinting. Examining billions of data points across a catalogue of sixty million songs, researchers synthesised the information into intelligence readily usable by music services. If you liked song x, it would find you song y with extraordinary accuracy.

The Echo Nest have, for example, a danceability index that, they allege, transcends genre. They have a side project called Every Noise At Once, which is building a complete profile of the world's music genres. Unlike other data-analysis firms they focus only on music; their clients include MTV, Vevo and Spotify rival Rdio. Earlier services like Pandora and Last.fm had developed sophisticated audio fingerprinting, but with this acquisition Spotify was aiming to take the lead. Founder Daniel Ek made clear the reason for the acquisition: 'You will see the quality of our recommendations increase,' he said.[4] Before long Spotify launched 'Discover Weekly', a new service that, every Monday, sent users a new batch of songs tailored to their listening habits.[5] Playlists have become sophisticated, knowledgeable explorations of micro-styles and offbeat genres. They are also influential: playlist Rap Caviar has 2.1m followers.

But others weren't standing still. Pandora's Music Genome Project continued to innovate, looking at between 400 and 2,000 traits per track to identify what people might like. Soon after Spotify bought The Echo Nest, Google, moving rapidly into music streaming, bought a start-up called Songza which examined contextual data relating to users to suggest tracks. Apple had bought Beats and started piling into the space. They hired DJs like Trent Reznor of Nine Inch Nails and Zane Lowe from BBC Radio 1 to build playlists and run a new station, Beats 1, 'the world's local station', operating from London, New York and Los Angeles. As the *Financial Times* argues, although music now only makes a small proportion of Apple's revenues it has a symbolic place in the company. Competing on streaming means competing on curation: 'One of the features that will be retained [from the Beats app] is designed to elicit as much information as possible about a user's individual music tastes by asking them to select favourite genres and musical styles when signing up to the service. It is hoped that this personalisation, alongside recommendations from artists, will help overcome difficulty in choosing what to listen to from a library of millions of tracks.'[6] In just three months the number of Apple Music users grew to eleven million, and the service epitomised the company's renewed focus on curation. Artists including Jay Z, Coldplay and Madonna launched their own competing service, Tidal. New entrants like Slacker Radio, Hype Machine, Patreon or evening DJing apps added to the mix, each with their own take on how to find and recommend songs.

In a little over a decade the business and consumption of music had become a space of competing curation, driven by the supply shock of the digital era. Whoever 'owned' music wouldn't just be the cheapest or most attractive service – they would solve the question of musical excess.[7] The precise tactics, metrics and outcomes are, for our purposes, less significant than the terrain of battle itself.

Nor is this only a question of tech giants playing DJ. Smaller services are finding a place. Ambie supplies music to commercial premises. Based on the assumption that most players use crude, one-size-fits-all selection models, Ambie instead tailors offerings for each client. 'We founded Ambie under a different approach,' says founder Gideon Chain. 'We brought together a unique blend of music experts and tastemakers with real tech superstars ... and all geared towards building a curated music service, that could scale.'

Ambie's competitive advantage is quite simply better curation: the opposite of Muzak. All music is chosen by experts for the client's space. This human curation is augmented by in-house technology. Combining the two means that every customer has the best experience while the service remains scalable. But crucially everyone gets an expert. While the competition sells pre-prepared packages, Ambie can offer something unique while still keeping costs down.

For Chain, this aspect, reflected in Apple's hires or Spotify's social emphasis, is critical: 'Our belief is that machine-driven curation can achieve a fair amount – essentially reducing the amount of work required by each curator. However, music is too subjective to be compiled by computers alone. There are aspects of curation (sequencing, brand-specific guidelines, elements of mood) that computers still find very difficult. At the same time, our music experts are tastemakers in their own fields, immersing themselves in the world of music on a daily basis.'

Ambie works with a strong sense of place and brand. How does this song work in this room? What brand considerations are needed? That's not just about filtering swearing, for example; it's engaging with the whole tenor of a track to see if it aligns with the client's expectations. 'Everyone thinks they can make great playlists but the ability to accurately source, process and sequence tracks for a specific brand or space is actually incredibly difficult,' says Chain. 'Good curation covers many different elements but always begins with an incredibly detailed profile of the customer or space the music is being curated for. This includes brand values, customer demographic, interior design and specific zones, trading patterns, price point, competition, desired ambience/s and other key factors. Then there is the balance between contemporary and traditional music and the balance between familiar, mainstream music versus unknown, underground or emerging sounds.'

Ambie's sales proposition is based purely on their ability as tastemakers, expert selectors, influencers and technologists. Businesses can easily source music; finding music to play in your bar or shop isn't the problem. Ambie is specifically designed to solve the inverse equation, to find the *right* music.

Music today is curated. First we simply listened. Albums gave us a set order and selection. Then we created mixtapes for our friends. Now we share playlists. Once we listened to bands; now we listen to DJs. We used to create all our sounds from scratch; now we pick and sample from old songs. DJ Mark Ronson even argues we live in the 'sampling era' of music, where sounds are heard and reincorporated over and over again.[8] One track, 'Amen, Brother' by The Winstons, has been sampled on a further 1,687 songs.[9] This may not be curation as such but it shows the extent to which the old creativity myth is breaking down and how far a more curatorial mindset has become embedded. The sampler or DJ is half creator, half curator. In music and across cultural forms, first- and second-order creative acts are becoming increasingly blurred.

When the tools to make music are everywhere and music itself, in its extraordinary scope and diversity, is a click away, curation isn't a luxury add-on – it's a necessary component.

Play it again

What are the implications for culture?

First. The Broadcast Model of culture and media is dying. Earlier we saw how the Industrial Model of retail ceded ground to a Curated Model. The cultural and media corollary is the Broadcast Model giving way to a Consumer-Curated Model. In music the system of a few radio stations, labels and shops, which collectively dictated what was listened to, has given way to a complex mixture of algorithms and curated playlists. In television the shift is just as noticeable. Mid-twentieth-century America had a network oligopoly of NBC, ABC and CBS: The Big Three. In Europe state television predominated. As recently as the 1970s a British viewer would have chosen from three channels. Over time, with the satellite revolution, more and more channels came on screen. Television became abundant. VHS gave viewers more freedom. Then came the Internet: YouTube, peer-to-peer file-sharing networks, Netflix, Hulu, BBC iPlayer, all meant that the traditional model of scheduled broadcasts started to crumble. While the Broadcast Model was itself curated, what has changed is that we all now curate.

The power to decide who watches what and when has flipped from broadcasters to audience. Now we have to decide what we want to watch – from a vast menu. The same goes for reading, listening, playing, viewing. In museums the old style of exhibition started to give way to more interactive and collaborative programming. Albums and radio are Broadcast; playlists are Consumer-Curated. TV schedules are Broadcast; your to-watch list is Curated.

In publishing editors and imprints once held power. Then booksellers and review pages became key intermediaries. All of them lost ground to readers. You and I are now the most important suggesters and curators of books. Books don't correlate exactly to Broadcast, but the pattern is the same. In contemporary culture and media, sequencing and discovery are devolved away from old power bases. We don't listen to the radio as scheduled; we catch up at will on our podcast player. Young audiences find the idea of cinematic release schedules in different territories baffling and frustrating. Individual tracks – not albums – are the prime unit of musical consumption. We're as likely to listen to a playlist assembled by ourselves, our friends, a celebrity or a site like Pitchfork as one from a band or record label. We no longer expect news to be parcelled into a complete package, delivered at the same time every day. We dictate which video games get distribution through user-driven services like Steam Greenlight. The shift from top-down industrialised organisation to a user-centric Consumer-Curated Model is here.

This 'post-broadcast' media is hardly news. But its ramifications are still playing out. Cultural scarcity is not the problem. Adapting to the new reality is. Organisations that cling on to the old will see their influence, popularity and market share eroded.

It's not plain sailing. In the Broadcast Model we had no

choice but to enjoy a shared culture. In the Consumer-Curated world that's impossible. Moreover as we curate our own media, and choose the curators we will allow to help us, the potential for disappearing down the rabbit hole of our own tastes, beliefs and preferences increases.

It's a risk, and it highlights one of the differences between good and bad curation. Good curation helps the new, the unexpected; bad curation just confirms what you already want. This is why tastemakers have started to make a come-back against personalisation algorithms. Good curation is about adding value – not appropriating it.

Nevertheless, gatekeepers are not going away. Despite the rise in Consumer Curation, and contrary to popular myth, gatekeepers of all kinds are still around. In fact, they may be more important than ever before. It's easy to believe that because power has been devolved, gatekeepers are becoming redundant. They aren't – but their role is changing.

If gatekeepers used to be dictatorial figures, now they're guides. The fact that choice is so overwhelming, that every time we look for content, media or culture we are bombarded with options, means that despite Consumer Curation we still want trusted guides. Trusted is the operative word – one that explains why so many legacy brands have, despite the gleeful predictions of the digerati, managed to thrive.

XL Recordings, like many in the creative industries, made gatekeeping an integral part of their business model. The artists whose music they put out are worth considering because of all the others who were rejected. While XL would never put their own brand at the centre of a marketing campaign, because they focus on so few artists they are able to fully support everything those artists do. Their selection has a meaningful impact on the presentation of the artists and, in turn, on the likelihood of those artists being listened to.

Many traditional newspaper brands have found new online audiences. Publishers have not disappeared but become part of a validation process for writers: writers crave recognition; readers crave trusted signposts suggesting what to read.

Of course, gatekeepers aren't just legacy organisations. New gatekeepers spring up all the time. Spotify and the other music sites are as much gatekeeper as a traditional radio station or MTV. Vice, inasmuch as they direct attention here and not there, are gatekeeping as much as *The Washington Post*. Influential individuals who send tweets are still gatekeeping. New niches and gatekeeping roles are evolving all the time. The question for these new gatekeepers changes: how do you become trusted as a curator?

The truth is there is no shortcut. Authenticity, consistency, excellent selections – it's very hard to fake. It's why so many corporate attempts to become media curators fail. Gatekeepers of any kind have to be patient. They need a clear vision and they have to stick to it. The best legacy organisations have spent decades or even centuries building and augmenting that vision. Which is why the *Financial Times* and Penguin, Gagosian and William Morris Entertainment are all gatekeepers that remain influential, profitable and relevant. For the new emerging gatekeepers, building credibility is the challenge – but they do, and that's why we have things like Laughing Squid, Vox Media and Wattpad.

Cultural and media gatekeepers saw their old Broadcast Model crumble. But this didn't mean they were useless. Such is the excess of material available, they still have a role, no longer as the monopolists but as partners. In the attention economy, the key is who controls our attention. While gatekeepers are more numerous and no longer have total control, they still funnel attention, the oxygen of culture.

The change in creativity is part of a wider pattern: creativity

is shifting from its mythical phase towards curation. By now
the line between the two is ever more indistinct. Moreover –
and surprisingly – it's broadly accepted.

Perhaps the roots of this change lie in the move towards
what in the 1970s was termed postmodernism. Whereas previous art movements had distinct features, postmodernism,
whether in art, fashion, literature, architecture or philosophy,
was built around a playful, magpie attitude to the very idea
of distinct features themselves. Bricolage and recombination
would be the hallmarks. While this was once considered
advanced, we now take it for granted.

Architecture, for instance. Postmodern architecture was
a reaction to the modernist formalism of the mid-twentieth
century. Modernism had a functional aesthetic – the so-called
International Style, a visual language of severe blocks. It
was arrestingly up to date and serious. Against the militant
purity of modernism, postmodernism would playfully combine historical forms, cheekily picking motifs from across the
architectural lexicon.

The classic case is New York's Sony Building (see Figure
13), originally the AT&T Building. Designed by Philip
Johnson, begun in 1978 and completed in 1984, it was controversial from the start. Unlike modernist skyscrapers it
used classical forms on a grandiose scale; where they rejected
historical decoration, Johnson supersized it. The idea of putting a 'Chippendale'-style bookcase on a skyscraper seemed
outrageous to Manhattanites used to crisp right angles and
sleek monoliths. Moreover Johnson himself had once been an
arch-modernist, working with Ludwig Mies van der Rohe on
the Seagram Building, an iconic functionalist skyscraper in
the International Style which eschewed ornamentation. For
much of his career, history wasn't part of Johnson's design.

Like fellow postmodernists James Stirling and Robert

Venturi, Johnson neither bought into a single school nor rejected history – instead he and his contemporaries saw schools and periods alike as a menu. The giant pediment, the granite cladding, an enormous seven-metre arched entrance – these were taken from classical buildings, while the boxy form stayed true to the International Style. This visual sampling was echoed in Johnson's One Detroit Centre (again see Figure 13). Constructed on a similar scale to the Sony Building, it had over-elaborated Flemish-style gables – 1990s meets 1690s. PPG Place in Pittsburgh was another skyscraper, this time with spires reminiscent of a Gothic castle. Facades and

Figure 13. Left, the Sony Building; right, One Detroit Center

rooftops became spaces for decoration. By being too rigidly defined, modern architecture had become boring. Now columns and plinths, gables and spires were back – but as things to be chosen and combined, not stylistic essentials as they would once have been. Adherence to one doctrine was replaced by a whimsical medley of form.

Postmodern architecture then was, more than ever before, a curatorial exercise. It was perhaps another curation effect, another familial resemblance to the creativity of DJs and sampling or the rise of the curator as the central figure in the art world. We have an entire culture based on the referencing and reuse of cultural memes. Creativity as a force of originality is decentred, unmoored. What constitutes a classic second-order practice like curation is complicated as core tenets of the activity are brought into the heart of what it means to produce.

The modernists had, in the words of the poet Ezra Pound, wanted to 'Make It New'. Although they often reused old fragments of culture, there was something radically original about their literature, dance, music, visual art, architecture and cinema. Now the postmodernists wouldn't even try to Make It New. They'd just Make It. If the modernists were already living in an age when the encrusted layers of older culture meant the possibility of newness was difficult, they still wanted to challenge it. By the time we got to the age of postmodern architects, megastar DJs and curators curating curators at biennials, no one was even pretending 'pure' creativity was a possibility any more.

We have undoubtedly gone beyond the identifiable artistic movement of postmodernism prevalent in the 1970s, 80s and 90s. Yet nothing particularly definable has emerged to replace it – indeed, postmodernism even predicted this situation when it talked of the breakdown of 'grand narratives', including, one supposes, that of postmodernism itself.

Postmodernism is gone, is now a historical relic, but its legacy of 'neo-eclecticism' – anything goes, pick and choose, mix everything – is still here. Its mode of recycling bits and pieces of culture has apparently become permanent. Emotionally we may still be attached to the creativity myth – but in practice it seems we've already left it far behind. Today memes are recycled through every area of our culture: films are endlessly remade, books rewritten; TV programmes reference other TV programmes; remixes and samples dominate the charts. Pop Art self-consciously took its forms from mass consumer culture. Now art self-consciously takes from Pop Art.

This is not an unprecedented state of affairs. Shakespeare didn't write the plots for most of his plays *ex nihilo*; he recomposed them from a medley of sources. This was regarded as normal. Only when Shakespeare was later deified by a generation of writers, poets, actors and publishers as the epitome of creative genius would this be seen as somehow odd. Until the Romantic era, to emulate classical or religious sources of perfection was often more of an imperative than originality.

But, nonetheless, are we devaluing creativity? Producing a weakened, emaciated version of creativity where the critic, the curator, rather than the original is the hero? We can see these trends playing out in that media staple – the news.

The new news

In the first weeks of 2011 events that became known as the Arab Spring burst into the world's consciousness – and nowhere more so than in Egypt. Ruled for decades by Hosni Mubarak, Egyptians, inspired by their neighbours, started to protest. Then on 25 January, the situation intensified. Cairenes in their hundreds of thousands descended on Tahrir Square at the city's heart – a huge traffic intersection and ceremonial space surrounded by national museums and party headquarters. Chaos ensued. Tahrir Square itself became a giant encampment. Violence was never far from the surface as protesters, armed militias and the police engaged in shadowy running battles. By 1 February, Al-Jazeera reported, there were one million people in the square. During the protests, which eventually resulted in the collapse of the Mubarak regime when the army refused to intercede, there were thousands of deaths. Ninety police stations were burned to the ground.

Three years later the situation in Kiev, Ukraine, was equally combustible. As in Egypt, tension had been rising for years. In Ukraine it centred on the country's direction – would it turn west, towards the EU, or east, to Russia? After President Viktor Yanukovych pivoted towards Russia widespread protests sprang up, activists descending on Kiev's main civic space, the Maidan. Protesters were based there from December 2013, but vicious clashes between police and demonstrators in February 2014 became pitched battles. At first police fired rubber bullets but soon they moved to live ammunition, tear gas and flash grenades. There were even snipers on surrounding buildings. Events were complex, involving columns of protesters, behind-the-scenes political machinations, street clashes, subterfuge and a lack of 'objective' reporting. The timeline for 18 February alone is still hotly disputed.

In both Tahrir Square and the Maidan, traditional news operations struggled to stay on top of events. Both situations were immensely dangerous for reporters. In the fissile atmosphere of revolution, it was never clear who was on which side, who might present a violent threat, or what might happen next. Both situations were also complex, with both sides making the most of propaganda and the participants, dispersed across massive cities, becoming entangled in webs of enmity and allegiance. In previous years journalists would have done what they could – but this would have been after the fact, partial and incomplete. Only in hindsight would it have been possible to properly understand historical events.

Now journalists could try a different approach. Social media offered the possibility of citizen journalism – ordinary people recording the news. While citizen journalism never took off as its proponents had hoped, connected devices meant that more information than ever before was emerging from dangerous, complex events. Status updates and, perhaps most powerfully, mobile video were now in protagonists' hands. On-the-ground journalists would still be essential, but news desks could sift through a mass of uploads, verifying and collating material before inserting it as part of their own coverage. In Cairo and Kiev, as well as in even more difficult situations like the Syrian conflict, the character of journalism changed from writing the narrative to weaving the narrative from existing sources: amateur footage, once the supporting act, became the main event. If news organisations wanted to keep up, they needed new models of news gathering in which piecing together existing sources played a greater role than finding those sources in the first place. CNN no longer needed to shoot the footage itself, always a partial process using as it did single camera crews; it needed to find material for recomposing into its stories. And of course, this did not mean news organisations were redundant. Finding, verifying and contextualising the mass of information that was emerging in real time on the ground took authority, expertise, infrastructure and an existing audience. When CNN quoted a tweet or embedded mobile footage, we wanted to know what was happening, who was speaking and why; we still wanted the news to give us a coherent narrative of what was occurring, but the means to do so was shifting from reportage to collage.

The Egyptian and Ukrainian revolutions show how news is changing. It used to be about collecting and transmitting information. Now it is about parsing vast amounts of noise for the signal. It's what a report on the future of news from Columbia University's Tow Center calls 'post-industrial journalism': journalism not oriented to churning out mass product, but more focused, niche, flexible and curated.[10] A journalism where journalists will look more like editors – or curators.

Xavier Damman, the founder of curation service Storify, told me that 'In a world where everyone can publish, curation is an important part of making sure that real information isn't just data.' This distinction is crucial to reporting today. Storify is one example of a company built around helping others manage it. But unlike many digital entrepreneurs, Damman recognises this is a necessary but also an evolutionary trend, building on an existing base: 'Journalism has always been about curating sources, packaging them as a story and then distributing them to people. Now witnesses and experts – those same sources – are on social networks. We still need to listen to repackage them. But before journalists would have access to twenty sources – now it's two thousand. We need these people – journalists, bloggers, curators of any type – I call them information engineers – to optimise this output for large audiences, to filter through all the noise.'

One obvious change is that news sites link to each other as never before. This started with the new breed that began in the 1990s and 2000s: outlets like The Huffington Post, The Drudge Report and Slate. Whereas traditional news focused on being a complete package, these websites faced outward. They didn't see themselves as monolithic slices of content so much as connectors to the growing mass of interesting material on the web. Then the second generation of news sites like Buzzfeed and Quartz came along. Whereas the HuffPo's linking was innovative, for the new breed of 'digital journalism' it was standard. Floating on a sea of content, we dart in and out of publications.

Indeed, Buzzfeed, which was recently hiring for the new position of News Curation Editor, often consisted of embedded tweets, gifs and photos from elsewhere on the web. Its signature form, the 'listicle', was simply a selection and arrangement of existing material. Half of Quartz's famous daily email consists of links. The value proposition went from writing and delivering the news, to finding the most interesting content. What Quartz discovered and linked to was almost as important as what it produced. Before long embedded tweets, links to other sites and YouTube films were filling up pages on the sites of *The Guardian*, the *New York Times* and every major news outlet. The idea of the single story started to give way to rolling coverage composed from a mosaic of sources. On the margins of journalism and the web a new breed of business was finding space to grow. TheSkimm created detailed newsletters; This was building a social network that forced users to choose carefully what they shared; Longreads selected the best longer writing from 'hundreds of publishers'.

None of this should be a surprise – we can hardly expect the information explosion to leave activities like journalism, information provision and non-fiction writing and entertainment unscathed.

Partly this reflected the explosion in the amount of material. Everyone was now a 'content producer' and so the original content producers – news and media – had to adapt. Transaction costs associated with the production and distribution of content (of all kinds, of course, not just journalism) plummeted. Now in almost any niche there were clusters of published expertise outside industry confines. Companies and brands, personal blogs, influential tweeters, non-profit organisations, NGOs and university research centre newsfeeds all started producing high-quality material. The well-regarded SCOTUSblog had more in-depth coverage of the United States Supreme Court than traditional media. Britain's Westminster political bubble was covered with verve and scurrilousness by upstarts like the Guido Fawkes blog. Quite often, it was realised, a random tweet or a bystander with a smartphone encapsulated a situation better than any journalist – so why not co-opt them?

Not only was there more comment, but there was more potential news in the first place. A connected world bred stories. Then there were new models, goals and media for journalism: philanthropic and profit-driven; online and offline; crowd-sourced and professionally edited; video, audio, interactive and text-based. It meant more need for curation and more curation, that core interdependence we see time and again.

It means gatekeepers are still there. Their importance is reflected by the careers of two stars of the new journalism environment, Ezra Klein and Nate Silver. Klein left *The Washington Post*'s Wonkblog and Silver left the *New York Times*'s The Upshot; they went to start Vox and FiveThirtyEight. Both indicate that individual curation of the news is becoming more important in that both considered they had sufficient audience, clout and expertise to leave their institutions and start from scratch. Yet both Wonkblog and The Upshot have carried on, expanded and, according to the *New York Review of Books,* doubled in readership in the years since their two superstars left.[11] The value of big old gatekeepers, just like the value of new forms and superstar curators, has risen. Again this goes back to a familiar motif:

the amount of news information has increased so much we need more filters than ever before, trusted brands *and* new start-ups, those professionally produced *and* those devolved to us. We want new and personalised filters like Klein and Silver; we also want great legacy brands. In the new information environment, the more curators the better.

News organisations must also curate themselves. In their leaked Innovation Report, the *New York Times* claimed to publish well over 300 new URLs every day. Even the most ardent readers would struggle to keep up. The report also argues that the homepage has declining importance in funnelling readers to stories – they are coming from elsewhere (from links on social media for example). They manage this with projects like NYT Now, an app that presents a small, selected dose of *Times* stories. Hence there is a dual curation: the *New York Times* curates the news through its editorial selections. Then it curates itself. The use of the moniker NYT rather than *New York Times* is part of a push towards brevity and completeness often missing in the content abundance of the web. It gives the online news the feeling of what Craig Mod calls 'edges'.[12] NYT Now reintroduces a hierarchy; it's about summing up and categorising. The same impulse is behind new algorithmically driven services like Summly that digest the news.

News today means curating people out in the field, in the squares, on the ground of the revolution, not airlifted into it business class. It means wading through published material, much of it brilliant, at least as much awful, irrelevant or misleading, to present us with content that is varied, interesting and informative. And it means self-curation – selecting the most essential snippets for busy readers. This then is the new news: journalism in an information-rich era.

But it is not without serious problems. A Gallup report

concludes that trust in the news media has declined for decades and is plumbing new lows. In 1979 51 per cent had confidence in newspapers; by 2014 that had plunged to 22 per cent.[13] Those questions about ethics and curation are keenly felt here. Does the person adding the link garner more benefit than the producer? Do aggregators from Google to Flipboard appropriate the value of those creating the content? When your video of the revolution is on CNN, who benefits? Companies like Prismatic are able to data-mine the news for actionable investment insights – but again, the value of production is questioned.

In news, amongst certain of our cultural producers and on the Internet, some claim this shift in the locus of value actively harms production. Whether this is the self-interested squawking of an elite unwilling to adapt or a serious threat to free and accurate reporting remains to be seen. Either way, it needs monitoring.

No one can have missed the curatorial drift in culture and media. A process of cultural accumulation dates back centuries. The weight of culture, of media overload – their sheer copiousness, accessibility and diversity – creates a qualitative change in our interactions with the multifarious cultural forms that surround us. Our relationship becomes disaggregated, democratically splintered. Moreover, the convergence of those forms onto screen-based media only compounds the issue – the sum of it all competes for attention on nothing more than a small piece of glass.

Where once we created and consumed, intermediary roles are now legion, more visible, more structurally integral to our interactions with cultural products. Aesthetic, ethical and economic considerations aside, this is the reality of our cultural life. Down to our operating notions of creativity, our culture is geared towards second-order roles: DJs, A&R execs and even bouncers; editors, critics and curators; remixers, bloggers and commissioners. How to navigate the new reality? Taste and sensibility will play ever larger roles. The ethics of culture and the economics of media will continue to be challenged. Whether you are a publisher, an art gallery, a music platform or a digital journalism start-up the best curation will be a leading competitive advantage – especially for those, like Spotify or Apple Music, who effectively blend technological prowess with personal and aesthetic judgements.

Curation began with art and museums, as a property of culture, before spreading to the Internet. And it was on the Internet, rather than in culture, that it went global.

9

Curate the Internet

The world beyond marketing

However large you think the Internet is, it just keeps getting bigger. Just as we get comfortable with the idea of petabytes we find ourselves entering the Yottabyte Age, having skipped the intervening exabyte in the rush. The Internet only recently received a new IP (Internet Protocol) standard, IvP6, without which it would have ground to a halt – for the mathematically inclined IvP6 has $7.9 \times 1,028$ more locations than the previous standard, IvP4. This is all underwritten by a staggering and fast-growing physical infrastructure. Writing on *The Economist* website, Virginia Rometty, CEO of IBM, claims that 'There are more than a trillion interconnected and intelligent objects and organisms – including a billion transistors for every person on the planet.'[1] Moreover vast regions of the web remain hidden. The Deep Web, that portion beyond the purview of search indexing, represents up to 96 per cent of all digital data, whether it's company intranets, the anonymous Tor communication system or the 'darknet' of criminal transactions. Social, mobile and wearable technology have all exacerbated the ballooning of the Internet, as do the growing range of connected devices that form the nascent Internet of Things. As the cost of producing, publishing and storing data of any kind collapsed, so they flourished (thank you Moore's Law, thank you Tim Berners-Lee).

The Internet is now vast beyond comprehension. The story of Silicon Valley and its so-called Unicorns, all those billion-dollar start-ups, is the story of services that navigate the infinitude. These are the master aggregators who, by making the Internet work, by managing this excess, command our attention: and by commanding our attention, they command advertising dollars.

It's easy to see why curation became part of the Internet. Of all the overload we experience, the Internet, with its explosion of data and information, its density of connections, its speed, is the most obvious.

Nor is it solely a matter of volume. It's about the curious flattening of information. If the President of the United States sends a tweet, it is no different in form than an utterance sent by you or me. If the President of the United States gives a speech it happens in a vastly different context than if you or I did. Sure, the impact of the tweets will be different, but their substance is equivalent, unlike in the bumpy offline world. Online curation isn't just about whittling things down, it's also a qualitative parsing amidst far finer distinctions.

Earlier on I described curation as a kind of interface. On the Internet this is literally true – all our interactions have to be mediated through interfaces, and this involves necessary patterns of selection and arrangement. If curation has become so prominent in recent years, it's in large part down to this process; humans on one side of the screen, a mass of data on the other. Throughout this book many examples have already been web-based, and that should be no surprise.

The Internet's curatorial mix is multifaceted. Individuals,

services and protocols all play a role. At the higher levels new disciplines of curating build reputations and market companies. New kinds of celebrity, known for their sharing, dominate new media. And new kinds of business facilitate curation on an industrial scale.

One of the best known is Paper.li, a start-up which grew out of the Swiss Federal Institute of Technology. Co-founded by Edouard Lambelet, Paper.li lets users filter the Internet and repackage its contents in a digestible form. Every day they process 144 million websites. Their users collect what's interesting, helped by Paper.li's technology which does the heavy lifting and then publishes their choices.

When I spoke to Lambelet he explained the reasoning behind the site: 'The idea is to facilitate the discovery of the long tail of content. We all have this feeling of content overwhelming us, of drowning in content and information, in the news. I believe people are part of the solution.' Lambelet's vision of curation is one of a human process built on top of their technology. He sees this as integral – in that long tail human whims can find something different, something unexpected and worth sharing. The fusion is key: 'A lot of people don't actually want to create content, but they are engaged enough to recommend it. If they need to spend three hours a day in order to do that though, they can't, it's too much – so we bring web technology and semantic technology to make the job of curation easy on a daily basis.'

Ultimately Lambelet is building a business based on information overload and its solution. He recognises this, and indeed the way both have formed a central dynamic of the Internet: 'Because of this massive noise we are experiencing on the Internet, content filtering is more and more valuable to users. If I find someone who can help me filter this noise out, I will. Consumers are concerned by the noise. So it's not just about the creation of content – content filtering is also of value. From the beginning of the Internet we have always needed filtering – from portals and directories to websites and pages and then to search engines. Now it's overwhelming again, with social media and the nomadicity of content, we need to filter again – and this time the filtering is crowdsourced and curated.'

Dedicated curation services have found their place. Damman's Storify and Lambelet's Paper.li have both gained considerable traction. But we could equally have discussed Curata or Trap.it, Scoop It or Swaay, enterprise-level software aiming to turn businesses into worthwhile curators.

Paper.li and the others specialise in 'Content curation'.[2] This has become a discipline in its own right, a method built around the content-curation life cycle. Loosely, the process works as follows:

- **finding** content (from newspapers, Twitter, email newsletters, feed readers, keyword monitoring, the trade and speciality press, power social media users and influencers);
- **selecting** and organising the content. This often includes commenting on the work or excerpting, putting into context or collections;
- **sharing** it with others.

Most explicit web curation is based on this pattern, although as we will see, the implicit curation of the web is altogether more complex. What's striking about the discussion around content curation is how much of it comes down to marketing.

Marketers see content curation as a way of pulling in new audiences, establishing credibility, creating deeper engagement with existing customers and even boosting search engine optimisation – SEO – and return visits. Once, marketers typically saw themselves as media producers. They wanted to funnel everything on to their own products and spaces – not other people's. Content curation feels radical as a marketing strategy because it overturns both maxims.

Curation marketing recognises that buyers have changed – they don't expect marketing to be simple messages broadcast through the obvious channels. It doesn't work. Information about products used to be scarce and markets were less saturated with product. Purchasers have grown more discriminating; they don't want crude sales messages, they want high-value content.

It's also part of a change in marketing: an evolution from straightforward sales to the building of brand affinity and customer retention: 'thought leadership', not just the generation of leads. It's marketing-as-a-service, useful and interesting in its own right. It also comes back to that perennial of curation – expertise. Good content curation demonstrates expertise and builds trust. Lastly, content curation may take a lot of intelligent selection, which itself is a resource, but it requires less up-front spend than classic advertising.

So businesses from Microsoft to Lego to, famously, America's oldest flour mill, King Arthur's, have self-consciously become curators. I've followed O'Reilly Radar for years, a regular dose of curated links from the technology publisher O'Reilly Media.

But the term is often used weirdly. Websites advise people to 'curate in the morning' or curate their way to success. Curation is seen as a shortcut, a defined thing, not a process. Curata, for example, have a twelve-step checklist for content marketing. It makes sense on one level, but reduces curation to a formula. Content curation isn't that simple, can't be slotted in as another routine task. Good curation is more difficult and subtle than that. This is why many such strategies feel hollow. Curation felt radical and different to some marketers, hence the understandable focus. But equating curation with marketing misses not only all the worthwhile curation beyond marketing (e.g. much of it) but also how integral curation has become to a wide variety of activities.

This isn't to deny that curation can form part of an effective strategy for marketing and community building. It absolutely can, and it is an essential ingredient. By some measures content marketing is the fastest-growing marketing segment for consumer brands.[3] At its best content curation marketing builds trust, is useful and interesting, and demonstrates that companies are working unselfishly as part of a wider conversation. But at its worst it's a meaningless buzzword trotted out to fill blanks in corporate strategy meetings.

We need to go beyond the idea of content curation – which is fine for describing newsletters, blogs, and playlists on Spotify, but doesn't really encapsulate what curation means on the Internet.

Instead we should look at it all as part of a Curation Layer.

The Internet is often regarded as a stack consisting of layers, from the physical layer of cables and servers, through various protocols up to the application layer – the bit we users generally encounter in the form of web browsers and so on. The Curation Layer doesn't sit formally within this framework, but in its spirit, alongside other layers like the content layer, the social layer or even the game layer. Given the limited amount of information any human can engage with, there are always filtration and selection mechanisms. Collectively these filters form the Curation Layer.

We are cloaked in curation and everywhere encounter the Curation Layer. It's just that it's much easier to spot in the digital world.

Perhaps one reason why curation is regarded with such

suspicion is the so called 'stack fallacy', the mistake of believing that the layers above yours are easy to build. It's just curation, choosing; it's easy, anyone can do it. This rarely proves to be the case. Just because you're good at building databases, distribution centres or even web platforms doesn't mean you're good at expert selection.

How do we work with and in the Curation Layer? Businesses use it as part of their marketing offering in the form of content curation. Curators like Maria Popova, Matt Drudge or Jason Kottke develop sizeable audiences through idiosyncratic curation. Start-ups like Paper.li or Bundlr develop tools to augment the curation of others. Websites like Pinterest make everyone a curator of cakes, cats and, for me, book jackets. The point is that Internet curation happens on a grand scale. Not only is it concentrated in pockets of content curation, but it's also something much bigger – an integral part of our core technology, business and informational environment.

It does however beg a further question. Throughout this book I have looked at algorithmic and human curation together. Large web services have been called curators. Can we really talk about these as curation, or is that stretching the term beyond breaking point?

Of machines and men

Sitting in his office at Oxford University's Internet Institute, Luciano Floridi, Professor of Philosophy and Ethics of Information, is quite clear: speaking with rapid clarity, he argues curation cannot be ascribed to the big web platforms. 'Curation implies responsibility for what you curate,' he says. Responsibility is a human trait. 'Curators are experts – you have to have a say to be a curator. There is a practical side to curation that means algorithmic curation should be joined by a sense almost of ownership or custodianship. The ability to intervene, to follow on, to ensure your curation has an impact, is key. It is a pragmatic relationship.' The point for Floridi is that curation has ethical overtones that go back to its root *curare*. Curation doesn't just mean selecting and arranging, it means doing those things for a purpose grounded in helping.

We broadly agree on why curation matters. 'Curation comes as a consequence of abundance,' he says. 'You don't need to curate papyrus or rolls of script.' But Floridi sees curation as having a very specific role. 'It puts the entity, the thing curated, at the centre. The curator has a mentality, a sensitivity that looks at what is good for something. The good of the entity comes first, before the curator.' Curation, he argues, 'is altruistic towards what is being curated'. And this is where the idea of machine-driven curation runs into problems. Automated programs that simply direct users elsewhere, that don't have custody of information or content, cannot do this. Floridi argues that Google is more likely to curate advertising, of which it is a direct custodian, than content, which it merely pushes people towards. It's what author Carmen Medina calls curation's 'moral lens'.[4]

There is then a big question about what constitutes curation. This is more than just a semantic question – it is about the economy's direction, business strategies that will succeed or fail. Throughout this book I have looked at algorithmic and human curation side by side, arguing that both should be seen as part of the curatorial drift. However, many assume that curation is explicitly human, while the plainer 'aggregation' is machine-driven. Most discussions of content curation, for instance, rest on this distinction.

Content farming, mass aggregation – these don't have the unmistakable human touch which curation seems to imply. That touch which becomes so valuable in a world governed by machine-made systems.

David Byrne, the musician and commentator, makes a similar point in an article about curation for the *New Statesman*: 'What I and other "experts" offer is surprise,' he writes.[5] Byrne argues that his experiences 'being a wee bit outside the norm, are a little more biased, skewed, pre-edited and peculiar than what those herd-based and algorithmic services come up with'. The result is that it helps people in 'encountering an idea, an artist or a writer outside the well-trodden and machine-predictable paths'. This person-centric curation is 'a potlatch process', a 'social glue', an exchange of information among friends. Byrne, like Floridi, makes the point that perhaps curation is valuable precisely because it avoids the algorithmic and the aggregative and is instead imbued with human values, quirks and all.

So why do I see curation as spanning both the algorithmic and the personal? Before I answer, one proviso: the dividing line between curated and not curated is still fluid and malleable. It's not always clear and will take time to settle.

But the reason I think both work is that, first, this is how we use the word. Some discussions assume curation can never be performed automatically, others assume it can and is. As with the word curation generally, the genie is out of the bottle and attempting to legislate language is pointless. Follow the trends out there, on blogs and social media, in the traditional media, in books and podcasts, and plenty of people are comfortable using the word with the suggestion that algorithms suffice as curation. It's not neat, and it raises all kinds of conceptual difficulties; but for better or for worse this is how the English language moves forward.

Second, I think it applies as there is no neat divide between what people and machines do. Every time we use the Internet our interactions are substantially guided and governed by programs and protocols. Yet they themselves are ultimately created and controlled by people. Something as basic as a search enquiry is a complex dialogue of human decision making and automation. At one end are the decisions of users; at the other those of search engineers. In between lie various technologies that mediate between the two with a dizzying level of complexity. Automated processes now offer experiences and selections so advanced they go far beyond what we commonly label a filter. And we saw earlier how, at Amazon, Apple and Netflix, machine-driven and human-driven curation dovetailed. While many Big Data processing tasks would be impossible if done by humans, these systems are still designed, maintained, monitored, governed, changed and consumed by people.

Indeed, while tech companies are known for pushing machine-driven systems, Google will use personal recommendations in highlighting restaurants on its explore feature in Google Maps and Samsung is, like Apple, employing editors (and partnering with Axel Springer) for its news aggregation app. The service will be divided into a 'Need to know' section curated by an editorial team and a 'Want to know' section driven by algorithms.[6] Algorithms factor in human 'up votes' or engagement metrics; and we respond to these and shape them in turn. When discussing curation we have to acknowledge this complementary reality, seeing the blend as one of the signature forms of our time. We should recognise that there are now no hard and fast lines between what is machine-driven or algorithmic and what is human. In the words of the investor and technologist Peter Thiel: 'Computers are tools, not rivals.'[7] Just as we use all manner of machines when we put together a new building but don't say the building is 'machine-made', so curation often happens in amalgams of the automated and the personalised. Moreover we are still interested in the subjective; just because automation is required, doesn't mean we don't want extra, personal filters layered on top. Serendipity has not been retired. As one of the leading writers on web curation, Steven Rosenbaum, puts it: 'In an era of data abundance, the thing that is scarce is taste.'[8]

The next book you read may well have been recommended to you not by a person, and not by an algorithm – but by a strange emergent cyborg that combines the two ... However this isn't to say that distinctions don't exist. Along with the axis of explicit and implicit curation is a further distinction within the Curation Layer. There isn't a uniform level of curation. In some areas curation is especially thick or dense; and in other areas it is much lighter, the layer is thin:

- **Thick curation:** by and large this is what marketers talk about when they discuss curation. It's about humans; it's the curation of Canopy.co or Boing Boing; Instagram and O'Reilly Radar; a store on Etsy or the front page of Arts and Letters Daily. It's the Discover section on Kickstarter or the Public Domain Review. It's intense, fully realised, based on detailed personal choices, often for smaller audiences; it discusses its choices and comments on them, adding extra spin to its decisions. It works as an additive part of the Curation Layer.

- **Thin curation:** a lighter, often machine-driven form of curation – the network of cataloguing and filtration mechanisms, recommendation and discovery algorithms, that we find throughout the Internet. We wouldn't necessarily always call it curation as it works automatically or semi-automatically, generally without commenting on or explaining its processes. At its fringes it melds with tagging systems and folksonomies (the results of social tagging), search indexing and retrieval algorithms, database architectures and version control systems like Git. It is the underlying and necessary curation of the Internet, the suite of

systems that by deep selection and arrangement make
managing the superabundance of information a practical possibility.

As with the Curated and Industrial Models of Selection,
there isn't a hard divide between the two – it's again a spectrum. Thick curation is often explicit curation, thin curation
often implicit curation. But this needn't be the case. Retailers
like Eataly, for example, don't explicitly call themselves curators but they are undoubtedly an example of thick curation.
Pinterest is much closer to explicit than implicit curation. But
Pinterest is, like most such services, a composite – people's
personal curation fills their own boards, while the site as a
whole uses various machine-driven mechanisms for finding,
recommending and sorting that material. So its users make
Pinterest a thickly curated space; but Pinterest has built its
own thin curation to help. And for those who might think
Pinterest a trivial example, it has seventy-three million users,
a valuation of around \$11bn and an application program-
ming interface – API – for major business users.[9]

Moreover, while this division of thick and thin works most
obviously in digital environments, it's a general phenomenon.
Art galleries, boutique record stores, specialist cycle cafés,
libraries, brand-name hotels, film sets, festivals and even investment portfolios are thickly curated. Meanwhile department
stores, sculpture parks, shopping malls, trade fairs, markets
and even some neighbourhoods (think New York's Nolita or
London's Marylebone) are still curated, but more thinly.

The two are also complementary. Thin curation makes
the Internet governable and its content discoverable. Thicker
curation breaks beyond search. It answers subjective questions, the questions you didn't even know you wanted to
ask. By introducing random human elements, it bursts the

'filter bubbles' of automated systems, taking us beyond what Upworthy CEO and writer Eli Pariser calls the 'search and retrieval Web': an echo chamber of our own preferences augmented through behaviour-tracking recommendation algorithms.[10] That mesh of machine-driven filtering technology creates a 'city of ghettos' to which thick curation, of wide-ranging material, is one answer. Unpredictable, messy and strange, human judgement can go beyond this canalised, automated version of the web. It leaves room for random epiphanies and takes us beyond our blind spots. We need algorithms, but we still need ourselves.

On a wider level, without a blend and balance of different kinds of curation we will fall into self-reinforcing loops of taste and opinion. Rather than open up and explore the world, curation would close it down. One form of curation – let alone one curator – represents a totalitarian vision. A diversity of models and curators mitigates the risk. It opens rather than closes.

As with the move from the Industrial to the Curated Model of Selection, so we are seeing the 'thickening' of the Curation Layer. Internet businesses understand that more curation offers more value to users. This tendency to move towards more curated experiences and denser discovery protocols is one of the long-term trends of the Internet.

Prizefight: Facebook v. Twitter

Take those giants of social media, Facebook and Twitter. Big Curation. Their respective strategies and performance over their maturing years (roughly 2010–2016) encapsulate this movement towards thicker curation. By looking at them I am not trying to pick winners or suggest who will do well in future – the sector moves much too fast for that. I'm looking backwards to see what happened.

Twitter CEO Dick Costolo was worried. It wasn't meant to be like this. When Twitter debuted on the NASDAQ its market capitalisation was a hefty $24bn. Despite making a loss, Twitter was worth more than most media businesses in the United States. But Costolo's earnings calls with Wall Street investors were taking on an uneasy tone. Metrics were bad. User growth had stalled. New people were turning away in droves, alienated by a system that seemed incomprehensible and stacked in favour of existing super-users.

Since launching in 2006 Twitter had enjoyed massive growth. In 2007 it hosted around 5,000 tweets a day; by 2013 that figure was approaching 500 million. But the fundamental interface remained the same: it was still an unending 'firehose' of real-time tweets in a single feed. The mechanism for finding content hadn't evolved. What's more, the three most significant user interface touches designed to help manage this – the @ sign to signify someone, # to denote tweets around a topic, retweeting to share someone else's tweet – had been driven by users. Only later were they formally adopted. All of which meant that despite becoming one of the largest and most active sites on the Internet, Twitter devolved curation to its users.

Journalist Nick Bilton's account of Twitter's history hints at why. From the start Twitter suffered from a confused identity. Each of the four co-founders had a different vision, resulting in years of internecine squabbling that hobbled efforts to build a workable product (early users will remember the Fail Whale which featured on regular outages). Ev Williams, the imaginative Nebraskan who had previously founded Blogger before selling it to Google, saw Twitter as a communications network. He thought Twitter should be a place to share news and find out what was happening. Meanwhile the first programmer, and later CEO, Jack Dorsey, thought it should be personal – about what you were doing. Dorsey was wilful and intense, a match for Williams. The other founders could barely keep the peace. Even when they had all moved on, Twitter was stuck between competing imperatives and there was a certain stasis in product development. Was it an evolved RSS feed and syndication platform? A chat system and social network? A real-time opinion aggregator?

Then, once the company had gone public, came the increasingly awkward investor discussions. On one such call even the Chief Financial Officer at the time, Anthony Noto, confessed that the site 'isn't the most relevant experience for a user'.[11] He went on to admit that 'putting [interesting] content in front of the person at that moment in time is a way to organize that content better' as against the firehose, where it's lost. It was an admission from the top that, for many, spewing 350,000 tweets a minute needed better curation.

Down the road in Palo Alto things couldn't have been going better for Mark Zuckerberg and Facebook. Having made a rocky start, Facebook shares performed strongly after the company went public. Their value quadrupled between July 2013 and July 2015, by which time the business was worth $245bn – the world's seventeenth-largest by market capitalisation, increasingly seen as an essential part of advertising and with user numbers continuing to grow. At the time of writing Facebook has 1.5 billion users, meaning if it were a country it would easily be the largest on earth. Twitter meanwhile has a shade fewer users than the population of the US, around 315 million. Starting around 2009–10 Twitter's user growth has been stalling, while Facebook's powers ahead. Facebook realised much earlier that a more curated experience was essential. Curation would make Facebook friendly; the lack of it made Twitter intimidating.

One pivotal change was the introduction of a filtered News Feed, a controversial measure pushed through by Zuckerberg himself. Facebook users would no longer see everything posted, but instead would have a more managed experience. Engineer Lars Backstrom explained Facebook's reasoning on the company blog:

> The goal of News Feed is to deliver the right content to the right people at the right time so they don't miss the stories that are important to them. Ideally, we want News Feed to show all the posts people want to see in the order they want to read them. This is no small technical feat: every time someone visits News Feed there are on average 1,500 potential stories from friends, people they follow and Pages for them to see, and most people don't have enough time to see them all.[12]

Backstrom claimed that those 1,500 stories were digested to 300 pieces of content per user per day. For heavy users of the site, these numbers would be blown out of the water – without the new system they might be exposed to 15,000 posts per day. Moreover Backstrom reported that because of better targeting, posts that had previously been viewed only 43 per cent of the time were now viewed 70 per cent of the time.

While (like the Google search algorithm) Facebook's News Feed examines thousands upon thousands of factors, at its core the process is quite simple. Something is likely to be shown on your feed roughly according to the following:

interest in the poster

x

track record of the post

x

track record of the poster

x

type of post (status update, image)

x

when it was posted

=

likelihood of appearing on your feed

This is thin curation indeed. But, crucially, compared with Twitter, it gave users a curated experience beyond their own decisions.

The algorithm is constantly evolving powered by detailed qualitative research, Facebook's enormous dataset and rigorous testing. One addition (along with recording likes, shares, comments and so on) was factoring in the time users spent looking at particular posts. Even this has an algorithm that ensures you really are looking at the site and not waiting for it to load or wandering off. It's part of Facebook's battle to stay ahead. At times this has backfired – when they were found conducting a study into the emotional impact of curation, which included seeing if they could alter people's emotions, there was an outcry. But experimentation continues. Facebook Moments, launched in 2015, auto-curates photos (say from a family party). Time stamps and facial-recognition software build profiles of who was at an event and then aggregate and share associated pictures. Facebook Instant Articles works with news providers like the BBC and *Der Spiegel* to select quality content targeted at individual users – all hosted by Facebook.

At an extreme Facebook are building a walled-garden Internet – neater, safer and more curated, with all the positive and chilling aspects that implies. As its growth shifted to emerging markets, Facebook realised it had a pivotal role to play in shaping the Internet's future. In Asia, Africa and Latin America it launched internet.org, for example, a charitable push for cheap data and a simplified web enabling more people to access the Internet.

As part of internet.org users have free access to services like Wikipedia and health information – and also of course to

Facebook and Facebook Messenger. There are Facebook-only data plans, while countries like Ghana and the Philippines have hugely discounted Facebook data plans (e.g. you pay very little or even nothing for using Facebook). The upshot is that in parts of the world people use Facebook without realising they are on the Internet. In Asia and Africa researchers noticed an interesting trend: surveys of Internet use showed people claiming not to use the Internet. Yet when followed up in focus groups, they would claim to use Facebook. News site Quartz investigated further and found that 11 per cent of Indonesians and 9 per cent of Nigerians on Facebook claimed never to use the Internet.[13]

This, then, is the Internet of the next four billion. People gravitate towards the dually curated world of Facebook – curated by their friends and curated by Facebook itself. Highly curated walled gardens were already the trend with apps, but Facebook, as the super app, intensifies that trend. What's more this system wasn't just easier for new users but it seemed to work especially well in mobile, which had rapidly become the most important segment in tech. It takes us back to the portals of the early web, like AOL, which featured a vanishingly small button called 'Go to internet'. Not only does it make the Internet more palatable, but it has helped them better target adverts. They know more about users and how best to target material. Whether you think this is good or not it's certainly been good for someone – Facebook.

Twitter had to respond. On one investor call Costolo acknowledged that Twitter needed to 'curate' more. One idea was the logged-out homepage – a curated version of the site. Another was the 'While You Were Away' feature, which aimed to take the best tweets people might have missed. They added an Instant Timeline feature for new users. They even launched a new product for media publishers – curator.twitter. com. It was a mixture of their most advanced filtering technology, a mechanism for building new Curated Collections, a way of curating multimedia content including Vines, real-time data insight into what was happening on Twitter and a broadcasting channel Tweets. Another innovation is the Highlights feature – this updates twice a day and creates a feed of twelve or so tweets the algorithm thinks will interest you. Bloomberg called it 'a significant step outside Twitter's comfort zone in pursuit of new users' – and one towards Facebook.[14]

Perhaps the most significant venture is Moments – a move into direct curation. Twitter builds collections of Tweets, Vines and Periscopes around live events. These include both scheduled events – the Superbowl or Glastonbury, say – and breaking news like natural disasters or election results. Or it could just be interesting stuff – they envisage a channel for 'Throwback Thursday', but also focus on big-ticket headlines like Business and Sport. Users swipe through narratives built in real time around these events, looking at one Tweet (or Vine or Periscope) at a time. Moments is meant to distil the best content – and few now deny there is a mass of great stuff on Twitter – into coherent, easily digestible packages for basic users of the site.

What's more, there is a human element to decision making – collections are curated by a team with newsroom experience. Those editors will be able to embed relevant tweets into people's timelines. In addition Twitter is partnering with trusted brands like the *Washington Post*, *Vogue* and NASA to select content. Twitter is turning itself from a quasi-random firehose into an edited media outlet. This is new – how will they deal with atrocities? To what extent will paid events gain prominence? This needs new competencies. Twitter are pushing the service hard, integrating it into their desktop and mobile interfaces. But they also want to decentralise it – the tool could be pushed out to all Twitter users, allowing them to better curate their output. Indeed, the launch of Moments came with an explicit 'Moments curation policy' on the main Twitter website.

There is no easy fix. Twitter haven't solved all their problems. When in early 2016 a rumour spread that Twitter might transition to an algorithmically driven timeline, there was an immediate and ferocious backlash. The company backed down from wholesale change but, still facing the wrath of growth-hungry investors, persisted in attempts to create more algorithmically filtered experiences. Suddenly not only the financial future of Twitter but its passionate relationship with millions of users was at stake – over the issue of curation.

Twitter, having fallen behind, is now aiming for thick curation. Facebook has built tools and programs to curate itself. The direction of travel for both has been to add more and more into the Curation Layer; to offer users more value through more curation; to respond to the overload enabled by their own platforms; and to use curation as a means to better understand those users. Corporate strategy in big West Coast tech (but also in the phenomenal success of a product like WeChat from China's Tencent) can be read through the prism of curation as finding more ways to let people curate and find better-curated environments amidst the excess.

Take Yahoo!, a company whose relationship to curation – explicit and implicit, thick and thin – has been inconsistent. They haven't been sure where or how they should fit into the Curation Layer. Founded by Jerry Yang and David Filo, Yahoo! was originally a hand-selected directory of links, the original web-curation site. In those feverish early days it was enough to get them noticed. Led by the energetic Jeff Mallett, Yahoo! enjoyed a rollercoaster few years, building an early search engine and riding the dotcom bubble like almost no one else: its share-price spike on going public was, at the time, the third-largest in history.[15] They also bought GeoCities, as we saw earlier, the idea being that Yahoo! would become synonymous with managing the Internet.

But it went wrong. Yahoo! tanked in the dotcom crash. So began twelve years of soul searching and a succession of CEOs (from Hollywood, from the tech industry, Yang again). Missed opportunities became commonplace: the times they failed to buy Facebook, the bungled acquisition by Microsoft, bad deals with Google. Under the leadership of Terry Semel Yahoo! expanded into a direct media company. Unlike Google or Facebook, which had clear missions (to manage the world's information, to connect people), Yahoo! now had a conflicted identity – was it about search or media, technology or content?

Despite failing to keep pace with Google's search and advertising technology, Yahoo! made some astute acquisitions in the mid-2000s that should have put it in the curatorial vanguard. Del.icio.us and especially Flickr, sites for storing and sharing links and pictures respectively, were at the time hot property and pioneers of the new system of distributed tagging that let users produce taxonomies and cataloguing mechanisms for large datasets. They were early and successful examples of how web platforms grew powerful by enabling users to become curators in their own right. I recall Flickr's tag cloud as a revelation, a whole new way of engaging with content that made maximum use of what was hyperbolically (but not incorrectly) known as 'the wisdom of crowds'.

Yet even these services never reached their full potential. Del.icio.us was spun out of the business some years later. Flickr remained in the stable, but was eclipsed by other photo-sharing sites, often better optimised for mobile. That classic of web curation – photos – may have started on Flickr but it quickly moved elsewhere. Meanwhile Yahoo! relied increasingly on its legacy users, its large Yahoo! Mail base and a fortuitous investment in Alibaba, a ferociously expansive Chinese web business whose rising value undergirded precarious Yahoo! stock.

Then in July 2012 they hired Google executive Marissa Mayer as the new CEO. Mayer was one of the earliest and most influential Google employees. She pioneered data-driven user experience, relentlessly focusing on making the interface simple and backing it up with hard facts (recall the significance of Google's arrangement of information). Mayer's pitch was based on her vision, her tech experience and her leading sense of platform and product. Mayer would have two years before Alibaba went public. Two years when a floor was placed on Yahoo! stock; two years to turn the business round and fashion a consumer technology company to rival Google or Facebook. What would she do?

Mayer was going to remake Yahoo! as a product not a media company – the latter being the favoured approach of the internal candidate she pipped to the post. Having started with hand-curated links, Yahoo! had lost out as one of the Internet's curators in chief. All those missed opportunities and lack of focus meant they had time and again misunderstood the direction and significance of curation on the web. Mayer would change that. She had some quick successes – award-winning apps; product teams working on great stuff; a turnaround in aspects of the culture; thousands of job applications. But saving Yahoo! required much more.

So she embarked on a two-year acquisition binge. Tumblr was founded by David Karp, a young New York-based CEO. He had a huge audience of young people, billions of page views a month, high user engagement. Above all Tumblr was part of the new way of curating the Internet. While earlier blogging platforms let users produce their own content, on Tumblr it was more common for users to repost videos, images and text from elsewhere in a kind of endless collage. In response to the growth of web content, services like Tumblr were offering a personalised curation of all those trillions of images and minutes of film. Mayer went in big, for $1.1bn. Like Flickr it was going to have in Tumblr a focused, grounded curation at the heart of its new strategy. Tumblr acted as the filter for a generation. While its audience was valuable, the curatorial aspect, getting back into being part of the Internet's curatorial mix at the social level, made sense in terms of the wider corporate strategy.

Mayer acquired over sixty companies in that time, the vast majority of them based on curation. They included, for $30m, Summly, a start-up founded by seventeen-year-old Briton Nick d'Aloisio, Snip.it, which allowed people to make collections of links, and social recommendation services like Jybe, Alike and Stamped. The product revamps, from new weather apps to new 'digital magazines' led by famous names like former *New York Times* tech correspondent David Pogue, curated sites built into verticals on top of Tumblr, were about curation – if Yahoo! was to stay in media and keep pursuing a Janus-faced tech/media strategy, the media element would also be highly curated. Search technology and user interface (or selection and arrangement) were back as an in-house priority. Mayer wanted Yahoo! to reclaim a central role in selecting and arranging the Internet. At the time of writing, the omens aren't looking great.

What happens next is an open question. There are reports Yahoo! could be broken up or sold.[16] It isn't the point. Mayer's career, Yahoo!'s history, strategy and future all hinge on working within the Curation Layer – how well they do it, whether people like it and how many users they can empower to curate in their own right. The value of the web today is contingent on the tools and capabilities available to curate it. It's not only why Mayer will spend $1.1bn on Tumblr but why she would want to methodically re-gear the whole company around curation.

Curator takes all

So much value has been created by the technology boom that difficult ethical, legal and financial questions about how that value gets shared are unavoidable. Curation has become so central to how we navigate the web, and the value of attention it attracts and enables so great, that we should question whether the skew has gone too far. Are we disproportionately rewarding curators over creators? It's the same question that dogged the cultural debate, but here writ large – tech companies are so vast that entire sectors are impacted by their whims; the value of creation itself is potentially eroded by business models. How can that be a good thing?

What are the ethics of this new reality? For example, how credit and reward are apportioned might increasingly be out of whack – hence the outsized rewards that go to curators and gatekeepers, whether that's Hans Ulrich Obrist rather than new artists or Eataly rather than micro Slow Food producers. The Copyright Wars and debates around the apportionment of revenue from digitised culture have been done to death, but the issue doesn't go away.[17]

A few years ago Maria Popova launched online the Curator's Code – an attempt to ensure that fair deserts were shared. Using new Unicode symbols, the code indicated links of direct and indirect discovery – the equivalent of acknowledging 'via' and giving a 'hat tip'. Attribution would be universal and clear; boundaries between creator and curator respected; the 'creative and intellectual labor' of both acknowledged.

Only it immediately ran into controversy. Commentators objected, as they often do, to the use of the word curation. But beyond that they claimed that not only was the code unnecessary, since typing *via* was easy enough, but that it didn't go far enough: curators were still leeching off the production of others.[18] The writer and technologist Jaron Lanier has written extensively about the problem.[19] For him the issue is quite clear, and is financial in nature: in this great curatorial edifice creators no longer see the full monetary rewards because they get creamed off whilst descending through the Curation Layer.

I well understand this problem. As someone who earns a living producing books and apps in the expectation of selling them, making any kind of money, let alone luxuriating in non-financial attribution, is difficult. The more people need to be supported by an individual product or service, the greater difficulty there is in making the numbers add up. Unless you hit a gusher, factoring in each cost layer of production and the newer additional curatorial layers is tough. A $10 cheque from Google Ads or Spotify doesn't a new economy make.

Yet somehow we have to find ways of squaring the excess production and its declining yields. Somehow we have to navigate the overload; to make things discoverable. Those people that do inevitably create and appropriate value. To rail against this, to think it is the height of decadence, parasitism, piracy, pretentiousness, is all very well – but it solves nothing when production itself is often not the problem. Selecting and arranging from it is.

We need to find an accommodation that remunerates creators – rewarding them with more than just a hat tip – but also produces the full diversity of thick and thin curation we need to operate. Part of this will involve an evolving appreciation of creativity as a second-order activity. Again, I don't expect this to be popular.

We all want to buy into the creativity myth and I for one hope it never goes away. Ours would be a grey and shoddy world without its romance. But as the context changes, so must our concepts. Over the next decades the challenge for

Internet curation – from Facebook down – is to share value. Even if we don't call it curation, patterns of selection and arrangement dominated the Internet's early years; they've driven our experience.

The Argentinian writer Jorge Luis Borges wrote a story about the Library of Babel. His library was composed of a near-infinite labyrinth of hexagonal rooms, which contained every possible combination of a 416-page book, randomly sorted. Yes, somewhere in the library was every useful and brilliant possible book. But in reality the library was endless and entirely useless. Without curation, or aggregation, or filtering, the Internet would be such a Borgesian nightmare. The overload would render all production and creativity pointless – it would be lost, undiscoverable and buried. We should remember the Internet isn't just an evolutionary stage of the gathering excess but a radical inflection point that completely alters the terms of engagement. To use another literary example, the critic Neil Postman contrasted two dystopian visions of the future, those of George Orwell and Aldous Huxley:

> Orwell feared those who would deprive us of information. Huxley feared those who would give us so much we would be reduced to passivity and egoism. Orwell feared the truth would be concealed from us. Huxley feared the truth would be drowned in a sea of irrelevance.[20]

The future we have come to inhabit is Huxley's. The question is not whether or not curation is needed. It's how we build a system that financially accommodates the new diversity of activity.

And we shouldn't forget that the creativity myth *is* a myth – creativity has always involved recombination. There has never been a clean division between creativity and what we now call curation. Negotiating the two has always been complex.

Curation will remain central. It will encompass a series of interlocking or nested interfaces, from the most refined human judgements to great underlying architectures that govern all our digital interactions. Over time the drift within the Curation Layer has been towards thicker curation. This is why, despite powerful technologies, human curation has a place. While many believe curation precludes machine-based mechanisms, thin and thick allow us to have both.

While the examples here happen to be businesses, of course, swathes of curation, perhaps even the majority, happen in nominally non-market, personal activities. More of which soon. Yet, it is striking how businesses of all kinds have become selectors and arrangers – implicit curators.

10

Curate Business

The commanding heights

Next to Hong Kong Island's Star Ferry terminal is the International Finance Centre. At 412m its Tower 2 is the second-tallest building in the Special Administrative Region and an instantly recognisable landmark. Nestled beneath it, part of a complex including blue-chip offices and a Four Seasons hotel, is a shopping mall, the IFC Mall.

This is not your run-of-the-mill emporium.

With many of the world's biggest-spending consumers on its doorstep, the IFC Mall sees sales numbers most retail businesses would kill for. For the upmarket brands packed into the mall this is amongst their most important outlets. When I speak to the bullish general manager, Karim Azar, he tells me many of the shops sell double their counterparts in New York. 'The saturation of brands is high in Hong Kong,' he says. 'But the most successful stores for many brands are in Hong Kong. For Chanel or Ferragamo or Armani – for any shop on the Canton Road for example – it will be the number one in the world for that brand.'

Hong Kong is a ruthlessly competitive retail market. As late as the mid-90s China was a backwater for luxury goods firms. Twenty years later, China was, in many cases, their most valuable market and the largest luxury goods market on earth – by some estimates up to half the global market consists of Chinese consumers, although much of this is money spent abroad.[1] With its longstanding *laissez-faire* philosophy, frothy stock market and Rolls-Royce-driving super-rich, Hong Kong is the luxury entrepôt to China and Asia – their first port of call, where reputations are made and unmade. In turn, Hong Kong views itself as being at the apex of fashion and taste. Azar says: 'The Hong Kong consumer is the most sophisticated in Asia and most Asians are emulating Hong Kong. They [people from Hong Kong] have been exposed to fashion for longer than any other Asian nation and so the brands are developed here.' It all means that when it comes to fashion, luxury and high-end retail, Hong Kong – with its elite shopping malls like the IFC and equivalents of Bond Street like Canton Road, is where the action is.

Azar knows his business has to be cutting-edge. Anyone visiting Hong Kong can testify it's not short of places to buy luxury goods. If you haven't bought your Ferragamo shoes or Hermès tie at your hotel or in the mall beneath your office, don't worry! There's one just next to your departure gate at Chek Lap Kok. When Azar uses the word 'saturation' he means it. If IFC wants to maintain its position as the leading destination in the territory, it can't just follow the old real estate strategy of going to the highest bidder and jamming shops in. Azar may speak the hard-and-fast talk of a classic businessman, but his business shades surprisingly close to the work of a curator.

'I am very fussy. I travel the world looking for the coolest brands, the next big thing. I get hundreds of requests from brands looking for space. We meet with the CEOs of the biggest and the best and we tell them what we want. We say no to people all the time.' With the pick of the world's brands at his feet, Azar's job is to identify those that are newest, the most different, interesting and valuable. Those putting in extra to create an amazing experience; the brands of tomorrow on the bleeding edge of global culture, not two steps behind the West. 'We can pick and choose the brands we work with – we want to keep it very selective, we were the mall that brought tons of new things to Hong Kong. Tom Ford, Zara, Club Monaco, Zanotti, Givenchy, Tory Burch, Moncler – we brought more than fifty brands to Hong Kong, including cosmetics brands like Estée Lauder who never had a standalone presence before.' Azar's point is that IFC isn't just a place for spending large quantities of money on luxury goods – it's about pioneering taste on the whole continent.

While Hong Kong's retail market is uniquely ('fiercely') competitive, with some of the highest rents per square foot to be found anywhere, the wider regional context is also in play. Sitting at the foot of the Pearl River Delta, Hong Kong forms part of the world's largest urbanised region. Between sixty and one hundred million people live there. Moreover this area was the initial engine of capitalism in China and today has the second-highest per capita GDP of the People's Republic after Shanghai. The upshot is serious regional competition.[2] Across the mouth of the delta lies that other Special Administrative Region and former colony, Macau, with its glittering casinos. Just across Hong Kong's mainland border lies Shenzhen, the original Special Economic Zone and now a sprawling megacity and manufacturing hub, home – as we saw earlier – to a vast Foxconn plant. Then there is Guangzhou, capital of Guangdong province, a wealthy mercantile city of some eleven million. Even lower-tiered cities like Dongguan or Foshan have populations equivalent to large European capitals. As some of the richest and most developed cities in China, they are racing to catch up with Hong Kong.

Which means that, more than ever, Azar's proposition of IFC as the area's leading shopping mall relies on a considered curation. If everyone has the latest luxury brand, Azar wants to find the next big thing and put it in a new context. He won't let stores get complacent. They have to constantly refresh their offering and keep their premises looking sharp.

'We want to enrich the retail experience. It's about visiting eight shops the customer enjoys, rather than just three big shops,' he says. Much of this involves making the retail experience as attractive as possible. He cites huge investment in stores, elaborate plans from the top architects. Shops go to lengths they never normally would to get into the IFC. They produce unique goods for that store. For them it's status and access to top consumers; for IFC everything is about an offering that will keep them at that apex. In Azar's words, this is about 'chasing everything' – finding the cutting edge and then shaping the selection and arrangement of shops around it.

Hong Kong's government is alive to the dynamic as well. It's part of the reason why, like Abu Dhabi, they are investing in large cultural infrastructure projects like the West Kowloon Cultural District. Situated on the harbour waterfront, this will be an arts complex of seventeen institutions including museums, concert halls and theatres. If Guangzhou can have a shiny new opera house, Hong Kong can go one better.

We wouldn't usually think of a real estate and retail manager as a curator. Yet what Azar does bears an uncanny relationship to curation. In the super-saturated world of Hong Kong's high-end retail the value is shifting from supply (owning a mall, opening a store) to curation. As work changes, this pattern is becoming increasingly prevalent in unexpected places.

Like Hong Kong, Silicon Valley is a focus of abundance. Change, innovation, a multitude of start-ups, talented engineers, exciting ideas, media gossip, billions of dollars of venture capital (VC) money and numberless data collide at the digital world's nerve centre. We tend to think VC firms are making mega-bucks. This is a myth. A few VCs, like Sequoia Capital, Kleiner Perkins Caufield & Byer or Andreessen Horowitz, take an outsized chunk of the rewards. They make selections that beat the competition amidst mass uncertainty and information overload. Many VCs only track the S&P 500 – if they are lucky. Many go bust.

Sequoia are one of the oldest firms in the region and have a near-unrivalled reputation. Perhaps their most legendary VC is the Welsh-born Sir Michael Moritz. Moritz was there in the dotcom boom. He considered dozens of investments on a weekly basis. He would look at areas that were already crowded. When he invested in Google, the space was already busy. Firms had billions in cash and all the market share. Getting in late, like he was, is not the classic VC strategy – which aims to be ahead of the curve, investing in nascent sectors and riding their growth from risky early foundations. When Moritz looked at Google he would have seen a college-based and inexperienced management team, a crowded sector and a garage operation. Numerous Valley VCs had already passed.

Moritz bucked the trend and invested $12.5m. This stake would, in just a few years, be worth billions.

Moritz is different in the Valley. He is not a Stanford computer science PhD. Instead he has a history degree. Moritz doesn't start with technology, so much as with the overall situation and how a company slots in. It's not just this or that tech – but how is the market moving? What are the founders like? What's that design movement? What's the price of processing power? Where are consumers spending their time? What are the problems people face? Where might software be in ten years' time? Moritz adjusted his companies to the reality as he saw it. He realised that you shouldn't just select the right start-up, you then needed to continuously mould, adjust, rearrange it for reality, for constant change. You didn't just invest in Google, you worked with the company to help it *become* Google.

Moritz realised that blind faith in technology led to bad investment decisions. He developed an investment philosophy that was flexible, not a mechanical process but one that grew from deep expertise, experience and consideration of the environment. Moritz reads voraciously around his investments. He wants to know everything. It's understanding in the round, iterating, pushing, pivoting, that makes those investments a success. It is an art. Moreover, as he tells Joshua Cooper Ramo, most of his best investments have come from a profound ability to empathise with the hopes, dreams and fears of the founders – he fully admits that investments that didn't work or were missed came from a lack of empathy.[3]

Moritz's approach to VC is different. In the process he has become a billionaire. Sequoia's investments are worth 20 per cent of the value of the entire NASDAQ.[4]

Moritz resembles a curator as much as an old-style investor. The skills involved substantially overlap. In a complex scenario he found a new way of doing business that reacted to change. It's a skill replicated by the best investors like Warren Buffett. Moritz claims it's hard to find new VCs. It's an exceptional skill set of selecting and arranging that is not easily replicable. Understanding the tech or having a Harvard MBA doesn't mean you see things in the round. Many VCs, unlike Moritz, did not survive the dotcom crash. If the tech boom pops, many more will go to the wall.

Moritz and Azar occupy quinary roles – roles in the commanding heights of the world economy. They are superstars influencing global trends. While neither would be called a curator, what they do, the skill set they share, has a close familial resemblance. Their ability to select in crowded fields and to add value by doing so; to follow up and carefully arrange those selections for maximum success; their expertise and understanding of their fields; all these make them irreplaceable.

When jobs get pushed upstream in crowded, difficult markets, they become curatorial. Whether it's luxury brand outlets or tech investments, distilling complex, overloaded markets into clear and successful selections is one of the defining abilities of our time. Understanding this change explains how work has already altered over the last thirty or so years – and will continue to alter. Sure, such jobs have always existed. Newspaper editors, interior designers and retail buyers, for example, have always worked by selecting and arranging. It's their increased prevalence, scope and potential to create value that has changed. And if for the time being they are concentrated in privileged but significant enclaves, they will, I believe, rapidly percolate into more business sectors and geographical areas.

Whenever I spoke to art or museum curators, the suggestion that venture capitalists might be family was anathema. That, they scoffed, isn't curating. Speaking to a lecturer teaching a master's degree course in curation, I argued that surely this was great for curating? Curating has become a kind of advanced prototype for the future of work. Curators' core skills have never been more desirable. Isn't this something to embrace? The business of art and the art of business have never been closer.

Shut up and take my money!

Piggly Wiggly changed retail forever. It may have been incongruously named but the Memphis, Tennessee store founded in 1916 by Clarence Saunders ushered us out of the formal nineteenth-century world where goods were kept behind counters into a brave new twentieth-century reality: self-service shopping. Saunders let customers browse and pick items at will, rather than wait for harried assistants to pluck them off segregated shelves. They then took the goods to a centralised cash desk and paid. Walking through those turnstiles customers had agency; they walked into a new kind of experience. Suddenly layout, mix and brand communication took centre stage. These new stores spread through America and hit Europe in the 1950s. This was when shoppers became shoppers as we know them today.

Saunders created a new model of shopping for a new kind of industrialised economy and consumer. His template would reign for a century.

Now that model is crumbling. Driven by overlapping trends – the supply shock from China and new technologies; the extraordinary expansion in stock availability engendered by ecommerce; the dramatic growth of luxury as a retail force, with its high margins and greater vertical integration; changing consumer preferences and purchasing behaviour – the experience of shopping is undergoing a shift comparable to that of the early twentieth century. We have already seen this: the shift from an Industrial Model of Selection to a Curated Model. It's worth exploring in more detail.

Imagine an Industrial Model fashion store. It has a reasonable selection. At most there may be a few thousand different lines in the store, but most likely there will be fewer.

Contrast this with shopping online. A search for 'dress' on

Amazon returns 947,000 results; narrowing this to 'black dress' returns 244,000 (numbers which, if anything, clearly indicate the extent of the Long Boom's legacy). If shopping on the Internet had a killer app, it was this – everything was available. But of course, in the familiar pattern, that expansion required an overlaid compression of choice: 947,000 dresses is of use to no one. Size of catalogue becomes irrelevant compared to finding people the right garment; a more difficult task as options proliferate. This is one reason why Amazon hasn't (to date) dominated fashion, that most personal and self-expressive of categories. In contrast, think about a company like Opening Ceremony. In the words of the *LA Times*, 'if there is one store that has shaped fashion retail in the 21st century, it's Opening Ceremony.'[5]

Founded by Carol Lim and Humberto Leon in New York's SoHo in 2002, Opening Ceremony was inspired by a visit to Hong Kong, that same retail pressure cooker Karim Azar works so hard to maintain. Their idea was to show brands from all over the world, featuring a given country every year. At the same time they would break and showcase new American designers. Every item was carefully chosen and each new store opened after careful thought. It's always blended styles, from the high to the low, from the utterly exclusive to the offbeat and punk. They work with mainstream brands like Vans or Topshop, artists, film stars and directors; they revive tired old labels; and they discover completely new designers. Installations and collaborations are key.

Opening Ceremony became the ultimate in a new kind of fashion store that was global, almost like an art gallery, built around its selections and partnerships. It's no accident that Opening Ceremony became an icon just as fashion became infinitely available. As designers spring up; as clothing factories increase production, often in terrible conditions for the workers; as clothing becomes something we can order at the click of the button; the value, aesthetic and pecuniary, moves into Opening Ceremony territory: the curation of the offering. Let's face it. The average Opening Ceremony customer willing to spend $500 on a shirt doesn't want for clothes, or for places to buy clothes. These privileged consumers want only for the latest and best fashions.

Saunders and other retailers expanded customer choice so much that a renewed and strengthened intermediary process is now required. What's changed is not that retailers are curating, for at some level they have always done so; it's the focus on curation as retail's *raison d'être*. Production, supply chains and logistics have all been to some extent 'solved'. While admittedly still complex and difficult, they aren't the central challenge or purpose for a retailer (although for ecommerce companies, solving the 'last mile' question of getting goods into people's hands quickly is still a defining task).

Earlier we saw how a new kind of 'box subscription' food business enables you to have selections sent to you. The model is spreading. OwlCrate sends a monthly delivery of hand-selected young adult books, while Faithbox sends out Christian-influenced products and materials. My Little Box selects lifestyle goods. Not Another Bill picks surprise gifts. Cratejoy, based in Austin, Texas, is a company designed to provide the infrastructure for such box subscription businesses in anything from toys to T-shirts. Birchbox, one of the leaders in the area, does something similar in cosmetics. For $10 a month users sign up to receive five new samples. On signup the customer inputs their preferences and requirements and subsequent packages are carefully chosen based on their 'beauty profile'. This service is invaluable for niche or start-up luxury brands. Birchbox is, around this curated offering, building both a media business, creating content, and a traditional retail business.

Birchbox and Opening Ceremony embody many of the most important trends in retail. They both have a curated offering at their heart. This means they not only select intensively, but they talk about it. Opening Ceremony is producing more videos for its websites and Birchbox has become an online publication. Customers want more information about the products they buy. The 'research phase' before purchasing has increased dramatically. People are more likely to turn to trusted curators, especially those that discuss products and processes in detail.[6] Getting the balance right is crucial. Retailers have seconds to win or lose a customer. Much rests on how information is displayed. Are there price comparisons? If so, how many? Do you need to put not just badges and reviews but a physical location (even if just the head office) on every single page? Is there information about the packaging? Do you link to other sites' reviews? How many off-site reviews do you need? Do you have a downloaded data sheet and if so, what data does it include? Is there background product information and technical specs?

They also combine ecommerce with bricks and mortar. Birchbox is, on the face of it, an ecommerce business. But it has segued into the physical realm, opening an outlet in Manhattan. At a Fast Company conference, Birchbox co-founder Katia Beauchamp estimated that the lifetime value of a customer who visited the store was two and a half times greater than that of an online-only customer. The opposite trend applies for Opening Ceremony – its chic stores are replicated by a substantial online presence. This is what Professor Scott Galloway of New York University's Stern Business School calls the end of 'pure play'.[7] He argues that it's no longer viable to be purely a physical or ecommerce retailer. You need both. Ecommerce transmits rich content and information, lets you maximise range. But you also need a physical store. In part they are convenient, flexible warehouses, but they also force you to narrow the range. Galloway's research shows that most in-store purchases have been researched online anyway. Hence the necessity of a multichannel offering.

Getting the curatorial mix right across physical and digital environments will be a key competence for retailers. Moreover, he believes the 'vanity economy' of luxury, beauty and apparel will be at the forefront of further changes in retail – exactly as might be expected from Birchbox and Opening Ceremony.

Recently I attended a talk by James Daunt, boss of the UK's largest dedicated book chain, Waterstones. Going into the 2010s, Waterstones was in trouble. The high street generally had been hit hard by recession and digital commerce. For retailers trading on price, new discounters and the Internet had proved painful. In books the challenge was particularly acute. Amazon's market share had grown rapidly as it became the dominant force in bookselling. Already operating on thin margins, Waterstones was in a battle for survival. Its loss would be more than a shame – it would be a catastrophe for writers, British publishing and the book-buying public.

Parachuted in after a Russian takeover in 2011, Daunt, who previously ran an upmarket chain of eponymous bookshops, set about reconfiguring the business. He realised it could never compete with Amazon on range or price. Instead he had to capitalise on Waterstones' existing strengths.

Waterstones' range went from passive to actively chosen; every book is judged, selection size and arrangement is constantly changing, driven by expert choice rather than publisher payments. Staff are empowered to choose, display and engage with books. Centralised buying has been banished in favour of selections made by individual stores. Daunt sees curation as the breakthrough change. Waterstones is happy to stock fewer books, but they should be finely chosen. Booksellers have accountability as curators, rather than passive receivers of orders. Making bookstores interesting and having their selection based on judgement, rather than what publishers pay, for example letting booksellers and not publishers dictate the front of store, was how Waterstones fought back against a 25 per cent collapse in sales in favour of the Amazon Kindle. Even where central buying remained important, it was better allocated, recognising that different geographical areas and shops had different requirements.

In other words, personal curation and bookselling, beautiful environments, the chance of serendipitous discovery or conversation – these are what give Waterstones a fighting chance in the digital age. They have, in other words, moved from an Industrial Selection Model driven from HQ and by supplier contributions to a more Curated Selection Model, buttressed by the humanity and diversity of their physical stores and booksellers. In Daunt's presentation he reported a significant uplift in sales and a return to profit. The business was secure. It again shows the complex relationship between machine-driven and human-driven curation. Amazon pioneered algorithmic recommendations ... but years later Waterstones is building a great business on the back of human, personal selections, carving a niche against the Seattle behemoth through explicit and thick curation based on its legion of passionate booksellers. What's more, as Amazon piles into same-day delivery, urban lockers for after-work collection and even swarms of delivery drones, the physical convenience argument disappears and all that's left is curation. Curation may have grown on the web, but its impact spreads far beyond. After all, even Amazon responded to the landscape with an old-fashioned bricks-and-mortar bookstore, Amazon Books, which opened in Seattle in late 2015. This is just the start of a plan to roll out hundreds of such bookstores.[8]

The Curated Model is still in its infancy. But start-ups

indicate the direction of travel. Lyst, for example, is a popular retail aggregator that lets users browse among 11,500 designers and stores from Alexander McQueen to Valentino. They then create, share and purchase from 'lysts'. Lyst extensively mixes algorithmic recommendation with personal curation, is growing fast and has raised over $60m in financing from luxury goods giant LVMH and venture capitalists Accel Partners, amongst others.[9] If you want furniture the curated model can be found in start-ups like made.com and Dot and Bo. Electronics? Have a look at Grand St. Talk about fashion and cosmetics? Tech? A little over eighteen months since going live, the brilliant Product Hunt was sending 2.5 million users a month to new launches. Kit.com was designed to change the way we discover 'things worth getting'. We've not even mentioned the merged fashion giant of Italian ecommerce star Yoox and Net-A-Porter, or Refinery29 – places that seamlessly combine content, curation and retail.

Nonetheless it would be a mistake, as Waterstones and any number of retailers illustrate, to elide the Curated Model with start-ups. Galloway cites companies like Gap and Apple – vertically integrated, selective with their product, seamlessly crossing digital and physical retail – as great examples of companies who have succeeded in the new retail landscape by doing both. Both in a sense curate themselves – at the level of manufacturing *and* retail. Shopping mall company Westfield has opened a large Labs operation in the Bay Area to build the new technologies retailers will need – as have Walgreens, Walmart, Target and American Eagle Outfitters, among many others.[10] So-called 'legacy' retailers have been growing their ecommerce efforts at a phenomenal pace for years. The truth is that in today's world there is no online or offline. There is a blend.

High-end retail was always curated – these were always

pleasant, hushed environments, museum-like in their selection and presentation. Now the new dynamic pushes mass access to the Curated Model of Selection, out from its deluxe redoubts and on to the high street.

For most of the twentieth century the way we shopped remained consistent. Producers made goods; shops sold them. We browsed freely, discovering products through shop aisles but also via advertising or word of mouth. Clarence Saunders created a robust system that delivered enormous rewards. But, faced with an increase in possible supply and the new content environment, retail is changed. Utilising to maximum benefit the mix of digital and physical, providing information around selections and products, building trust as a curator and recognising that how we discover, recommend and filter goods in abundant markets is irrevocably altered – these are the rules of curated retail. Neither Walmart nor a small boutique on the Marais's Rue des Francs-Bourgeois will duck the challenge: that discovery, not supply, is now the major obstacle in the consumer economy.

Bazaars, now and then

What we have come to call curation isn't some recent innovation. It has existed for centuries. The innovation is that we have come to label it curation. The word has travelled, the activity has always been present and it's carried on evolving – yes, becoming more prevalent with time, but coming from a clear lineage of practice. In what might be called the bazaar economy – the world of markets – curation has always held a key role. In any market, price competition is always going to be important. But beyond that comes the selection and arrangement of goods. What you have; whether it is exclusive or not; how finely sourced; where it sits in the market; how the wares are displayed – long before there were any ideas of curation these were day-to-day concerns.

Take that classic of world trade – the Silk Road. While it is usually associated with Chinese traders, Indian mer- chants also played a prominent role. Before the Industrial Revolution, India and China dominated world commerce. Up to 1750, they controlled just over 40 per cent of global wealth. All merchants on the Silk Road faced enormous chal- lenges, but for those from India they were acute – not only did Indian merchants face deserts and bandits but this was a trans-Himalayan trade, traversing the highest and remotest mountain fastness on earth. To reach their markets, for mil- lennia caravans travelled from the subcontinent, across the Indus and Oxus rivers, over the Hindu Kush mountains and through the Khyber Pass.

Textiles were the most significant items to be traded, but there were also spices (pepper, cinnamon, nutmeg, cloves, ginger and mace), jewels, dyestuffs like indigo, weapons, sugar, rice (Indian rice was considered superior) – travelling hundreds, even thousands of miles to the markets of central Asia in Bukhara, Samarkand, Tashkent or Isfahan. Roman togas and Turkic turbans alike were made from Indian cloth (Indian cotton was cooler than wool and was considered a mark of exotic distinction). India's advantage was that, com- pared with the arid steppe, it was a fertile land that could support a large population which in turn produced plentiful cloth. Ancient Greece and Rome were already major export markets for Indian cottons; Pliny the Elder claimed that 550 million sesterces were sent to India by Romans every year.[11] In return traders would travel back from Inner Asia with thousands of steppe-bred horses, but also with leather and wool, furs from Siberia, paper, silks and porcelain from China triangulated through Inner Asia.

Indian merchants, living in their caravanserais, were at the heart of an integrated transcontinental network of trade and banking. Multan, in modern-day Pakistan, was a key hub city located between the mountains and the riverine plains, the Islamic and Hindu worlds. Under the Mughal Empire (1526–1707) this trade flourished from northern India, the Punjab in particular. In the early modern period, Scott C. Levi estimates, there were 35,000 Indian merchants working the Silk Road; Isfahan in Persia alone had an Indian population of around 12,000 in the late seventeenth century. From there merchandise could be sent to the Mediterranean or the Caucasus and Muscovy.

There was an infrastructure not only of caravanserais but of roads and passes, trees for shade, wells, bridges, fortresses to suppress armed attacks. The Mughal emperor Akbar the Great alone ordered the construction of 1,700 caravanserais and worked with his Persian Safavid counterpart, Shah Abbas, to protect the trade routes even during times of conflict. Caravans needed unloading every evening and reloading in the morning, the work being managed by Afghan nomads. The process became so efficient that fresh fruit from Central Asia could be carried as far as the Deccan plateau in the heart of the Indian subcontinent.

Caravan merchants nevertheless had to be careful. Their journey was arduous. They faced cold, heat, shortages of food and water, bandits and wars as they traversed the barren mountain passes. Everything was strapped to camels or loaded onto precarious carts. By the late seventeenth century up to 30,000 animals were each carrying 180 kilos of merchandise. Each caravan transported hundreds or thousands of bolts of cloth, to be sold in stages so as not to flood the market.

By the eighteenth century, fuelled by European bullion plundered from the New World, a quarter of the world's textiles were produced in India. This created jobs for farmers growing cotton, skilled spinners, weavers, dyers, printers, artists, logistics specialists and, at the fulcrum of it all, wholesalers. The Punjab in particular became a global centre of textile production, but Sind, Gujarat and Bengal were also significant producers. There were many different kinds of cloth. Basic materials, but also cotton blended with linen and silk. There were calicoes, chintzes and muslins; Kashmiri shawls, turbans and towels; numerous patterns, prints and colours. India had an edge in production and hence price; but then it also had the diversity and quality of product to go with it.

Indian merchants had to carefully select what they were going to take. Due to the means of transport and the terrain there were huge limits on what could be packed. Although some intelligence was available from their network, information about distant markets was often a matter of guesswork. Logistics, fulfilment and financing were core areas of competence for the merchants – the indispensable basis of their trade. But success also required two further elements: having the right balance of goods in the limited space of the caravan, and the ability to sell them effectively at the other end. Matters of selection were, then, critical to the operation of the trans-Himalayan Silk Road. Balancing the selection of goods was central to the success or failure of these enterprises. Get the mix right – one blend of textiles, spices and weapons for this town, another for that – and the rewards were enormous. Get it wrong and years', even decades' worth of work and capital would be wasted.

This then is the truth of the merchant. They either compete on price or they compete on their selection and arrangement. Or more likely both. This is true of the caravan merchants of Mughal India; the Renaissance cloth traders of Florence or Leipzig; in the Grand Bazaar of Istanbul; or at contemporary markets from London's Columbia Road flower market to Tokyo's Tsukiji seafood market to wares on Etsy.

What has changed is that as time goes on, the elements of selection and arrangement become ever more central. The Multani merchants of the seventeenth century faced a Herculean challenge in moving their produce to market. Choosing the balance of spice and calico – which quantities, which products – was always bounded by the incredible difficulties not only of production but of distribution. Today, in a world of just-in-time integrated supply chains, that element is less important. Being able to access textiles is no longer a competitive advantage; choosing them is.

All of this can still be found today in India's burgeoning economy. While it's a truism that, since the so-called Licence-Permit Raj was lifted in 1991 with a raft of economic liberalisation, the Indian economy has been growing fast – at an average rate of 6.8 per cent for 1991–2011[12] – it's also true that India, like most of the world, is seeing a shift in the nature of value towards curation-style activities. This isn't to deny or even underplay the challenges – for most of India's population life is still crushingly hard. It is nevertheless a recognition of how growth is occurring in the world's second-largest country by population.

Today it is a mistake to think of India's population simplistically as a mass market. In fact, focusing in this way on the country's 1.2 billion people, up to 300 million of whom are middle-class consumers (and 56 million of whom own a car), creates an error. For example, Tata launched the Nano – a people's car designed to be cheap enough for millions. But it didn't catch on. The market simply didn't want a one-size-fits-all car. People would either stick with motorbikes or wanted to trade up and have more of a differentiator. It was, argues analyst Dheeraj Sinha, a misunderstanding of Indian consumers to think of them as an undifferentiated mass.[13] A focus on cost at the expense of aspirational and other higher-end values was a category error. Stripping things down to the bare minimum, thinking only about cost, was a strategy that failed to win converts. Moreover it meant that focus moved away from careful curation and differentiation, which harmed brands in the affluent areas as well as those attempting to move upmarket. While the Nano failed, Mahindra and Mahindra, which focused on well-fitted SUVs, continued to flourish.

Indian consumers are, after two decades of growth, on the upgrade cycle – of their phones and cars for example. While the 1990s were about rolling out products like TVs, fridges, microwaves and cars in ever greater numbers, more sophisticated consumers are now becoming the norm, with the associated offerings and retail environments. Shopping malls, retail chains, experts and consumer spending have all mushroomed. A curation-oriented approach is proving more successful in India than the mass market many businesses thought they would find. In Dheeraj Sinha's words: 'The Indian consumer is done with the expected stuff. He wants some shock value – a break away from the routine. He wants bang for his buck, he wants his money to show itself. The desire cuts across social strata.'[14]

Because of the size of its market, scale was prioritised over differentiation in India – whether in telecoms, airlines or retail. This is now changing. Picking up on the bazaar theme, the retail chain Big Bazaar launched by the Mumbai-based Future Group (India's second-largest retail conglomerate) was an attempt to create a mass-market Indian retail destination – its slogan *Isse Sasta Aur Achcha, Kahin Nahin* translates as 'nowhere is cheaper and better than this'. Big Bazaar was an attempt to create a 'carefully curated' version of the street market. It was an attempt to bring the best of the old together with the best of the new in a highly curated setting. This is also the driver behind initiatives like Foodhall. While it hasn't been plain sailing and the group has more recently hit trouble, it shows how those at the forefront of Indian business are going for curated approaches to what was traditionally seen as the definitive mass audience.

Many of the largest Indian businesses are themselves highly curated entities. Conglomerates are a common form, often built up around powerful business dynasties from traditional groups like the Parsis of Mumbai or the Marwaris from rural Rajasthan. Marwari families like the Birlas grew up in and through the bazaar economy; today they manage vast diversified portfolios of businesses. The Hinduja brothers, who own assets amounting to around $35bn, are descended from Indian traders who worked in Iran. The trick with such groups, now aped by the founding of a portfolio business like Alphabet, the parent of Google, is to balance elements within the whole; to have hedges built into the mix to ensure overall flourishing is possible. Moreover, such businesses can, thanks to their mix, be resilient. While Western firms have often pursued a strategy of divestment and focus, these sprawling familial empires are growing on the back of melding elements together.

And of course at the grandest level India is an act of managing diversity, of language (thirty languages and thousands of dialects), religion and culture. A new breed of Indian entrepreneur is putting together pan-regional versions of fashions and food. The salwar kameez has spread to south India, while dosas can be found in the north. The need for Indian businesses to micro-target is growing and is becoming ever more possible. This explains the flourishing of a website like Craftsvilla, India's largest ethnic crafts marketplace, which retails unique handcrafted items from sarees to candles. It can match diversity with scale, targeted curation with the mass and complexity of Indian produce. A complex interplay between regionalism and the national is creating a series of overlapping, nested and interlocuting markets. Weddings for example have become a $40bn industry where every element – themes, Bollywood-style dances and costumes, sangeet ceremonies (like a wedding shower) – is pored over in great detail, and a different regional elements are spreading throughout the country.

Bazaars – markets – are a constant of history. They remain as relevant today as ever. Throughout history we have expected to find curators of various kinds. The librarians who organised information; the critics who picked out and praised works that stood out from the crowd; the collectors who amassed work and the custodians who looked after it. But there were also the merchants, wholesalers and buyers. These roles have never been synonymous with curators, but they always shared much of the skill set. Curation is not the explicit goal of these businesses; it's folded into them, a vital part of the proposition but not its most obvious aspect. This was true in the time of the Mughals and it remains true. India's economy today has a large element that is living in poverty; a large middle that is getting used to consumer life; and a fast-growing upper segment that is redefining itself around curation.

Curation-type skills are not as limited by time and space as we might be inclined to believe.

The curation scientific

Information businesses of any kind are also transformed. We've already seen this at work in our cultural life and on the Internet. But, thanks to that incredible increase, it reaches everywhere that touches information.

Scientific enquiry is one such area. The journal *Nature* is today the world's most highly cited, according to Thomson Reuters.[15] For researchers, having their name in the journal can make careers. When epochal discoveries are made – anything from the ozone hole to cloning Dolly the sheep or sequencing the human genome – *Nature* publishes the findings.

From the seventeenth century science became more formalised, its newly established methods at last enabling humankind to understand the world. As the nineteenth century began, most scientific apparatus and infrastructure was still that of the late Renaissance – a realm of amateur experimentalists and dilettantes. Even great names like Humphry Davy, Michael Faraday or Antoine Lavoisier, for example, effectively worked on their own, outsiders ploughing their own furrow. As the nineteenth century wore on, however, things began to change. German university research laboratories were increasingly professionalised and their American cousins began to catch up. But scientific communication was run by bodies like Britain's Royal Society. Attempts at new journals tended to fail.

Founded in 1869, *Nature* reflected the new reality of science as an increasingly professionalised and socially significant discipline (just ten years earlier Darwin had forever changed humanity with the publication of his *On the Origin of Species*). Norman Lockyer, its founder, was a scientist and thinker jointly credited with the discovery of helium. A member of the exclusive X Club, a group of liberal thinkers aiming to modernise science and the popular mind, he formed a coterie that would contribute extensively to the new journal. Published by the Macmillans, *Nature*'s stable backing and prominent researchers, guided adroitly by Lockyer, ensured it quickly became a settled part of the scientific firmament.

Its mission was simple. First, to 'place before the general public the grand results of Scientific Work'. Second, 'to aid

Scientific men themselves, by giving early information of all advances made in any branch of Natural knowledge throughout the world'.[16] Although the first aim was fairly normal for a publication, the second was (perhaps unsurprisingly) forward-thinking: *Nature* wasn't just a publisher, it wanted to integrally support, 'aid' the work of science. It gave them room to go beyond publishing.

Nature soon cemented itself as the foremost scientific journal. Meanwhile science, the original progenitor of the Long Boom, was undergoing a huge inflation. The number of articles published in scientific journals has been doubling every thirteen years. By the mid-2000s over 1.35 million peer-reviewed articles were published every year. In 1950 there were around 60,000 recorded journals. Fifty years later it was one million.[17] *Nature* itself has recorded even more bullish figures, talking about a 9 per cent trend growth rate in articles, which equates to a doubling of global output every nine years.[18] On top of this, innovative means of publishing science have been established, bypassing the slow pace of traditional peer review and dissemination – in physics, for instance, the repository arXiv lets researchers post work (early stage, pure data) inadmissible in *Nature*. The situation is just as bad in the humanities: research suggests that 93 per cent of humanities journal articles are never cited.[19]

Scientists have an abundance problem. Wading through even a fraction of the available research is impossible. Long gone are the days of an Aristotle or Erasmus, when one individual could master the entire field of knowledge. Staying abreast of material even in your niche is difficult. Moreover, as the speciality and the depth increase, so does the complexity of the work.

Which is where *Nature* comes in. *Nature* is the arch-curator of science. As the most trusted and prestigious curatorial brand in the game (although the journal *Science* might object), its selections for inclusion in the main journal are arbiters of quality and significance. As science grows, far from losing their importance top-end journals like *Nature* have only seen it increase. Its editors, a phalanx of scientists armed with PhDs from the world's top institutions, decide what matters and why. As with curation everywhere, the value of a good curator increases with production. *Nature* remains a flourishing business, premised on expert curation, the jewel in the crown of the newly merged Holtzbrinck and Springer group.

But there is now another angle to this story. *Nature*'s parent company had been busy in areas that highlighted another trend within curation, one that has been apparent throughout this book. They set up Digital Science, a cross between an old-fashioned VC and an incubator for scientific communications technology. *Nature* is an old-fashioned curator, still a publisher at its heart. Digital Science would try something new: it would build a new suite of tools allowing scientists themselves to become curators. So, for example, they created products for managing data; for producing and sharing references; for sifting through the welter of citations; for publishing and filtering scientific work in new ways. The mission, note, still chimes with *Nature*'s original purpose – aiding scientists. Digital Science is a recognition that adding journals to boost top-line growth is a strategy that is running out of road; instead, providing people on the frontline of information overload with imaginative tools offers a better opportunity. Others agree – Mendeley, for instance, a London-based start-up which aimed to transform scientific communication, was snapped up by journals giant Elsevier.

Today we see two parallel tracks of curation. First there is the model of the firm itself as curator. *Nature* curates scientific research; Opening Ceremony curates fashion; Ambie curates music.

Then there is the firm as an enabler of others' curation. Companies build tools allowing – empowering – people to become curators in their own right. Spotify spends vast amounts improving its own curation, but, through its playlists and sharing of functionality, allows anyone to create and broadcast their musical taste. Facebook has in place thin films of curation – but the whole point is that it's we ourselves who curate it, through our connections and what we choose to post. WeChat, Tumblr and Pinterest all enable others to be curators. It's what powers the self-curation of sites like Wikipedia or TripAdvisor – powerful curators in their own right, but driven by a distributed curation amongst the users.

Creating means for others to *curare* is a signature business model of the digital age.

Magazines more widely, for example, are changing. At some level they were always curators. Now a company like Stack curates them, sending out different magazines to users. And then comes the next level – distributing that curation everywhere. Flipboard makes selections, but it also disaggregates content and lets users rearrange it into collections of their own making. Flipboard shifts magazine curation from editors to readers; from Broadcast to Curated. Having raised hundreds of millions of dollars, the expectation of investors is that, one day, this combination of Flipboard and reader-centred curation (or its equivalents like promising Dutch start-up Blendle) will be worth more than magazine giants like Hearst or Condé Nast.

Having a strategy for letting others curate, for outsourcing to those on the frontlines, will be more and more essential. It's a model we have seen time and again on the web and it's not going away. Social media relies on networks of trust, intimacy and knowledge, amplified by connectivity – given how much curation is about personality and connection, it's hardly surprising this model is so prevalent.

Again, this needs to be placed in the wider context. That the locus of value has moved is recognised by those suffering the consequences. The boss of Taiwanese electronics manufacturer Acer, Stan Shih, coined the term 'smiling curve' to describe the problem facing his business. If the curve represented value, he could see a depression in the middle of the supply chain among producers, a depression creating the 'smile'. Upstream intellectual property owners like chip designers and down-stream sellers with consumer brands and access were hogging value. Middling players like Acer were trapped between them, their margins squeezed. Manufacturing alone, without those benefits of IP or glossy brand, wasn't cutting it any more. It lost value. Apple and Gap experienced the reverse. Likewise, in educational or scientific publishing, value is shifting from the middle of the curve – that great mass of journals – to high-level curators like *Nature* or tools enabling others to curate. We saw in Part II how many retailers were struggling, caught in their own version of the smiling curve. At the same time a new generation of retailers who understand the curatorial landscape is emerging, and platforms like Etsy, Popshops and Datafeedr drive highly curated niche offerings.

Science generally is tending towards curation. Biocurators, for example, continue the legacy of Linnaeus in curating the natural world, now at the level of genetics. Finance too is becoming richly informationalised. Earlier we saw how Lisa's problems boiled down to an excess of information. Everything from a Bloomberg terminal to new offerings like StockTwits (which aims to derive market data from Twitter) or Symphony provide tools for traders to sift the maelstrom of information, with greater and lesser levels of success. Look through the promotional literature of venture capital or private equity funds and you'll notice the word 'curated' with surprising regularity.

And at a high level there are curious echoes between finance and art. Both, for example, revolve as much around secondary selections as primary productions. In the late nineteenth and early twentieth centuries, art became ever more self-involved – successive waves of art grew more abstracted, commenting on themselves. In the same way, towards the close of the twentieth century finance became abstracted and self-referential; derivatives, securities based on other securities, were, like movements in art, built on top of one another, getting further and further away from the underlying reality they were meant to describe. At the same time art became ever more lucrative, traded as just another fungible asset by a breed of wealthy buyers looking for good returns. Deloitte's Art and Finance Report claims that three-quarters of art buyers made their purchases for investment purposes.[20] Firms like Cadell & Co are art advisers, but are regulated as financial advisers: their brief is to combine collection know-how with market savvy. Deutsche Bank has extensive collections and an in-house art department. I hesitate to draw any conclusions from this, but it's an interesting parallel.

Curation, as a word, may have started far from business. But its attributes have long been central to many companies and roles. Now, in a world where services and intangibles play ever more central roles in the generation and distribution of wealth, they are integral.

Many nineteenth-century economists believed in something called Say's Law, named after the French economist Jean-Baptiste Say. Roughly speaking his law suggested that production equalled demand; that the more was produced in an economy, the more demand and consumption there would be. Production created wealth, which created demand. John Maynard Keynes and others disputed this. In blunt form Say's Law fell out of favour. But it's nonetheless true that we have an extraordinary capacity to soak up, manage and profit from rising production. Even if Say's Law doesn't hold at the macro level, close up we can see how rising production has spawned new industries designed to manage and modulate growth. Business is creating what I call ecosystems of curation. These are new networks where a multitude of specialised firms collectively curate a sector. That these ecosystems have grown so much, and support such a diversity of commercial life, is testament to the change discussed in this book.

Centuries ago fashion was governed by the twin poles of artisan producers and local gossip – who was wearing what in Florence, what the lord and lady stepped out in and so on. As time went on further elements were added – shops and media. They became key filters and trend setters. By the middle of the twentieth century, fashion was dominated by powerful designers and ateliers, the growth of influential magazines like *Vogue*, and retail outlets on the smart streets of global fashion capitals. Today all this still exists, but has become vastly more complex – and the complexity has become more intermediated in order to manage it. For a start, the differentiation within each category has been immeasurably increased. We have a huge range of designers from global brands to tiny experimental boutiques. Then there are the new curatorial roles – fashion bloggers, amateur and professional photographers, trend watchers (one firm alone employs 3,000 of them),[21] personal shoppers, stylists, brand strategists, retail architects, algorithm coders. Even shopping mall managers! Just as human and algorithmic curation work together, so in these ecosystems do we also see the coexistence of professional and amateur, big brand and local niche.

As the rag trade grew and diversified, more elements of the industry, which was always amongst the most intensively curated, came to involve curation. Together it now produces an intricate network, linking producers and reporters, online and offline, selecting and arranging the right garments for the right people. Localised regions of the broader Curation Layer involve overlapping curation ecosystems whose increase in size and diversity is underwritten by significant economic and social change. It reflects the fact that searching for what you know you want has, in this arena as in so many, become trivial. Finding what you don't know you want has, conversely, become ever more valuable. The ecosystem – whether in food, or news, or scientific communication – is the difference.

The question for many businesses is, I believe, now about their strategy for navigating the ecosystem they are entering. If you are an established player, how can you entrench your position or diversify into new parts of that ecosystem? And if you are new, where do you fit into the elaborate existing structures? Getting the answer right is one of the business challenges of our time.

The distributed Curation Model indicates something vital. It is now we, you, I, everyone, who are the most important curators of all.

11

Curate Yourself

I, Curator

For most of human history identity hasn't been up for grabs – it's been foisted upon us. Where you grew up, your gender, race and class all effectively channelled your options, your projection of and sense of self. Identities were taken off the shelf: the peasant or the knight, the dowager or the besuited banker, the coal miner or even the consumptive poet, were all archetypes people could readily buy into. This isn't to say people had no agency – of course they did. But their social identity was more often than not, wherever they were, quite clearly laid down, something they had to buy into and live completely. With many large caveats and exceptions, we tended to receive our identities direct from our parents and our place in society.

Over the past fifty or so years, for the first time in history, this doesn't hold. Earlier on I spoke about how curation usually has a performative or service role; how it is directed out, towards an audience. Now we reach the limits of this interpretation, the frontier of curation: ourselves.

There has been a dramatic qualitative shift in how we approach the tricky business of being. Where we used to take identities off the shelf, now we delicately pick and choose those elements we like and want. We make ourselves up. In the words of the novelist Neal Stephenson, 'Our cultures used to be almost hereditary, but now we choose them from a menu as various as the food court of a suburban shopping mall.'[1] For want of a better word, and at the risk of sounding ridiculous, we curate our identities. Curation is no longer directed solely towards others as a performance or presentation; it's internalised. This marks not only a change in how we relate to our lives, but also a further shift in what it means to curate.

This works on two levels. First we curate ourselves outwardly. This isn't simply having certain clothes and being seen at the right parties. It's about subtle, tacit signals composed as a signifying mosaic drawn from the rich and varied sources of the contemporary world. Second, we curate our experiences. We don't want to lead linear and predictable lives – instead, the very stuff of reality is treated by the modern consumer like an art exhibition, a series of contrasting, surprising, thrilling and thought-provoking items whose uniqueness and sequence give meaning to the whole.

This might sound highfalutin', but really it breaks down into a concrete sense most of us have experienced: the craving for variety, newness and difference amply catered for in the modern economy, whether it's literally entry to an exhibition, adventure holidays or a new kind of work. In short, our attitude to ourselves internally and externally has been caught up in the same dynamic we've been looking at all along. As might be expected, this has positive and negative dimensions.

In the last chapter – as we have done throughout the book – we saw how businesses empower people to curate for themselves. This would never have come about had not there not been a willing audience, keen to share and curate their music or photos. For this model to work, there had to be demand – one that often appears madly self-absorbed and absurd, but whose influence and reach is growing even as it is decried.

Choose life

Over the twentieth century children took their cues less and less from their parents. Where once this would have been a near-automatic process, by the middle of the century, with the dawning of specific and mainstream youth cultures, the hold of previous generations was loosening. New subcultures emerged: mods and rockers, punks and skinheads, rastas and metallers, goths and New Romantics. Each had an internally coherent look and cultural form. It would be wrong to say that these cultures were not a hotch-potch – they were. Teddy Boys, for instance, took Edwardian suits and combined them with intense rhythm and blues music.

Punk was one of the most easily identifiable such subcultures. It first hit Britain in the heatwave summer of 1976. Mired in widespread unemployment, the country struggled to comprehend the depths of its post-war decline. By 1977 punks had exploded into the mainstream, causing consternation among the respectable classes. Punks were angry, alienated, nihilistic and profane. They were, ironically, the perfect dramatisation of a country in crisis; the symptom of an ongoing slow-motion collapse, designed to provoke a reaction. Punks were recognisable above all for their stylistic challenge – like the mods and rockers before them, their very look was meant as a challenge and an appropriation of the dominant forms.[2] They cut up the Union Jack and spliced it about their person. With its quiffs, leather jackets, drainpipes, skinhead overtones, denim and 'bovver boots', punk was a medley of post-war styles literally held together by safety pins. The point about punk, as with all those post-war movements, is that for the first time on a mass scale people were choosing entirely new identities for themselves, and that moreover, those very new looks and identities were themselves carefully selected composites.

But there were nonetheless clear boundaries. It would be difficult to be a punk, for example, if you wore a plain business suit, had a conservative haircut, went home to the suburbs every evening and listened mainly to Bach. Punk was never as simple as we remember, but it nonetheless came as an internally coherent package, certain elements of which were necessary. Even rebellion, let alone the many more 'acceptable' identities, was carefully codified and consistent. Being a punk was a strange assemblage of self-selection, screw-the-system aggression and box-ticking exercise.

Compare this with that much maligned, possibly retired, contemporary subculture: the hipster. Originally hipsters were another post-war subculture, a 1950s movement like the Beats. Typically they were working-class to the Beats' middle class, dandyish in zoot suits, drapes, quiffs and attitude. They were the white working-class side of the vibrancy of black musical culture. They were identifiable.

Today we can still identify hipsters. We see them with their elaborate beards, fixed-gear bicycles, predilection for the bars of Brooklyn ... (where they are possibly drinking third-wave coffee). Yet the essential elements of hipsterism are non-existent. There is no set of defining traits. Instead, the defining trait is a kind of self-conscious curation of the self (and forgive me if that sounds like an incredible hipsterism). Take the attitude to vintage clothing. Whereas a Teddy Boy or punk sampled from specific eras, the hipster liberally takes from across the spectrum: a 1950s jacket, 1920s trousers, sneakers from the 1980s, a T-shirt emblazoned with a 1990s cartoon. There is no governing narrative, image or identity beyond the mash-up of them all; beyond the ability to choose and recombine there is nothing that necessarily defines the hipster. In the 1970s both the accountant and the punk had clear expectations of their image and demeanour; they understood who they were and how they fitted into a picture of the world. With the hipster this disappears. They are people of pure bricolage – assemblages self-consciously picked from across the entire spectrum, artfully, ironically put together into a globalised kind of non-identity whose shared elements are more in the spirit of curation than any of the things that go into them.

Before you scoff, and yes, well you might, like third-wave coffee this is the thin end of a wedge whose significance extends beyond its metropolitan roots. To some extent the last fifty years have seen all of our identities take this curatorial turn. We make things up far more than we used to. The guy sitting next to you at the football in jeans is probably an investment banker about to fly off to his yacht. The woman in pearls sitting next to you at the opera is a nurse just finished her shift. We all have more freedom and opportunity to make up who we are going to be; to put together different contrasting elements.

This all goes back to the expansion of choice. There are *tout court* more options. We can all find products from across the spectrum – vintage, high-street, ultra-cheap, luxury. The media is always on, beaming us images of lifestyles and cultures. No sooner has a subculture developed than it has been globalised and co-opted by major brands. Again, this is a qualitative shift. Think of fan culture. To be a fan in the pre-Internet days took devotion. If you were collecting Star Wars figurines say, you'd have to laboriously hunt them down. You'd make contacts at your local shop, around which you'd spend inordinate amounts of time. Tracking down new titbits of knowledge took time and effort. On the Internet it's easy to be a fan. You can find those models, rare comics or costumes with ease. Arcane information is a few clicks away. Everyone can be a fan whenever they want. Fan culture, as a result, has boomed: just look at the growth of events like Comic Con in San Diego.

The curation of identity is built on growing individualism. But it is all undergirded by the growth in choice. The fact that we can pick clothes from across the decades, that we have so many films, games and TV shows, means that we are forced to select. In the face of the slowly accreted accumulation of personal choices, the kind of complete social forms and identities which used to predominate break down. In their place comes the Curated Model of Selection and its personal equivalent. When consumerism, pluralism and selection are foundational, we become curated entities. In this way – I'm sorry to tell you – we are all hipsters now.

As consumerism continues its march, so it spreads. In Eastern Europe and large parts of Asia, what were until recently collectivist societies have given way to individualism. In a single generation choice has gone from limited luxury to ubiquitous presence. For older generations in China, their experience was rooted in communism. Within living memory they experienced the deprivations of the Great Famine and forced collectivisation; they went through the extremities and violence of the Cultural Revolution. They lived lives of brutal sparseness where any kind of choice was a rarity. Fast-forward to their children and grandchildren and, for the middle classes at least, things couldn't be more different. Until recently consumerism in China had a near-transgressive aspect that demarcated the generations. Young Chinese consumers were a new breed, smothered in love from the so-called 4-2-1 structure of a typical family (thanks to the one-child policy, every child is the focus of attention for their two parents and four grandparents). In the words of one commentator, 'competitive and lonely, wealthy and not afraid to flaunt it, this generation of children began to define themselves and their position through their consumption choices'.[3]

Young Chinese are, unlike their elders, able to sample from the global menu just as much as their Western peers. They too are used to eating McDonald's one day, traditional Chinese the next, just as their equivalents do in Los Angeles or Milan. They too will happily select from this or that musical tradition, cinematic genre or stylistic mode; for them too the world, its history, culture and art is a grand shopping mall to be sampled from at will. Maoism this is not.

Club Tropicana

Several years ago I watched a programme about the hotel Claridge's. The manager said something interesting. His guests, he implied, wanted to 'curate their experiences' – and this was where Claridge's came in. Once this grand hotel, marked at every turn by deep layers of decorum and the kind of understated elegance for which English brands are known, was the natural habitat for its guests – everyone would have felt quite comfortable and at home. His throwaway comment revealed a change; now few of his guests would feel quite at home. Instead, for them, it was an experience; one that formed part of the 'curated' whole which was their lives; that fitted into a rich blend, rather than being a seamless part of a coherent whole. Claridge's recognised that it was a particular kind of experience for a particular kind of experience-chasing consumer.

Tourism trades in experiences. Inasmuch as it is about consumption of a good, we should expect to find here the familiar pattern of curation. And vacations, like fashion, like our consumer lives, reflect who we are – they are not only about what we like and choose but what we wish others to perceive us liking and choosing. We have now built a marketplace for experiences that reflects a change in how people want to parcel their experience.

Tourism too has been part of the Long Boom – and has hit overload. Tourism was once a set of clearly defined experiences. Everyone knew what tourism consisted of, and who would experience it. The Grand Tour around southern Europe specialised in sights from antiquity and the Renaissance – the perfect education for louche aristocrats keen to explore the continent's classical heritage and have some adventure. In the later nineteenth century those same aristocrats began travelling instead to the beaches and waters of the French Riviera – the Promenade des Anglais in Nice, for example, was built for wealthy English tourists. Spa towns had always been tourist destinations; places like Bath or Baden-Baden were frequented by those looking for recuperation. For most, tourism happened to other people.

In a clear echo of the post-war period's changing identities, and as a result of the strong growth of those years, tourism became available to a wider group. Relatively affluent northern Europeans started visiting places like mainland Spain, Majorca and Rimini in Italy. Britons, Germans and Scandinavians soon descended in their millions: the number of international tourists in Spain grew from six million in 1960 to thirty million by 1975.[4] From Iberia and the Balearics tourism spread fast, in the process enabling previously isolated and impoverished communities in remote coastal areas of the Canary Islands, Greece, the former Yugoslavia and Turkey to develop.

Such tourism was based around the charter tour week: a structure designed to fill northern European aeroplanes flying to a limited number of sure-fire destinations. The planes would take out one load and pick up another on the way back, a weekly tempo that became part of the social fabric of tourism in the Mediterranean. It worked well for the tourists: guaranteed flights and hotels made for low prices, which expanded the numbers who could afford to go. The week had a rhythm: tour guides, local fiestas, standardised excursions to local sights, sunbathing and organised barbecues on the beach. It even explains why, despite cosmetic differences, almost all Mediterranean hotels look the same: they are designed to be functional and cheap, while directing as many rooms and balconies towards the sun as possible. Companies like Club Med and the tour operators have become much slicker and more sophisticated, but many elements of their holidays would be recognisable to a packager of the late 1960s and early 70s.

Orvar Löfgren argues that the Mediterranean, from the Grand Tour to the package holiday, created the modern tourism archetype: sun, sea, sand and sex, coupled with some 'sights' and culture.[5] Clichés of the Med sunbelt became the tourist ideal from Thailand to the Caribbean, in the process reshaping poor and distant parts of the world into hub destinations and motors of national growth. Like identity, tourism was taken off the shelf. It meant offering a limited range of known elements. Tourism's transition to mass activity rode on the same tide of increasing wealth, rising choice and widening options. A new breed of discerning consumer, less interested in traditional holidays than in new experiences, arrived just as computerised booking systems liberated them from the constraints of the packaged tour, the falling price of air travel threw open the map and, later, Airbnb and others strapped rocket boosters to room supply.

Packaged holidays began to suffer: overhasty development, overcrowding and badly behaved tourists created the so-called Torremolinos Effect, tourism's particular species of overload named after the Costa del Sol resort that suffered from loutish Brits, a crippled infrastructure, pollution and homogeneity, where old cultures and cuisines were elbowed aside in favour of crowded beaches and cheap booze. This was precisely what the new breed – who called themselves travellers as much as tourists – didn't want.

Now people wanted something unique, secluded, 'unspoilt' and original. An experience. So began the boom in niche and experiential travel. 'Travellers' weren't content seeing the Eiffel Tower; they wanted, with only traces of self-awareness, a tour round a Rio favela. They didn't want to roast on a beach; they wanted to scuba-dive a shipwreck. They wanted to go clubbing in Ibiza one weekend and have tea at Claridge's the next. Tourism was unbundled. Places and experiences were now to be curated, not taken as a generic package. Over the last thirty years the old pattern of tourism gave way to the independent traveller, the backpacker, the explorer. Traditional resorts started to lose out – rather than go clubbing in Magaluf people wanted to run with the bulls at Pamplona's San Fermin festival; rather than sunbathe in Benidorm they wanted to attend the Tomatina, that extraordinary food fight in the Valencian town of Buñol. While, say, Thomas Cook was always curated, the trend is yet again evolutionary, towards a more prominent and intense curation.

Tourism is big business. Every year over 1.1 billion people (up from only twenty-five million in 1960) travel for pleasure, in an industry supporting up to one in eleven jobs worldwide.[6] Tourism has a huge impact on the economy, the environment and local culture. Changes in tourism, as in many of the industries we have examined, have a larger ripple effect than might be supposed. Travel agents have, for instance, by and large given way to aggregated review sites like TripAdvisor (which acquired the curated travel site Wanderfly). While they may have disappeared from the middle of the market they have reappeared strongly at the top. Tourism is no longer packaged. Rather it is designed, or 'tailor-made', in the industry parlance; from something we passively accept to something we actively curate; from a limited set of clearly defined experiences to a kaleidoscope of options. In London an agency like Black Tomato will design your holiday down to the T – turning it into a curated series of bespoke experiences. Australian firm ATP offers trips that are, according to the *Daily Telegraph*, 'curated to the nth degree'.[7] Meanwhile a new service called Peek has backing from Jack Dorsey and Eric Schmidt amongst others. As its founder Ruzwana Bashir (echoing the usual mantra of curation businesses) told Fast Company: 'We're not showing you absolutely everything. We are showing you the best things.'[8] As we have seen time and again, the pattern is for new curatorial positions to open at the top of the market, selecting and arranging for, in this case, a new nomadic elite hungry for exclusive experiences, before rippling out through wider contexts.

As adventure sports and ashrams, yoga retreats and mountain hikes ease their way into the traditional sun and sea mix, new infrastructures of hospitality, entertainment and transportation are needed. In parallel new breeds of experiential businesses and cultural forms are emerging. These aren't just bungee jumps for student backpackers in New Zealand. Cinema and theatre have both, for instance, been changed by the advent of immersive versions like Secret Cinema or Punchdrunk. Watching a film is transformed into a live, interactive experience – you are thrown into the fiction. It's memorable, different, absorbing and exciting. It's cinema for people saturated in cinema; for people whose Netflix habit means that choice of films is less important than choice of experience.

The new market for experiences means that we prize those brokers who can get us tickets for Bayreuth, Wimbledon or the Kentucky Derby; who can arrange for us to visit the Venice Carnivale or Coachella. These days corporate lawyers are more likely to talk about their weekend endurance sailing than afternoons on the golf course. Just as we view culture as a tapestry from which to sample at our leisure, so we regard leisure itself. Sophisticated event discovery services like YPlan and Dojo, or new offerings from Time Out Labs, are built to cater for this trend, using data around location, preferences, timing and a multitude of event-creation and indexing tools to wade through the thousands and millions of events put on each year. YPlan pitch themselves as curators for the wealth of experiences offered by modern life; the idea being there is so much happening, discovering it all is impossible. Live events are a $22bn-a-year industry in the US alone, while the share of expenditure on live events relative to general consumer spending has risen 70 per cent since 1987.[9] What we want even more than the latest designer outfit (incredible, I know) is the latest designer experience, whether it's Punchdrunk's production in a half-forgotten warehouse or a one night only pop-up bar. Experience itself slots into the pattern of Long Boom and overload, and, just as we have seen elsewhere, it's developed its own Curation Layer, its own ecosystem for managing it.

This isn't a bad thing and taps into several significant trends. As we saw in Part I, James Wallman, author of *Stuffocation*, argues we already own too much stuff and it doesn't make us happy.[10] The trouble with new things is that we quickly adapt; the initial boost wears off. What's more, things degrade. Meanwhile experiences have a host of benefits – far from getting worse over time, they only become more burnished in the memory. That disastrous camping trip? Character-building! Unlike material goods, experiences are difficult to compare, so they don't make us feel inadequate. You could spend a fortune on a fortnight in the Maldives and for all I know my wet week in a tent was more fun. Not only are our experiences objectively harder to measure, but research shows we are much less inclined to do so in the first place.[11] Experiences, unlike material things, tend to be inherently social – they get us out of the house and let us meet new people.

Experiential purchases are also at the forefront of the economy. Eventbrite, a live event discovery and ticketing platform with annual sales of over $1.5bn, conducted research suggesting that, driven by the 'sharing' opportunities afforded by social media, 78 per cent of millennials (18–34 year olds) would choose desirable experiences over desirable material products.[12] A report from the Boston Consulting Group concluded that experiences were growing 4 per cent faster than goods purchases at the upper end of the market.[13] Worth $1.8 trillion and $1 trillion respectively, over the long term experience will overtake goods in the higher-end bracket and it's likely a similar pattern will play out throughout the wider consumer economy.

All of this equates to a change in the tenor of the self and of experience. It's a subtle change. I'm not arguing that until recently people didn't pick and choose the elements that went into their holiday; or didn't piece together experiences for the way they contrasted. People have always done these things. Yet again what's changed is the prevalence and intensity. As with everything about this book, it's less about sudden pivot points and more about the larger-scale direction of travel.

Making a statement

Like retail, entertainment, information, consumer goods and art exhibitions, the self is curated. None of those businesses devolving curation to distributed groups would ever have got off the ground had they not found willing participants. These are the people – us – who spend hours carefully constructing a social media profile, choosing this and that photo, video or article to share. And then measure the results on Klout. The people for whom all aspects of our life, from our walk to work onwards, are measurable – and then compared with others, with Fitbit or our smart watch. We work for companies who employ someone to find and repackage the most interesting news in our sector, all in the name of brand building. We are even the people whose attitude to finding partners has become one of filtration systems, whether that's a swipe to the left on Tinder or complex and allegedly scientific mechanisms. Even romance is overloaded and requires curation, and before we get too upset it's we the users who asked for it.

Throughout this book we have seen the 'menuification' of the world – everything becomes a series of too many choices that require management. Overall I am neutral on the desirability or otherwise of this. It's the society and economy we have ended up with, and compared to having too little it's an excellent place to be. It provides new, interesting, fruitful opportunities for leisure and employment alike.

But one does have to raise a sceptical glance at this curatorial turn in our sense of self. It can lead to a flat, deracinated version of what it means to be. It's painfully self-conscious. Experiences and identity become calculations. The great

narrative arcs that once defined our lives are now chopped up
into unrelated sequences – what the author Douglas Coupland
calls 'denarration'[14] and the digital writer Douglas Rushkoff
calls 'present shock'.[15] Again, it should be stressed that I don't
see this as anything particularly new; just as more widespread,
more prominent.

The sociologist Pierre Bourdieu argued that all matters of
taste are matters of distinction: our tastes, judgements and
choices don't stem from any 'natural' or 'superior' aesthetic
or cultural preferences.[16] Rather, our tastes serve to define us
in relation to others. In his epic study of the French middle
class, Bourdieu saw even the smallest examples – the food
people ordered in a restaurant, the songs they would listen
to at home – as powerfully connected to class and what he
called cultural capital. It is those with such capital who define
what serves as good taste. Good taste is naturalised by those
with cultural capital. Taste is not about judgement; it's about
separation. About making statements that distinguish us from
those 'above' or 'below' us in the perceived hierarchy. Much
of the class system is built from aesthetic decisions. Having
internalised various elements of taste, we then 'self-select' into
a certain class.

So what happens now, when everything is on the table,
when the billionaire in a private jet wears jeans and a T-shirt?
When we approach our lives like a greatest hits playlist?
Despite widening inequality, the spread of a curation mindset
that deliberately picks from across the spectrum of options
changes the power relations implicit in our choices. We still
don't understand what it means when everyone is a curator.
I believe we are entering a new phase where curation itself
becomes cultural capital. The more curated a person is, the
more they are able to weave eclectic, rare and differing elements into their own life as experiences, as goods, the more

of a new kind of cultural capital they enjoy. It's no longer about eating this or that food in a restaurant; it's about how those restaurants blend together. Of course this is still about money – the more money you have, the more you can curate your life.

To quote another Left Bank thinker, Michel Foucault, we have become 'entrepreneurs of the self'.

It is often noted of Internet businesses, particularly ones that are free to use, that the user is the product. Just as those services enable us to become curators, so they turn us into a product for advertisers. So targeted are these systems, built on reams of personal data and sophisticated technology, that it's no stretch to say we are curated; we are carefully selected and unwittingly arranged for advertisers. As a publisher I've found these services very useful. But again, it all feeds into a changing dynamic of who we are and how we live.

The philosopher Matthew Crawford isn't the first to wonder whether all this is leading to a crisis of attention so severe it's undoing our sense of personhood, but he sums the problem up excellently:

> We are living through a crisis of attention that is now widely remarked upon, usually in the context of some complaint or other about technology. As our mental lives become more fragmented what is at stake often seems to be nothing less than the question of whether one can maintain a coherent self. I mean a self that is able to act according to settled purposes and ongoing projects, rather than just flitting about.[17]

No one has the answer to this. But I suspect that it will involve more curation and not less; that, as a society, we have gone too far down the road towards overload; that, quite simply, not curating is not an option. Whether we like it or not, whether we choose to call it curation or not, the modern world forces us to be curators. We will have to get used it.

Conclusion

A cabinet of curiosity

One of the most famous Renaissance *Wunderkammer* – literally wonder rooms – was that of the singularly named Dane, Ole Worm, a naturalist and antiquary born in Aarhus in 1588. A restless and lifelong learner, Worm travelled Europe studying in Germany, Switzerland and England before settling at the University of Copenhagen, where he entered the service of King Christian IV as his physician.

A polymath, Worm taught the arts and natural history, making advances in anatomy and identifying the small parts of the cranium now known as the Wormian bones. He was also a linguist, collecting and preserving runic scripts from ancient Scandinavia. But today he is best known for his *Wunderkammer* (see Figure 14), one of the most renowned of the early modern period. Here was Worm the natural philosopher, collecting arcane artefacts brought back from exploratory missions to the New World. Stuffed animals were blended with turtle shells; racks of antlers with totems and statues; mineral specimens with vials of potions. Squid, fossils, reptiles, skeletons and furs jostled for space in his

Figure 14. Ole Worm's cabinet of curiosity
from the mid-seventeenth century

bestiary. Worm collected clockwork mechanisms and autom-
ata including a mechanical duck: so-called 'artificialia'. His
research strayed from the natural world into ethnographic
and numismatic collections. One legendary piece was the
remains of a plant–animal hybrid called the 'Scythian Lamb'
or 'Vegetable Lamb of Tartary' – a woolly fern of Central Asia
that supposedly came alive as a kind of sheep tethered to the
plant and its roots.

But his collection was also used for empirical research –
Worm famously concluded that the long horn in his collection
was not that of the mythical unicorn, but from a narwhal.
He did this by poisoning his pets and then feeding them
ground-up horn – when they failed to recover this was, he
argued, because the horn was not bestowed with the magical
restorative properties expected of a unicorn. Worm spent

years not only collecting the most interesting specimens, but also cataloguing them, studying them, arranging them. He would personally guide visitors around the collection and claimed it was built so that people could learn. As a figure he stands at the junction of an extraordinary range of disciplines: anthropology and ethnography, biology and taxonomy, museology and archaeology, medicine and anatomy, classics and linguistics.

On his death in 1654 the collection was subsumed into that of the Royal Danish Kunstkammer. Posthumously published as the *Museum Wormianum* in 1655, a catalogue of engravings provides a rich insight into this unusual collection. It was the stepping-off point for further scientific advancements. *Wunderkammer* were strange menageries that came about at a time when the boundaries between art and science, the occult and the factual, enlightenment clarity and good old-fashioned kleptomania were still loosely drawn. They connected the new world of scientific learning, cataloguing, making sense of things, to an older world of hoarding and mysticism; they were part biological lab, part anthropological museum, part wizard's chamber.

Yet curating this display firmly pointed in the direction of modernity. The process of selection led Worm to think through what was important or unique. What was worth preserving and including? It led to a sense of expertise, history and empirical experimentation. *Wunderkammer* allowed for juxtaposition. They allowed people to focus on finding new and interesting things and then to compare them, study them. This helped them find analogies, discover order in the chaos of the natural world and parallels in the messy world of human culture. It created ideas of pedagogical display. As a contemporary of Galileo, Descartes and Sir Francis Bacon, Worm and other curators were helping to forge scientific understanding.

The process of creating the cabinet of curiosity – its curation – was closely intertwined with the development of a modern world view.

Curation became central to museums because, as a process, it required intense focus and wide knowledge. Curation, through its basic attributes, helped make sense of the world. It's still doing so to this day. Curation may be a second-order activity, but it's one whose reach and impact shouldn't be underestimated.

How curation works

Unfortunately there is no shortcut to good curation. It's always specific and rooted in trust and knowledge. You can't click your fingers and make it happen; it's hard work, an ongoing activity. Not curating, just letting things spill out and pile on one another, is in many ways the easy option; curating well is tough, patient stuff. There are however some messages worth keeping in mind:

- Whatever we call it, curation is already happening. It's a label that's been adopted for existing trends as much as a practice that spread. Getting het up about whether something is curation or not is a waste of time; while the term is often used carelessly, it's here.
- Nonetheless much curation is still unrecognised. Many businesses are predicated on curation-style activities – only they don't name it as such. Even in something like publishing, for example, it's rare indeed to find commissioning editors and publishers who call themselves curators.
- This ties into the concepts of explicit and implicit curation. We all know explicit curation, and can see the

fashion blogs and designer cocktail bars where something along those lines is obviously going on. But beneath lie swathes of implicit curation; curation going by any other name, helping to make the world manageable.

- To understand why curation shouldn't be dismissed as another pointless fad, we have to see its core tenets in the context of long-term rising productivity, the explosion of the digital revolution and the related phenomena of overload. This new environment requires a change in orientation for businesses and individuals alike.
- Older models, like the Industrial Model of Selection or the Broadcast Model of Culture, have been seriously destabilised in this scenario. In their place Curated Models, that go beyond basic search, optimised for complex and saturated markets, are taking over.
- Expertise, understanding and judgement have never been more important. But we are also seeing new assemblages of automated and algorithmically driven processes. Figuring out how best to combine the two is a major part of effective curation in the twenty-first century.
- Everywhere the direction of travel is towards greater levels of curation. Curation is becoming thicker. If this book could be summarised in an image it would look like this:

Less Curation **More Curation**

- We only appreciate the power of selection when we look at the full range of associated curation effects.

Whether it's about refining large sets, simplifying complexity while keeping nuance, contextualising and explaining, or bringing out the full innate power of things through clever arrangements, these curation effects have outsized impact.

- Gatekeepers are not going away – but they are changing.
- One of today's most important business models is creating the tools and means for others to curate. While boosting one's own (for want of a better word) brand as a curator will always be important, building platforms that empower others to become curators has started to take precedence as one of the signature business forms of our time.
- This new centrality of curation changes our attitudes to businesses like retail, indeed, even our attitudes to what businesses do. The firm as a curator is not a recent idea, but remains a force. But the changes go deeper – it changes our relationship to our cultures, to the idea of creativity and even to ourselves.

The bad and the ugly

Suggesting that all is well, that thanks to curation we are entering a Utopian world of excellent coffee, plentiful art and absorbing jobs for all, is obviously inappropriate. As I have hinted throughout the book, there are issues and limitations with curation.

Curation raises questions over intellectual property, credit and the apportionment of rewards, especially on the Internet. Curators cannot ignore the fact that they are, at some level, making a living or gaining an audience through the work of others. This is less the case now we have started curating for an audience of one – but all those presentational forms of curation are gaining through the work of others. Systems of distributing credit like the Curator's Code are on balance to be welcomed, despite the carping. They are better than nothing. But as Jaron Lanier and others point out, no one can eat on retweets. Lanier's own solution is to develop a new system of micropayments that allows for a better-distributed system of rewards; something that means the Siren Servers, Lanier's name for the big curatorial powerhouses from Google to Facebook et al., don't just clean everything up.

It's not hard to get behind Lanier's proposal, but it's a million years from becoming a reality. In the meantime creators have never had it harder, and even the long tail of curators find actually earning a living as opposed to gaining followers is difficult. Not curating isn't the answer – our world would quickly become unnavigable. But apportioning rewards correctly remains difficult.

The case for curation's place in the modern economy should not be overstated. My argument is that it's growing fast, but this still means it's limited. Look at the Fortune 500 and you will find a fair number of companies for whom curation is a major part of their proposition: retailers, technology companies, media businesses. But you will find many more that exist in realms far from those I have discussed here – energy, banking, pharmaceuticals, automotives. The truth is the world's biggest companies still look more like ExxonMobil and J.P. Morgan than Amazon or News Corp. However it is worth noting that most of these companies are locked into straightforward additive growth models and are hence compounding rather than alleviating the symptoms of overload. This creates opportunities for those businesses willing to tack the other way.

There are also question marks as to what kind of jobs

curation creates. On the one hand it should be an undiluted positive. Here should be the next generation of jobs, tailored to the new reality, suitable for the attention spans and habits of media-rich Gen Yers. These are jobs countries from Russia to Abu Dhabi are trying to create. Yet technology can change everything; the idea of the 'second machine age' that is upending our ideas of work and creating a new era of machine-dominated jobs has gained currency.[1] The authors of a book on the topic point out that in the mid-2000s self-driving cars were a joke; no one could make them work and the idea itself felt like science fiction. Ten years later they are becoming a common sight on the streets of California. What seems like a safely 'human' activity can quickly, in this environment, become technologised. The authors point out that communication and pattern recognition are, for example, now firmly the province of machines. Curation is meant to be at least partly human and this makes it valuable. But what if we realise we prefer the curation of ultra-advanced AIs that find us things and manage the world with uncanny accuracy and efficiency?

We just don't know where this is going. While we can be confident that the need for curation will increase, we don't know whether curation will hold out the promise of good new jobs or if a few dominant technology platforms will accrue all the rewards. As skilled and subjective labour, curation should be an employment redoubt in this emerging techno-economic nexus. But, since we have already come to rely on machine-driven mechanisms, nothing is certain. Even while it's unlikely we will need to create jobs that boost supply, will we create jobs that manage it?

Indeed, at one level curation has opened up a new and more democratic vista, in that being a curator has lower barriers to entry than being a creator. Sure, it doesn't mean everyone will be a good curator, but as the scales tip towards over-production it should create opportunities for new kinds of business or new forms of cultural engagement. Yet it's often remarked that inequality is on the increase – especially in places like the US and the UK, as well as being deeply entrenched in emerging economies. Pretty much everywhere, we are heading back to, if not already arriving back at, inequality levels last seen in the 1920s and before.[2] Curation may slot neatly into this dynamic. Certainly, the experience of the art world suggests that even as the number of curators booms, a few lucky individuals at the top rack up air miles and prestigious commissions while everyone else ekes out a meagre living. Superstar curators, whether in the art world or a Silicon Valley Unicorn like Pinterest, may take massively outsized rewards as, thanks to network effects and a star system, small opening advantages grow into unbridgeable gulfs.

Curators have power. And never more so than when attention itself is becoming the most valuable currency of all. There is no code though for how they exercise this power. There is no rulebook, no real laws, no governing structure or professional body for curation. It's too slippery and widespread for that.

So is this the nightmare? That we live in a world where creativity is devalued? Where not only do all the rewards go to second-order activities, but they go disproportionately to a small few, a small few who have survived or ridden a wave of extinction thanks to the frontiers of new technology? Yes, it's the nightmare. But it needn't happen.

Taking care

Curation is not without issues. Few things are. However, we cannot simply ignore it, or pretend it's not here, and that it's not already working. Curation is a structurally necessary part of contemporary life whose significance and value is growing.

What we shouldn't forget though is *curare*, curation in the sense of taking care of. Curation capable of incorporating a moral dimension, that has, as Professor Floridi indicated, a sense of custodianship. Whether that's through digital means or otherwise, it will, I believe, make a crucial difference. Curation that doesn't have the sense of taking care, preserving, nurturing is more likely to lead to negative outcomes. Having credibility and expertise may be necessary for good curation; but it's all too easy to forget about this side as well.

The ultimate question is not where curation is happening or what it is, but what's the difference between good and bad curation? Whether curation is explicit or implicit, thick or thin, is less important than whether it's useful.

Good curation, as we have seen, involves expertise, taste, judgement. But it also involves trust, empathy and considerations beyond itself. When curation is devoid of these elements, it descends into irrelevance. How we manage overload requires a sense of curation far beyond that of cupcake photos. But when curation is built around a sense of what others want, imbued with a service ethic, when it cares about what it curates more than the curation itself, those charges are unfair – curation here is rightly valuable. It becomes, to paraphrase the economist E.F. Schumacher, business as if people mattered.

We are only at the beginning of where these ideas could take us. Whether we get there or not depends on the choices of millions of curators large and small, traditional and new, professional and amateur, online and offline; but the opportunity is enormous if we are willing to go beyond our comfort zones and think big. Curation is adaptive, what Nassim Nicholas Taleb calls antifragile – the more you load onto it the stronger it gets.[3] The more stuff we as a society produce, the more we are overloaded and so the more valuable curation becomes. If our present trajectory continues we should, then, expect to see more of the kind of activity we have come to call curation.

It would astonish our ancestors that today we can build companies, institutions and livelihoods from the sifting and organisation of the sheer mass of material we produce. But this is the world we have come to inhabit. Selection and arrangement, refinement, display – these aren't afterthoughts or sideshows in the modern world; they at the vanguard of a practice whose roots run deep but whose future is more significant than ever. Learning how to make the most of them, to work with them effectively, to broaden and deepen their impact, is one of the core principles of working effectively in an age of too much and we'll be all the better for it.

From humming data centres to the trillions of hours spent in front of screens; from dusty street markets to glistening marble-clad shopping malls; from the logistics of the new tourism to prestige projects on newly minted islands; from Amazon engineers to fashion designers, Silicon Valley VCs to drinks entrepreneurs, sales assistants to CEOs, in all of it curation is here, it's happening and it's changing how we work and live, how we engage with the sprawling and multitudinous world we have created.

Thinking through careful selections. Cutting down the problems. Growing people's chances of understanding, or purchasing, or finding, or simply appreciating. Arranging to maximise – getting the most out of everything. Understanding how curation effects are diffused throughout our culture. Using that understanding to make wise choices on behalf of others: welcome, once again, to the curation economy.

Notes

INTRODUCTION

1 http://www-01.ibm.com/software/data/bigdata/what-is-big-data.
   html
2 http://www.mckinsey.com/~/media/mckinsey/dotcom/insights/strat-
   egy/mckinsey%20quarterly%2050th%20anniversary%20issue%20
   overview/mckinsey_quarterly_q3_2014.ashx
3 http://www.lexisnexis.com/applieddiscovery/lawlibrary/whitepa-
   pers/adi_fs_pagesinagigabyte.pdf
4 http://www.theguardian.com/books/2015/apr/18/
   david-balzer-curation-social-media-kanye-west
5 Obrist (2014), p. 24
6 https://www.youtube.com/watch?v=X4TuPAlQLcg
7 http://uk.phaidon.com/agenda/art/articles/2011/
   september/09/a-brief-history-of-the-word-curator/
8 http://www.forbes.com/sites/stevenrosenbaum/2014/03/29/
   is-curation-over-used-the-votes-are-in/
9 http://www.thedailymash.co.uk/news/society/
   tossers-curating-everything-2015041697425
10 http://www.pressgazette.co.uk/content/going-forward-here-are-te
   n-bits-jargon-journalists-would-most-prs-de-layer-their-ecosystem
11 Wooldridge (2015)
12 http://ebookfriendly.com/tokyo-bookshop-one-book-week-pictures/

First World Problems

1 Mayer-Schönberger and Cukier (2013), p. 9

1 The Long Boom in Everything

1 http://www.sleuthsayers.org/2013/06/
the-3500-shirt-history-lesson-in.html
2 See https://www.newscientist.com/article/mg22029430.400-
primeval-planet-what-if-humans-had-never-existed/
3 From *The Communist Manifesto*
4 Smil (2005)
5 Kaplan (2008)
6 http://www.economist.com/news/business/21568384-can-foxconn-
worlds-largest-contract-manufacturer-keep-growing-and-improve-
its-margins-now
7 http://english.caixin.com/2013-05-14/100527915.html
8 Arthur (2009), p. 193
9 Dorling (2013)
10 Chang (2014)
11 Figures from Prasad Rao and van Ark, eds (2013)
12 Ibid.
13 https://www.gov.uk/government/uploads/system/uploads/
attachment_data/file/443898/Productivity_Plan_web.pdf
14 https://orionmagazine.org/article/the-gospel-of-consumption/
15 Alpert (2013), p. 11
16 Rifkin (2014); Mason (2015)

2 Overload

1 Wallman (2014)
2 Simms (2014)
3 Figures from Wallman (2014)
4 http://www.voxeu.org/article/gdp-and-life-satisfaction-new-evidence
5 Skidelsky (2013)
6 http://www.slideshare.net/ActivateInc/activate-tech-and-media-
outlook-2016/8-The_total_tech_and_media
7 All figures from Schulte (2014)
8 Nisen (2014)

3 The Creativity Myth

1   For more detail, see for example http://www.gramophone.
    co.uk/features/focus/a-meeting-of-genius-beethoven-and-goethe-
    july-1812?pmtx=most-popular&utm_expid=32540977-5.-
    DEFmKXoQdmXwfDwHzJRUQ.1
2   https://www.youtube.com/yt/press/en-GB/statistics.html
3   http://static1.squarespace.com/static/545e40d0e4b054a6f8622bc9/t/
    54720c6ae4b06f326a8502f9/1416760426697/Peak_Stuff_17.10.11.pdf
4   Koestler (1975)
5   Mazzucato (2013)
6   http://archive.wired.com/wired/archive/4.02/jobs_pr.html
7   See for example http://lareviewofbooks.org/essay/
    post-scarcity-economics/
8   Harari (2014), p. 275

4 The Origins of Curation

1   http://www.newyorker.com/magazine/2014/12/08/art-conversation
2   Perry (2014)
3   For more on this and the history of curation in museums, see
    Schubert (2000)
4   http://www.telegraph.co.uk/culture/art/3671180/Duchamps-
    Fountain-The-practical-joke-that-launched-an-artistic-revolution.
    html
5   Perry (2014)
6   For more, see http://www.fastcompany.com/1702167/
    inside-wild-wacky-profitable-world-boing-boing

5 The Principles of Curation

1   http://techcrunch.com/2014/07/28/
    apple-to-buy-swell-for-30-million-per-report/
2   http://www.ft.com/cms/s/2/d72f0e14-27ab-11e4-be5a-
    00144feabdc0.html#axzz3fgNqiHFu
3   http://www.slideshare.net/ActivateInc/activate-tech-and-media-
    outlook-2016/120-120THE_APP_ECONOMY
    wwwactivatecomDespite_massive_number
4   https://stratechery.com/2014/business-models-2014/

5 http://www.hollywoodreporter.com/news/
   blockbuster-delays-424-mil-debt-25172
6 Christensen (1997)
7 https://redef.com/original/age-of-abundance-how-the-content-exp
   losion-will-invert-the-media-industry
8 http://variety.com/2015/tv/news/tca-fx-networks-john-landgra
   f-wall-street-1201559191/
9 http://mashable.com/2012/03/26/kaggle/
10 Mentioned in http://www.theatlantic.com/technology/
   archive/2014/01/how-netflix-reverse-engineered-hollywood/282679/
11 http://www.wired.co.uk/magazine/archive/2015/02/features/
   do-adjust-your-set/page/2
12 Ibid.
13 http://www.theguardian.com/commentisfree/2014/oct/26/
   supermarkets-reign-is-over-hail-the-independents
14 Iyengar (2011), p. 187
15 Iyengar and Lepper (2000)
16 Schwartz (2004)
17 Superbly summarised in Kahneman (2011)
18 Levitin (2015)
19 http://unhealthywork.org/classic-studies/the-whitehall-study/
20 Discussed in http://www.newyorker.com/magazine/2014/02/17/
   cheap-words
21 http://www.newyorker.com/magazine/2014/02/17/cheap-words
22 https://hbr.org/2015/11/how-marketers-can-personalize-at-scale
23 http://ben-evans.com/benedictevans/2015/6/24/
   search-discovery-and-marketing
24 Dormehl (2014)
25 Quoted in Brand (1994)
26 Catmull (2014)
27 Cited in http://www.newyorker.com/magazine/2012/01/30/
   groupthink
28 Quoted in http://www.neboagency.com/blog/
   art-curation-interview-maria-popova/
29 Shenk (2014)
30 Barden (2013)
31 Ibid.
32 Ibid.
33 Bateson, Nettle and Roberts (2006)
34 Levitin (2015), p. 6

35 See http://www.edwardtufte.com/tufte/posters and http://www.edwardtufte.com/tufte/minard

36 Schmidt, Rosenberg and Eagle (2014)

37 For more detail see https://www.uie.com/articles/three_hund_million_button/

38 Hidalgo (2015), p. 178

6 CURATION EFFECTS

1 http://www.telegraph.co.uk/finance/newsbysector/transport/10044827/Ferrari-tries-to-cut-car-sales-to-protect-brand-exclusivity.html

2 http://www.wsj.com/articles/the-summers-most-unread-book-is-1404417569

3 http://www.wired.com/2014/10/content-moderation/#slide-id-1593139&sref=https://delicious.com/ajaxlogos/search/wired

4 Tainter (1988), p.160

5 Ibid., p. 91

6 Ibid., p. 93

7 Richards (2014)

8 http://www.ft.com/cms/s/0/db2b340a-0a1b-11df-8b23-00144feabdc0.html#ixzz3V8OJ6Oaa

9 Siegel and Etzkorn (2014)

10 http://www.linnean.org/Education+Resources/who_was_linnaeus

11 Levitin (2015)

12 Guber (2011), p. ix

7 CURATE THE WORLD

1 All figures taken from an Abu Dhabi Tourism and Culture Authority press release and interview

2 Krane (2009)

3 http://www.clearias.com/sectors-of-economy-primary-secondary-tertiary-quaternary-quinary/

4 http://www.census.gov/foreign-trade/index.html

5 http://www.nytimes.com/2012/08/29/dining/eataly-exceeds-revenue-predictions.html?_r=0

6 http://www.entrepreneur.com/article/238389

7 http://www.oxfam.ca/there-enough-food-feed-world

8 http://www.britishcoffeeassociation.org/about_coffee/coffee_facts/

9 https://www.stumptowncoffee.com/producers/
   arturo-aguirre-sr-and-jr

10 http://www.ft.com/cms/s/0/bfce2878-c691-11e5-b3b
   1-7b2481276e45.html

11 http://www.forbes.com/sites/bruceupbin/2015/06/09/jack-ma-says-
   alibaba-has-no-plans-to-invade-america-its-the-other-way-around/

12 Wooldridge (2015), p. 14

13 http://www.wired.co.uk/magazine/archive/2014/06/ideas-bank/
   vinod-khosla

14 Kondo (2014)

15 http://chronicle.com/article/How-to-Curate-Your-Digital/151001/

8 CURATE CULTURE

1 http://www.theguardian.com/business/2011/feb/16/
   richard-russell-xl-recordings-dizzee-rascal-prodigy

2 http://www.theguardian.com/world/2014/aug/15/
   berghain-club-bouncer-sven-marquardt-memoirs-berlin

3 https://press.spotify.com/uk/information/

4 http://www.billboard.com/biz/arti-
   cles/news/digital-and-mobile/5930133/
   business-matters-why-spotify-bought-the-echo-nest

5 http://www.theverge.com/2015/7/20/9001317/
   spotify-discover-weekly-poersonalized-playlist-deep-cuts

6 http://www.ft.com/cms/s/f1d6e2ce-0b6b-
   11e5-994d-00144feabdc0,Authorised=false.
   html?_i_location=http%3A%2F%2Fwww.ft.com%2F-
   cms%2Fs%2F0%2Ff1d6e2ce-0b6b-11e5-994d-00144feabdc0.
   html%3Fsiteedition%3Duk&siteedition=uk&_i_refer-
   er=http%3A%2F%2Fwww.ft.com%2Fhome%2Fuk#axzz3cHpJzizM

7 And not everyone will survive; see http://qz.com/232834/
   streaming-music-has-become-a-pawn-in-a-high-stakes-chess-match-
   who-will-win-and-why/

8 https://www.ted.com/talks/
   mark_ronson_how_sampling_transformed_music?language=en

9 http://www.whosampled.com/most-sampled-tracks/1/

10 Anderson, Bell and Shirky (2015)

11 http://www.nybooks.com/articles/archives/2015/jun/25/
   digital-journalism-next-generation/

12 https://medium.com/message/coming-home-nyt-now-e3fc26f60a59

13 http://www.gallup.com/poll/171740/americans-confidence-news-
media-remains-low.aspx

9 Curate the Internet

1 http://www.economist.com/news/21589108-new-model-firm-its-
way-says-virginia-rometty-chief-executive-ibm-year
2 For more see Rosenbaum (2011), Curata (2015)
3 See https://www.youtube.com/watch?v=grU0xJ7JwLs
4 https://twitter.com/milouness/status/178595970639081473
5 http://www.newstatesman.com/2015/05/man-versus-algorithm
6 http://www.androidauthority.com/
samsung-curated-news-app-europe-638460/
7 Thiel (2014), p. 144
8 Rosenbaum (2011), p. 13
9 http://techcrunch.com/2013/11/14/pinterest-launches-its-first-apis-
partners-with-zappos-walmart-disney-nestle-random-house-hearst-
on-first-rollout/?ncid=twittersocialshare
10 Pariser (2011)
11 http://www.theguardian.com/technology/2014/sep/04/
twitter-facebook-style-curated-feed-anthony-noto
12 https://www.facebook.com/business/news/
News-Feed-FYI-A-Window-Into-News-Feed
13 http://qz.com/333313/
milliions-of-facebook-users-have-no-idea-theyre-using-the-internet/
14 http://www.bloomberg.com/news/articles/2015-04-23/
twitter-tries-to-tone-down-the-chirping
15 Carlson (2015)
16 http://www.theguardian.com/technology/2016/feb/19/yahoo-sal
e-goldman-sachs-jp-morgan-marissa-mayer-alibaba
17 See e.g. Taylor (2014)
18 See e.g. http://designnotes.info/?p=6823
19 Lanier (2011, 2013)
20 Postman (2005), p. xix

10 Curate Business

1 http://www.economist.com/blogs/economist-explains/2014/04/
economist-explains-17
2 http://cdn2.vox-cdn.com/uploads/chorus_asset/file/664128/

pearl_river_large.0.jpg

3 Ramo (2009)
4 According to Sequoia themselves, at least: https://www.sequoiacap.
   com/us/about/dentmakers
5 http://www.latimes.com/travel/fashion/la-ig-0907-opening-
   ceremony-20140907-story.html#page=1
6 See research from Interbrand cited by Jones (2014)
7 Ibid.
8 http://www.wsj.com/articles/amazon-plans-hundreds-of-brick-and
   -mortar-bookstores-mall-ceo-says-1454449475
9 https://angel.co/lyst
10 https://www.linkedin.com/pulse/20140619151046-6907-retail-
    innovation-labs-in-the-bay-area-indiana-seattle-illinois-austin-
    new-york-city and http://www.fastcompany.com/3039608/
    most-innovative-companies-2015/westfield-labs
11 Levi (2015)
12 Goyal (2014), p. 8
13 Sinha (2015)
14 Ibid., p. 117
15 http://www.nature.com/nature/about/
16 http://www.nature.com/nature/about/mission.pdf
17 All figures from Larson and Ins (2010)
18 http://blogs.nature.com/news/2014/05/global-scientific-output-
    doubles-every-nine-years.html
19 http://www.vox.com/2015/11/30/9820192/
    universities-uncited-research
20 https://www2.deloitte.com/content/dam/Deloitte/
    es/Documents/acerca-de-deloitte/Deloitte-ES-
    Opera_Europa_Deloitte_Art_Finance_Report2014.pdf
21 http://trendwatching.com/

11 Curate Yourself

1 Stephenson (2013), p. 265
2 For more see Hebdige (1979)
3 http://luckypeach.com/how-mcdonalds-started-in-china/
4 Löfgren (1999)
5 Ibid.
6 http://media.unwto.org/press-release/2015-01-27/
   over-11-billion-tourists-travelled-abroad-2014

7   http://www.telegraph.co.uk/travel/travelnews/10474809/
    Telegraph-Travel-Awards-2013-Favourite-escorted-tour-operator.
    html

8   http://www.fastcompany.com/3002093/jack-dorsey-eric-schmidt-
    back-peek-another-beautiful-curated-travel-startup

9   http://www.hughmalkin.com/blogwriter/2015/9/23/
    why-no-one-has-solved-event-discovery

10 Wallman (2014)

11 http://www.theatlantic.com/business/archive/2014/10/
    buy-experiences/381132/

12 http://eventbrite-s3.s3.amazonaws.com/marketing/Millennials_
    Research/Gen_PR_Final.pdf

13 https://www.bcgperspectives.com/content/articles/
    consumer_products_retail_shock_new_chic_dealing_with_new_
    complexity_business_luxury/

14 Obrist, Coupland and Basar (2015)

15 Rushkoff (2013)

16 Bourdieu (2010)

17 Crawford (2015), p. ix

Conclusion

1   Brynjolfsson and McAfee (2014)

2   Piketty (2014)

3   Taleb (2013)

Acknowledgements

As someone who works with books and writing every day, I well know how much work goes into making a book. Thanks are owed to too many people to list here, and apologies to those not thanked by name or who I have missed out.

First Alex Christofi and then Sophie Lambert have been incredible agents. Alex refined the proposal with a brilliant touch and placed the book; Sophie took things up without missing a beat and has been the sort of wonderful confidante, support and adviser that every author relies on to an almost crazy degree. Many thanks too to the wider team at Conville & Walsh. It's a huge privilege to work with them and I am incredibly grateful.

From the first meeting Tim Whiting of Little, Brown absolutely got the book and the ideas; it all clicked into place. He and Meri Pentikäinen have been the ideal critics, shepherds and visionaries that every book needs. Thanks to all of the wider team at Little, Brown and Piatkus for their hard work in bringing the book out. On all fronts it has been superb. Steve Gove did a brilliant job on the copyedit and greatly improved the book throughout.

There were many people I spoke to when writing the book. Huge thanks to all of them, in no particular order: Edouard

Lambelet, Xavier Damman, Gideon Chain, Lily Booth, Brian Armstrong, Daniel Kaplan, Shannon Fox, Karim Azar, Daniel Crewe, Emma Cantwell, 'Lisa' (you know who you are), Catherine Seay, Bobbie Johnson, Martin Gayford, Molly Sharp, Oriole Cullen, Simon Sheikh, Greg Linden, James Simmons, Luciano Floridi and the staff of the British Library and the Bodleian Library. On a wider level curation is now a much commented upon phenomenon and I have relied on the huge body of work represented in the bibliography and web links – this book would have been impossible without it.

Comments on the draft were immensely useful and have made it a much, much better book. For all their careful reading and attention – which blew me away – thanks are owed to Julian Baker, George Walkley, Anna Faherty, James Bullock and Stephen Brough. It should go without saying that all errors and infelicities are mine alone.

My co-founders at Canelo, Iain Millar and Nick Barreto, should also be thanked for putting up with me working on this book while we were also launching a new business. It's not a combination I would recommend if you value free time, but their support was invaluable.

Lastly, and above all, thanks to Dani for absolutely everything. It would take volumes to even begin. And I promise not to spend all weekend writing any more. For a month or two at least . . .

Bibliography and Further Reading

Alpert, Daniel (2013), *The Age of Oversupply: Overcoming the Greatest Challenge to the Global Economy*, London: Portfolio Penguin

Anderson, Chris (2013), *Makers: The New Industrial Revolution*, London: Random House Business Books

Anderson, Chris, Emily Bell and Clay Shirky (2015), *Post Industrial Journalism: Adapting to the Present*, New York: Tow Center for Digital Journalism

Arthur, W. Brian (2009), *The Nature of Technology: What It Is and How It Evolves*, London: Allen Lane

Balzer, David (2014), *Curationism: How Curating Took Over the Art World and Everything Else*, Toronto: Coach House Books

Barden, Phil (2013), *Decoded: The Science Behind Why We Buy*, Chichester: Wiley

Bateson, Melissa, Daniel Nettle and Gilbert Roberts (2006), 'Cues of being watched enhance cooperation in a real-world setting', *Biology Letters*, The Royal Society

Bilton, Nick (2013), *Hatching Twitter: How a fledgling start-up became a multibillion-dollar business & accidentally changed the world*, London: Sceptre

Borges, Jorge Luis (1970), *Labyrinths*, London: Penguin

Bourdieu, Pierre (2010), *Distinction: A Social Critique of the Judgement of Taste*, Oxon: Routledge

Brand, Stewart (1994), *How Buildings Learn: What Happens After They're Built*, London: Phoenix

Brynjolfsson, Erik, and Andrew McAfee (2014), *The Second Machine Age: Work, Progress and Prosperity in a Time of Brilliant Technologies*, New York: W. W. Norton

Carlson, Nicholas (2015), *Marissa Mayer and the Fight to Save Yahoo!*, London: John Murray

Catmull, Ed, with Amy Wallace (2014), *Creativity, Inc.: Overcoming the Unseen Forces That Stand in the Way of True Inspiration*, London: Bantam Press

Chang, Ha-Joon (2014), *Economics: The User's Guide*, London: Pelican Books

Christensen, Clayton M. (1997), *The Innovator's Dilemma: When Technologies Cause Great Firms to Fail*, Boston MA: Harvard Business School Press

Coyle, Diane (2011), *The Economics of Enough: How to Run the Economy As If the Future Matters*, Princeton: Princeton University Press

Crawford, Matthew (2015), *The World Beyond Your Head: How to Flourish in an Age of Distraction*, London: Viking Penguin

Curata (2015), *The Ultimate Guide to Content Curation*, Boston MA: Curata

Dobelli, Rolf (2013), *The Art of Thinking Clearly: Better Thinking, Better Decisions*, London: Sceptre

Dorling, Danny (2013), *Population 10 Billion: The Coming Demographic Crisis and How to Survive It*, London: Constable and Robinson

Dormehl, Luke (2014), *The Formula: How Algorithms Solve All Our Problems ... And Create More*, New York: Perigee

Economist, The, Introduction by Zanny Minton Beddoes (2014), *Debts, Deficits and Dilemmas: A crash course on the financial crisis and its aftermath*, London: Profile Books

Emmott, Stephen (2013), *10 Billion*, London: Penguin

Goyal, Ashima, ed. (2014), *The Oxford Handbook of the Indian Economy in the 21st Century*, Oxford: Oxford University Press

Guber, Peter (2011), *Tell to Win: Connect, Persuade, and Triumph with the Hidden Power of Story*, London: Profile Books

Harari, Yuval Noah (2014), *Sapiens: A Brief History of Mankind*, London: Harvill Secker

Hebdige, Dick (1979), *Subculture: The Meaning of Style*, London: Methuen

Hidalgo, César (2015), *Why Information Grows: The Evolution of Order, from Atoms to Economies*, London: Allen Lane

Johnson, Steven (2013), *Future Perfect: The Case for Progress in a Networked Age*, London: Penguin

Iyengar, Sheena (2011), *The Art of Choosing*, London: Abacus

Iyengar, Sheena S., and Mark R. Lepper (2000), 'When Choice is Demotivating: Can One Desire Too Much of a Good Thing?', *Journal of Personality and Social Psychology*, vol. 76, no. 6, American Psychological Association

Jarvis, Jeff (2009), *What Would Google Do?*, New York: Collins Business

Jones, Graham (2014), *Click.ology: What Works in Online Shopping*, London: Nicholas Brealey

Kahneman, Daniel (2011), *Thinking, Fast and Slow*, London: Penguin

Kasarda, John D., and Greg Lindsay (2011), *Aerotropolis: The Way We'll Live Next*, London: Allen Lane

Koestler, Arthur (1975), *The Act of Creation*, London: Picador

Kondo, Marie (2014), *The Life-changing Magic of Tidying Up: The Japanese Art of Decluttering and Organizing*, New York: Ten Speed Press

Krane, Jim (2009), *Dubai: The Story of the World's Fastest City*, London: Atlantic Books

Krogerus, Mikael, and Roman Tschäppeler (2012), *The Change Book: Fifty Models to Explain How Things Happen*, London: Profile Books

Kunkel, Benjamin (2014), *Utopia or Bust: A Guide to the Present Crisis*, London: Verso

Lanier, Jaron (2011), *You Are Not a Gadget: A Manifesto*, London: Penguin

Lanier, Jaron (2013), *Who Owns The Future?*, London: Allen Lane

Larson, Peder Olesen, and Markus von Ins (2010), 'The rate of growth in scientific publication and the decline in coverage provided by the Science Citation Index', *Scientometrics*, vol 84, no. 3, Springer

Leslie, Ian (2015), *Curious: The Desire to Know and Why Your Future Depends On It*, London: Quercus

Levi, Scott C. (2015), *Caravans: The Story of Indian Business*, New Delhi: Allen Lane

Levitin, Daniel J. (2015), *The Organized Mind: Thinking Straight in the Age of Information Overload*, London: Penguin Viking

Lindstrom, Martin (2008), *Buyology: How Everything We Believe About Why We Buy is Wrong*, New York: Doubleday

Löfgren, Orvar (1999), *On Holiday: A History of Vacationing*, Berkeley and Los Angeles: University of California Press

Lovell, Nicholas (2013), *The Curve: From Freeloaders Into Superfans: The Future of Business*, London: Portfolio Penguin

MacCannell, Dean (2013), *The Tourist: A New Theory of the Leisure Class*, Berkeley: University of California Press

Martin, James (2006), *The Meaning of the 21st Century: A Vital Blueprint for Ensuring Our Future*, London: Eden Project Books

Mason, Paul (2015), *PostCapitalism: A Guide to Our Future*, London: Allen Lane

Mayer-Schönberger (2013), Viktor, and Kenneth Cukier, *Big Data: A Revolution That Will Transform How We Live, Work and Think*, London: John Murray

Mazzucato, Mariana (2013), *The Entrepreneurial State: Debunking Public vs. Private Sector Myths*, London: Anthem Press

McKeown, Greg (2014), *Essentialism: The Disciplined Pursuit of Less*, London: Virgin Books

Mullainathan, Sendhil, and Eldar Shafir (2013), *Scarcity: Why Having Too Little Means So Much*, London: Allen Lane

Obrist, Hans Ulrich (2011), *A Brief History of Curating*, Zurich: JRP Ringier

Obrist, Hans Ulrich (2014), *Ways of Curating*, London: Allen Lane

Obrist, Hans Ulrich, Douglas Coupland and Shumon Basar (2015), *The Age of Earthquakes: A Guide to the Extreme Present*, London: Penguin

Offer, Avner (2006), *The Challenge of Affluence: Self-Control and Well-Being in the United States and Britain since 1950*, Oxford: Oxford University Press

O'Neill, Paul (2012), *The Culture of Curating and the Curating of Culture(s)*, Cambridge, MA: MIT Press

Pariser, Eli (2011), *The Filter Bubble: What the Internet is Hiding from You*, London: Viking

Perry, Grayson (2014), *Playing to the Gallery: Helping Contemporary Art in its Struggle to Be Understood*, London: Particular Books

Piketty, Thomas (2014), *Capital in the Twenty-First Century*, Cambridge, MA: Harvard University Press

Postman, Neil (2005), *Amusing Ourselves to Death: Public Discourse in the Age of Show Business*, 2nd edition, New York: Penguin

Prasad Rao, D.S., and Bart van Ark, eds (2013), *World Economic Performance Past, Present and Future: Essays in celebration of the life and work of Angus Maddison*, Cheltenham: Edward Elgar

Ramo, Joshua Cooper (2009), *The Age of the Unthinkable: Why the New World Order Constantly Surprises Us and What to Do About It*, London: Little, Brown

Rickards, James (2014), *The Death of Money: The Coming Collapse of the International Monetary System*, London: Portfolio Penguin

Rifkin, Jeremy (2014), *The Zero Marginal Cost Society: The Internet of Things, the Collaborative Commons, and the Eclipse of Capitalism*, New York: Palgrave

Rosenbaum, Steven (2011), *Curation Nation: How to Win in a World where Consumers are Creators*, New York: McGraw Hill

Rushkoff, Douglas (2013), *Present Shock: When Everything Happens Now*, New York: Penguin Current

Salecl, Renata (2010), *Choice*, London: Profile Books

Schmidt, Eric, and Jonathan Rosenberg, with Alan Eagle (2014), *How Google Works*, London: John Murray

Schubert, Karsten (2000), *The Curator's Egg: The Evolution of the Museum Concept from the French Revolution to the Present Day*, London: One-off Press

Schulte, Brigid (2014), *Overwhelmed: Work, Love and Play When No One Has the Time*, London: Bloomsbury

Schumacher, E.F. (1993), *Small is Beautiful: A Study of Economics as if People Mattered*, London: Vintage

Schwartz, Barry (2004), *The Paradox of Choice: Why More Is Less: How the Culture of Abundance Robs Us of Satisfaction*, New York: Harper Perennial

Shenk, Joshua Wolf (2014), *Powers of Two: Finding the Essence of Innovation in Creative Pairs*, London: John Murray

Siegel, Alan, and Irene Etzkorn (2014), *Simple: Conquering the Crisis of Complexity*, London: Random House Business Books

Simms, Andrew (2014), *Cancel the Apocalypse: The New Path to Prosperity*, London: Abacus

Sinha, Dheeraj (2015), *India Reloaded: Inside India's Resurgent Consumer Market*, New York: Palgrave Macmillan

Skidelsky, Robert, and Edward Skidelsky (2012), *How Much Is Enough?: The Love of Money and the Case for the Good Life*, London: Allen Lane

Smil, Vaclav (2005), *Creating the Twentieth Century: Technical Innovations of 1867–1914 and Their Lasting Impact*, New York: Oxford University Press

Stephenson, Neal (2013), *Some Remarks*, London: Atlantic Books

Studwell, Joe (2013), *How Asia Works: Success and Failure in the World's Most Dynamic Region*, London: Profile Books

Tainter, Joseph A. (1988), *The Collapse of Complex Societies*, Cambridge: Cambridge University Press

Taleb, Nassim Nicholas (2013), *Antifragile: Things That Gain From Disorder*, London: Penguin

Taylor, Astra (2014), *The People's Platform: Taking Back Power and Culture in the Digital Age*, London: Fourth Estate

Thiel, Peter (2014), *Zero to One: Notes on Startups, or How to Build the Future*, London: Virgin Books

Timberg, Scott (2015), *Culture Crash: The Killing of the Creative Class*, New Haven: Yale University Press

Timberg, Thomas A. (2014), *The Marwaris: The Story of Indian Business*, New Delhi: Allen Lane

Tripathi, Dwijendra, and Jyoti Jumani (2007), *The Concise Oxford History of Indian Business*, New Delhi: Oxford University Press

Wallman, James (2014), *Stuffocation: Living More With Less*, London: Portfolio Penguin

Weatherall, James Owen (2013), *The Physics of Finance: Predicting the Unpredictable: Can Science Beat the Market?*, London: Short Books

Weinberger, David (2007), *Everything is Miscellaneous: The Power of the New Digital Disorder*, New York: Times Books

Wooldridge, Adrian (2015), *The Great Disruption: How business is coping with turbulent times*, London: Economist Books

Wright, Alex (2007), *Glut: Mastering Information Through the Ages*, Washington, DC: Joseph Henry Press

Web links

'A Meeting of Genius: Beethoven and Goethe, 1812', *Gramophone*, http://www.gramophone.co.uk/features/focus/a-meeting-of-genius-beethoven-and-goethe-july-1812?pmtx=quarterly-dd (accessed 8 November 2014)

Allison, Chris, 'The Art of Curation: An Interview With Maria Popova of BrainPickings', Nebo (2010), http://www.neboagency.com/blog/art-curation-interview-maria-popova/ (accessed 14 October 2014)

'An Interview with Hans-Ulrich Obrist', *The Believer* (2012), http://logger.believermag.com/post/28845125847/an-interview-with-hans-ulrich (accessed 8 August 2013)

Ankeny, Jason, 'Eataly Elevates Food Retail, Tastes Success. What's Next?', *Entrepreneur* (2014), http://www.entrepreneur.com/article/238389 (accessed 12 July 2015)

Antonelli, Paola, 'A Curator's Tale', *Moma Salon: 1* (2014), https://www.youtube.com/watch?v=X4TuPAlQLcg (accessed 14 October 2014)

'Arturo Aguirre, Sr and Jr', *Stumptown Coffee*, https://www.stumptowncoffee.com/producers/arturo-aguirre-sr-and-jr (accessed 20 July 2015)

Auerbach, David, 'Twitter at the crossroads', Slate, 2015, http://www.slate.com/articles/technology/bitwise/2015/04/twitter_earnings_and_acquisitions_the_company_s_in_ trouble_and_its_options.html?wpsrc=fol_tw (accessed 3 May 2015)

Backstrom, Lars, 'News Feed FYI', Facebook (2013), https://www.facebook.com/business/news/News-Feed-FYI-A-Window-Into-News-Feed (accessed 16 June 2015)

Battan, Carrie, 'Johnny Depp Curates Pirate-Themed Compilation', Pitchfork (2012), http://pitchfork.com/news/48833-tom-waits-teams-with-keith-richards-patti-smith-teams-with-johnny-depp-courtney-love-teams-with-michael-stipe-for-depp-helmed-compilation/ (accessed 20 May 2013)

Blythman, Joanna, 'No wonder superstores are dying – we're sick and tired of their culture', *The Guardian* (2014), http://www.theguardian.com/commentisfree/2014/oct/26/supermarkets-reign-is-over-hail-the-independents (accessed 1 November 2014)

Bond, Paul, 'Blockbuster delays $42.4m debt payment', *The Hollywood Reporter* (2010), http://www.hollywoodreporter.com/news/blockbuster-delays-424-mil-debt-25172 (accessed 20 July 2015)

'Bowie to Curate New NYC Festival', *Billboard* (2006), http://www.billboard.com/articles/news/58498/bowie-to-curate-new-nyc-festival (accessed 20 May 2013)

Bradshaw, Tim, 'Apple looks beyond iTunes with launch of its streaming service', *Financial Times*, 2015, http://www.ft.com/cms/s/f1d6e2ce-0b6b-11e5-994d-00144feabdc0,Authorised=false.html?_i_location=http%3A%2F%2Fwww.ft.com%2F-cms%2Fs%2F0%2Ff1d6e2ce-0b6b-11e5-994d-00144feabdc0.html%3Fsiteedition%3Duk#axzz3cHpJzizM&sref=https://delicious.com/ajaxlogos/curation (accessed 6 June 2015)

Bradshaw, Tim, 'Growing Pains', *Financial Times* (2014), http://www.ft.com/cms/s/2/d72f0e14-27ab-11e4-be5a-00144feabdc0.html#axzz3fgNqiHFu&sref=https://delicious.com/ajaxlogos/curation (accessed 12 July 2015)

Bustillos, Maria, 'Why We Need Curators', Buzzfeed (2012), http://www.buzzfeed.com/mariabustillos/rise-of-the-net-jockey-why-we-need-curators#.brp04DYWnl (accessed 2 April 2013)

Byrne, David, 'Man vs Algorithm', *New Statesman* (2015),

http://www.newstatesman.com/2015/05/man-versus-algorithm (accessed 16 June 2015)

Chen, Adrian, 'The laborers who keep dick pics and beheadings out of your Facebook feed', *Wired*, 2014, http://www.wired.com/2014/10/content-moderation/#slide-id-1593139&sref=https://delicious.com/ajaxlogos/curation (accessed 29 October 2014)

Cheredar, Tom, 'NPR launches NPR One', VentureBeat (2014), http://venturebeat.com/2014/07/28/npr-launches-new-npr-one-mobile-app-for-curating-public-radio-news/ (accessed 29 July 2014)

'China's addiction to luxury goods', *The Economist* (2014), http://www.economist.com/blogs/economist-explains/2014/04/economist-explains-17 (accessed 18 July 2015)

'Coffee Facts', British Coffee Association, http://www.britishcoffeeassociation.org/about_coffee/coffee_facts/ (accessed 29 July 2015)

Collins, Glenn, 'At Eataly, the Ovens and Cash Registers Are Hot', *The New York Times*, 2012, http://www.nytimes.com/2012/08/29/dining/eataly-exceeds-revenue-predictions.html (accessed 16 May 2015)

Constine, Josh, 'Why Is Facebook Page Reach Decreasing?', *TechCrunch* (2014), http://techcrunch.com/2014/04/03/the-filtered-feed-problem/ (accessed 3 July 2015)

Crook, Jordan, 'Apple to Buy Swell for $30m', *TechCrunch* (2014), http://techcrunch.com/2014/07/28/apple-to-buy-swell-for-30-million-per-report/ (accessed 28 July 2014)

Curtis, Nick, 'Entrepreneur Kate MacTiernan on Danny Boyle's new film festival', *Evening Standard* (2013), http://www.standard.co.uk/goingout/film/entrepreneur-kate-mactiernan-on-danny-boyles-new-film-festival-shuffle-and-restoring-a-derelict-8673990.html (accessed 27 June 2013)

DeMers, Jayson, 'What Google's Knowledge Graph Means for the Future of Knowledge', *Forbes* (2014), http://www.forbes.com/sites/jaysondemers/2014/10/28/what-googles-knowledge-graph-means-for-the-future-of-search/2/ (accessed 8 February 2015)

Deshpande, Pawan, 'The Definitive Guide to Content Curation', Curata (2015), http://www.curata.com/blog/the-definitive-guide-to-content-curation/ (accessed 1 July 2015)

Doctorow, Cory, 'Clay Shirky on information overload and filter failure', Boing Boing (2010), http://boingboing.net/2010/01/31/clay-shirky-on-infor.html (accessed 17 February 2014)

Dredge, Stuart, 'Twitter boss confirms plan to expand curated experiences to all', *The Guardian* (2015), http://www.theguardian.com/technology/2015/apr/29/twitter-boss-curated-experiences-timeline (accessed 3 May 2015)

Dugan, Andrew, 'Americans' Confidence In News Media Remains Low', Gallup (2014), http://www.gallup.com/poll/171740/americans-confidence-news-media-remains-low.aspx (accessed 25 February 2015)

Ellenberg, Jordan, 'The Summer's Most Unread Book Is . . .', *The Wall Street Journal* (2014), http://www.wsj.com/articles/the-summers-most-unread-book-is-1404417569 (accessed 3 April 2015)

'Ethos', Sequoia Capital, https://www.sequoiacap.com/people/ethos/ (accessed 18 July 2015)

Evans, Benedict, 'Search, discovery and marketing', Ben-Evans (2015), http://ben-evans.com/benedictevans/2015/6/24/search-discovery-and-marketing?utm_content=buffer8ce71 (accessed 19 July 2015)

'Ferrari tries to cut car sales to protect brand exclusivity', *Daily Telegraph* (2013), http://www.telegraph.co.uk/finance/newsbysector/transport/10044827/Ferrari-tries-to-cut-car-sales-to-protect-brand-exclusivity.html (accessed 3 April 2015)

Fisher, Eve, 'The $3500 Shirt', Sleuthsayers (2013), http://www.sleuthsayers.org/2013/06/the-3500-shirt-history-lesson-in.html (accessed 18 July 2015)

Foster, Hal, 'Exhibitionists', *London Review of Books*, 2015, http://www.lrb.co.uk/v37/n11/hal-foster/exhibitionists (accessed 27 June 2015)

Freeland, Chrystia, 'What Toronto Can Teach London and New York', *Financial Times* (2010), http://www.ft.com/cms/s/db2b340a-0a1b-11df-8b23-00144feabdc0,Authorised=false.html?siteedition=uk&_i_location=http%3A%2F%2Fwww.

ft.com%2Fcms%2Fs%2F0%2Fdb2b340a-0a1b-11df-8b23-00144feabdc0.
html%3Fsiteedition%3Duk&_i_referer=&classification=con-
ditional_standard&iab=barrier-app#axzz3V8OFKGzd&s-
ref=https://delicious.com/ajaxlogos/curation (accessed 22
March 2015)

Galloway, Scott, 'The death of pure-play retail and impulse buys', L2
(2015), https://www.youtube.com/watch?v=grU0xJ7JwLs&-
feature=youtu.be (accessed 17 July 2015)

Gayford, Martin, 'Duchamp's Fountain', *Daily Telegraph*
(2008), http://www.telegraph.co.uk/culture/art/3671180/
Duchamps-Fountain-The-practical-joke-that-launched-an-
artistic-revolution.html (accessed 15 November 2014)

Good, Robin, 'Content Curation Visualized', Pinterest, https://
www.pinterest.com/robingood/content-curation-visualized/
(accessed 17 June 2013)

Goodhall, Chris, 'Peak Stuff' (2011), http://static1.squarespace.
com/static/545e40d0e4b054a6f8622bc9/t/54720c6ae4b-
06f326a8502f9/1416760426697/Peak_Stuff_17.10.11.pdf
(accessed 20 July 2015)

Groys, Boris, 'The Curator As Iconoclast', Bezalel (2006), http://
bezalel.secured.co.il/zope/home/en/1143538156/1143802471_
en (accessed 31 July 2013)

Hamblin, James, 'Buy Experiences, Not Things', The Atlantic
(2014), http://www.theatlantic.com/business/archive/2014/10/
buy-experiences/381132/ (accessed 29 July 2015)

'Henry Holland to curate Trinity Leeds launch', *Retail Gazette*
(2013), http://www.retailgazette.co.uk/blog/2013/03/23200-
henry-holland-to-curate-trinity-leeds-launch (accessed 20 June
2013)

Hern, Alex, 'End of the timeline? Twitter hints at move to Facebook-
style curation', The Guardian, http://www.theguardian.com/
technology/2014/sep/04/twitter-facebook-style-curated-feed-
anthony-noto (accessed 27 August 2014)

Honan, Mat, 'This is Twitter's Top Secret Project Lightning',
Buzzfeed (2015), http://www.buzzfeed.com/mathonan/twitters-
top-secret-project-lightning-revealed#.qkARmj57z&sref=https://
delicious.com/ajaxlogos/curation (accessed 20 June 2015)

'How Many Pages In A Gigabyte?', LexisNexis, http://www.lexisnexis.com/applieddiscovery/lawlibrary/whitepapers/adi_fs_pagesinagigabyte.pdf (accessed 13 February 2014)

Hudgins, Coley, 'Complexity Theory and System Collapse', The Resilient Family (2012), http://www.theresilientfamily.com/2012/03/complexity-theory-and-system-collapse/ (accessed 16 April 2014)

'Information', Spotify, https://press.spotify.com/uk/information/ (accessed 12 July 2015)

Ingram, Matthew, 'Twitter acquisition confirms that curation is the future', Gigaom (2012), https://gigaom.com/2012/01/20/twitter-acquisition-confirms-that-curation-is-the-future/ (accessed 23 January 2012)

Iyengar, Sheena, 'The art of choosing', TED (2010), https://www.ted.com/talks/sheena_iyengar_on_the_art_of_choosing#t-1378263&sref=https://delicious.com/ajaxlogos/curation (accessed 16 June 2014)

Johnson, Bobbie, 'Yuri Milner: Genius Investor or King of the Gold Rush', Gigaom (2011), https://gigaom.com/2011/03/16/yuri-milner-genius-investor-or-king-of-the-gold-rush/ (accessed 20 March 2013)

Jones, Dan, 'English clubs are left dazzled', *Evening Standard* (2014), http://www.standard.co.uk/sport/dan-jones-like-mowgli-as-he-faces-the-snake-our-english-clubs-are-left-dazzled-9141385.html (accessed 22 February 2014)

Jonze, Tim, 'XL Recordings, the record label that's tearing up the rule book', *The Guardian* (2011), http://www.theguardian.com/business/2011/feb/16/richard-russell-xl-recordings-dizzee-rascal-prodigy (accessed 6 June 2015)

Kaplan, Jeffrey, 'The Gospel of Consumption', *Orion Magazine* (2008), https://orionmagazine.org/article/the-gospel-of-consumption/ (accessed 15 October 2015)

Kaplan, Marcia, 'Celebrity Curators Help Personalize Ecommerce', Practical Ecommerce (2011), http://www.practicalecommerce.com/articles/3178-Celebrity-Curators-Help-Personalize-Ecommerce?SSAID=314743 (accessed 20 May 2013)

Karlsson, Per, 'The world's wine production 2000–2012', *BK*

Wine Magazine (2013), http://www.bkwine.com/features/winemaking-viticulture/global-wine-production-2000-2012/ (accessed 3 May 2015)

Kessler, Sarah, 'How Kaggle Solves Big Problems With Big Data Competitions', Mashable (2012), http://mashable.com/2012/03/26/kaggle/#C3APzntNGkqq (accessed 20 July 2015)

Kessler, Sarah, 'Jack Dorsey, Eric Schmidt Back Peek, Another Beautiful Curated Travel Startup', *Fast Company* (2012), http://www.fastcompany.com/3002093/jack-dorsey-eric-schmidt-back-peek-another-beautiful-curated-travel-startup (accessed 28 July 2015)

Kowalcyzk, Piotr, 'This unique Tokyo bookstore offers one book title a week', Ebook Friendly (2015), http://ebookfriendly.com/tokyo-bookshop-one-book-week-pictures/ (accessed 14 September 2015)

Kummer, Corby, 'The supermarket of the future', The Atlantic (2007), http://www.theatlantic.com/magazine/archive/2007/05/the-supermarket-of-the-future/305787/ (accessed 16 May 2015)

Kusinitz, Sam, 'An Exhaustive List of Google's Ranking Factors', Hubspot Blogs (2014), http://blog.hubspot.com/marketing/google-ranking-algorithm-infographic (accessed 7 July 2014)

Langer, Matt, 'Stop Calling It Curation', Gizmodo (2012), http://gizmodo.com/5892582/stop-calling-it-curation (accessed 19 February 2013)

Lawrence, Robert Z., 'An Analysis of the 1977 Trade Deficit', *Brookings Institution*, http://www.brookings.edu/~/media/Projects/BPEA/1978%201/1978a_bpea_lawrence_smeal_vonfurstenberg_gordon_houthakker_krause_cline_kareken_maclaury.PDF (accessed 30 April 2014)

Lehrer, Jonah, 'Groupthink', *The New Yorker* (2012), http://www.newyorker.com/magazine/2012/01/30/groupthink (accessed 8 February 2015)

'Lyst', *AngelList*, https://angel.co/lyst (accessed 20 July 2015)

Madrigal, Alexis C., 'How Netflix Reverse Engineered Hollywood', The Atlantic (2014), http://www.theatlantic.com/technology/archive/2014/01/

how-netflix-reverse-engineered-hollywood/282679/ (accessed 10 January 2014)

Madrigal, Alexis C., 'I Loved You, Blockbuster', The Atlantic (2013), http://www.theatlantic.com/technology/archive/2013/11/i-loved-you-blockbuster/281213/ (accessed 1 January 2015)

Malkin, Hugh, 'Why no one has solved event discovery', Hugh Malkin (2015), http://www.hughmalkin.com/blog-writer/2015/9/23/why-no-one-has-solved-event-discovery (accessed 12 October 2015)

'Malleable Malls', The Economist (2013), http://www.economist.com/news/britain/21571926-shopping-centres-are-proving-well-suited-digital-age-malleable-malls (accessed 22 January 2014)

Marshall, Kelli, 'How to Curate Your Identity as an Academic', The Chronicle of Higher Education (2015), http://chronicle.com/article/How-to-Curate-Your-Digital/151001/ (accessed 23 February 2014)

Massing, Michael, 'Digital Journalism', The New York Review of Books (2015), http://www.nybooks.com/articles/archives/2015/jun/25/digital-journalism-next-generation/ (accessed 7 July 2015)

Max, D.T., 'The Art of Conversation', The New Yorker (2014), http://www.newyorker.com/magazine/201–4/12/08/art-conversation (accessed 20 July 2015)

Mayer, Marissa, 'Tumblr + Yahoo!: It's Officially Official', Yahoo! (2013), http://yahoo.tumblr.com/post/53441093826/tumblr-yahoo-its-officially-official (accessed 20 June 2013)

McDuling, John, 'An epic battle in streaming is about to begin', Quartz (2014), http://qz.com/232834/streaming-music-has-become-a-pawn-in-a-high-stakes-chess-match-who-will-win-and-why/ (accessed 26 July 2014)

'Millennials', Eventbrite, http://eventbrite-s3.s3.amazonaws.com/marketing/Millennials_Research/Gen_PR_Final.pdf (accessed 12 October 2015)

Mirani, Leo, 'Millions of Facebook users have no idea they're using the Internet', Quartz (2015), http://qz.com/333313/millions-of-facebook-users-have-no-idea-theyre-using-the-internet/ (accessed 16 June 2015)

'Mission Statement', *Nature*, http://www.nature.com/nature/about/mission.pdf (accessed 27 July 2015)

Mod, Craig, 'Coming Home', *The Message* (2014), https://medium.com/message/coming-home-nyt-now-e3fc26f60a59#.frm70bk3c (accessed 20 May 2015)

Moore, Booth, 'Opening Ceremony Possibility', *Los Angeles Times* (2014), http://www.latimes.com/travel/fashion/la-ig-0907-opening-ceremony-20140907-story.html#page=1&sref=https://delicious.com/ajaxlogos/curation (accessed 20 July 2015)

Morton, Tom, 'A brief history of the word curator', Phaidon (2011), http://uk.phaidon.com/agenda/art/articles/2011/september/09/a-brief-history-of-the-word-curator/ (accessed 13 March 2013)

'Most Sampled', Who Sampled, http://www.whosampled.com/most-sampled-tracks/1/ (accessed 18 July 2015)

Munger, Michael, 'Market Makers or Parasites?', *Library of Economics and Liberty* (2009), http://www.econlib.org/library/Columns/y2009/Mungermiddlemen.html (accessed 7 July 2014)

Nisen, Max, 'Companies have turned killing time into an art form', Quartz (2014), http://qz.com/200725/companies-have-turned-killing-time-into-an-art-form/ (accessed 6 May 2014)

Nordmark, Jon, '14 retail innovation labs in the Bay Area and 5 other cities', Pulse LinkedIn (2014), https://www.linkedin.com/pulse/20140619151046-6907-retail-innovation-labs-in-the-bay-area-indiana-seattle-illinois-austin-new-york-city (accessed 20 July 2015)

Oltermann, Philip, 'Berghain club bouncer launches memoirs about life as Berlin doorman', *The Guardian* (2014), http://www.theguardian.com/world/2014/aug/15/berghain-club-bouncer-sven-marquardt-memoirs-berlin (accessed 15 August 2014)

'Over 1.1 billion tourists travelled abroad in 2014', World Tourism Organization (2015), http://media.unwto.org/press-release/2015-01-27/over-11-billion-tourists-travelled-abroad-2014 (accessed 5 August 2015)

Owens, Simon, 'One way in which Facebook is just like 1990s era AOL', Simon Owens (2015), http://www.simonowens.net/

one-way-in-which-facebook-is-just-like-1990s-era-aol (accessed 21 February 2014)

Packer, George, 'Cheap Words', *The New Yorker* (2014), http://www.newyorker.com/magazine/2014/02/17/cheap-words (accessed 27 September 2014)

'Parents treble time they spend on childcare since the 1970s', University of Oxford, 2010, https://www.ox.ac.uk/media/news_stories/2010/paren100407.html (accessed 6 May 2014)

Pasori, Cedar, 'Leonardo di Caprio Talks Art', *Complex Style*, 2013, http://uk.complex.com/style/2013/04/leonardo-di-caprio-talks-saving-the-environment-with-art-collecting-basquiat-and-being-named-after-da-vinci (20 May 2013)

Phillips, Matt, 'The slow sad decline of Radioshack', Quartz (2014), http://qz.com/263841/the-slow-sad-decline-of-radioshack-one-of-the-great-brands-of-the-80s/ (accessed 14 September 2014)

Popova, Maria, 'Curators Code', Curators Code (2012), http://www.curatorscode.org/ (accessed 12 March 2013)

Proto, Eugenio, and Aldo Rustichini, 'GDP and Life Satisfaction: New Evidence', *Vox*, 2014, http://www.voxeu.org/article/gdp-and-life-satisfaction-new-evidence (accessed 3 February 2014)

Rometty, Virginia, 'The year of the smarter enterprise', *The Economist* (2013), http://www.economist.com/news/21589108-new-model-firm-its-way-says-virginia-rometty-chief-executive-ibm-year (accessed 4 July 2015)

Ronson, Mark, 'How Sampling Transformed Music', TED (2014), https://www.ted.com/talks/mark_ronson_how_sampling_transformed_music?language=en#t-17584&sref=https://delicious.com/ajaxlogos/curation (accessed 29 May 2015)

Rosenbaum, Steven, 'Innovate – curation!', TEDxGrandRapids (2011), https://www.youtube.com/watch?v=iASluLoKQbo (accessed 27 May 2013)

Rosenbaum, Steven, 'Is Curation Overused?', *Forbes* (2014), http://www.forbes.com/sites/stevenrosenbaum/2014/03/29/is-curation-over-used-the-votes-are-in/ (accessed 31 March 2014)

Rowan, David, 'What do you do for the data disenfranchised?', *Wired UK* (2013), http://www.wired.co.uk/magazine/

archive/2013/04/ideas-bank/what-did-you-do-for-the-data-disenfranchised (accessed 3 June 2013)

Sargent, Mikah, 'Yahoo!, the Genghis Khan of the tech world', Medium (2013), https://medium.com/@mikahsargent/yahoo-the-genghis-khan-of-the-tech-world-66082ebcc1db#.7o6qkzbdw (accessed 5 August 2013)

Sawers, Paul, 'Blinkist for Android gives you the gist of books in 15 minutes', The Next Web (2014), http://thenextweb.com/apps/2014/09/01/blinkist-android-gives-gist-non-fiction-books-15-minutes/ (accessed 18 September 2014)

Seifert, Dan, 'Spotify's latest trick is a personalized weekly playlist of deep cuts', The Verge (2015), http://www.theverge.com/2015/7/20/9001317/spotify-discover-weekly-poersonalized-playlist-deep-cuts (accessed 20 July 2015)

'Shock of the New Chic', Boston Consulting Group (2014), https://www.bcgperspectives.com/content/articles/consumer_products_retail_shock_new_chic_dealing_with_new_complexity_business_luxury/ (accessed 29 July 2015)

Silver, James, 'Meet Netflix Founder Reed Hastings', Wired (2015), http://www.wired.co.uk/magazine/archive/2015/02/features/do-adjust-your-set/page/2 (accessed 12 July 2015)

Spool, Jared M., 'The $300m Button', User Interface Engineering (2009), https://www.uie.com/articles/three_hund_million_button/ (accessed 24 March 2014)

Starr, Oliver, '3 Reasons Curation is Here to Stay', ReadWrite (2011), http://readwrite.com/2011/05/09/3_reasons_curation_is_here_to_stay (accessed 20 March 2013)

'Statistics', YouTube, https://www.youtube.com/yt/press/en-GB/statistics.html (accessed 20 July 2015)

Stibel, Jeff, 'The Web is dead and the app killed it', Wired (2013), http://www.wired.co.uk/magazine/archive/2013/09/ideas-bank/the-web-is-dead-and-the-app-thankfully-killed-it (accessed 18 November 2013)

Streams, Kimber, 'Grand St, A Curated Online Consumer Electronics Store', Laughing Squid, 2013, http://laughingsquid.com/grand-st-a-curated-online-consumer-electronics-store/ (accessed 18 July 2013)

Streihorst, Tom, 'Post-Scarcity Economics, *LA Review of Books* (2013), https://lareviewofbooks.org/essay/post-scarcity-economics/ (accessed 5 August 2013)

Surtees, Michael, 'Curator's Code – No Thanks', Design Notes (2012), http://designnotes.info/?p=6823 (accessed 12 March 2013)

'The Pearl River Delta Megacity', Vox, http://cdn2.vox-cdn.com/uploads/chorus_asset/file/664128/pearl_river_large.0.jpg

'There is enough food to feed the world', Oxfam, http://www.oxfam.ca/there-enough-food-feed-world (accessed 3 May 2015)

Thompson, Ben, 'Business Models for 2014', Stratechery (2014), https://stratechery.com/2014/business-models-2014/ (accessed 6 November 2014)

'Tossers Curating Everything', The Daily Mash, 2015, http://www.thedailymash.co.uk/news/society/tossers-curating-everything-2015041697425 (accessed 29 July 2015)

Triggs, Rob, 'Samsung to launch curated news app for its Galaxy phones', Android Authority (2015), http://www.androidauthority.com/samsung-curated-news-app-europe-638460/ (accessed 12 October 2015)

Tufekci, Zeynep, 'Why Twitter Should Not Algorithmically Curate the Timeline', The Message (2014), https://medium.com/message/the-algorithm-giveth-but-it-also-taketh-b7efad92bc1f#.it5584ghn (accessed 14 September 2014)

Tufte, Edward, 'Minard Sources', Edward Tufte (2002), http://www.edwardtufte.com/tufte/minard (accessed 6 November 2014)

Upbin, Bruce, 'Jack Ma Says Alibaba Has No Plans to Invade America', *Forbes* (2015), http://www.forbes.com/sites/bruceupbin/2015/06/09/jack-ma-says-alibaba-has-no-plans-to-invade-america-its-the-other-way-around/ (accessed 20 July 2015)

Vanhemert, Kyle, 'Canopy: A Curated Site That Finds the Best Stuff You Can Buy On Amazon', *Wired* (2014), http://www.wired.com/2014/04/canopy-a-curated-select-of-amazons-most-awesome-products/ (accessed 18 September 2014)

Van Noorden, Richard, 'Global scientific output doubles every nine years', *Nature* (2014), http://blogs.nature.com/news/2014/05/global-scientific-output-doubles-every-nine-years.html (accessed 27 July 2015)

Vogel, Carol, 'At $142.4 Million, Triptych Is the Most Expensive Artwork Ever Sold at an Auction', *New York Times* (2013), http://www.nytimes.com/2013/11/13/arts/design/bacons-study-of-freud-sells-for-more-than-142-million.html?ref=international-home (accessed 13 November 2013)

Walker, Rob, 'Inside the Wild, Wacky, Profitable World of Boing Boing', Fast Company (2010), http://www.fastcompany.com/1702167/inside-wild-wacky-profitable-world-boing-boing (accessed 20 November 2014)

Warwick, Joe, 'Foxlow Review', *Metro* (2013), http://metro.co.uk/2013/11/21/the-hawksmoor-team-hits-another-high-with-neighbourhood-restaurant-foxlow-4194067/ (accessed 22 November 2013)

'West Kowloon Cultural District', Foster + Partners (2011), http://www.fosterandpartners.com/projects/west-kowloon-cultural-district/ (accessed 31 July 2013)

'What is Big Data?', IBM, http://www-01.ibm.com/software/data/bigdata/what-is-big-data.html (accessed 8 August 2015)

'When workers dream of a life beyond factory gates', *The Economist* (2012), http://www.economist.com/news/business/21568384-can-foxconn-worlds-largest-contract-manufacturer-keep-growing-and-improve-its-margins-now (accessed 22 September 2014)

'Who was Linnaeus?', The Linnean Society of London, http://www.linnean.org/Education%20Resources/who_was_linnaeus (accessed 20 July 2015)

Wigger, Erin, 'The Whitehall Study', Unhealthy Work (2011), http://unhealthywork.org/classic-studies/the-whitehall-study/ (accessed 19 July 2015)

Wolf, Gary, 'Steve Jobs', *Wired*, http://archive.wired.com/wired/archive/4.02/jobs_pr.html (accessed 18 July 2015)

Xuena, Li, 'Why Foxconn's Switch to Robots Hasn't Been Automatic', Caixin (2013), http://english.caixin.com/2013-05-14/100527915.html (accessed 22 September 2014)

Picture Credits

Figure 1. Abraham Maslow's hierarchy of needs. User:Factoryjoe / CC-BY-SA 3.0

Figure 2. Carl Rohling, *The Incident in Teplitz*. © SZ Photo / Blanc Kunstverlag / Bridgeman Images

Figure 3. Marcel Duchamp, *Fountain*. Kim Traynor / CC-BY-SA 3.0

Figure 13. Left, the Sony Building; right, One Detroit Centre. *Sony Building New York* by David Shankbone / CC-BY-2.5; User:V8americanpower / CC-BY-SA-3.0

Index

Illustrations are indicated by *italic* page references